Teaching STEM i
Secondary Scho_

The skills, knowledge and understanding of the subjects involved in STEM (Science, Technology, Engineering and Mathematics) are vital for all young people in an increasingly science- and technology-driven society.

This book looks at the purpose and pedagogy of STEM teaching and explores the ways in which STEM subjects can interact in the curriculum to enhance student understanding, achievement and motivation. By reaching outside their own classroom, teachers can collaborate across subjects to enrich learning and help students relate school science, technology and maths to the wider world.

Packed with ideas and practical details for teachers of STEM subjects, this book:

- considers what the STEM subjects contribute separately to the curriculum and how they relate to each other in the wider education of secondary school students
- describes and evaluates different curriculum models for STEM
- suggests ways in which a critical approach to the pedagogy of the classroom, laboratory and workshop can support STEM for all students
- addresses the practicalities of introducing, organising and sustaining STEM-related activities in the secondary school
- looks to ways schools can manage and sustain STEM approaches in the long-term.

This timely new text is essential reading for trainee and practising teachers who wish to make the learning of Science, Technology, Engineering and Mathematics an interesting, motivating and exciting experience for their students.

Frank Banks is Emeritus Professor of Teacher Education at The Open University.

David Barlex was Senior Lecturer in Education at Brunel University and directed the Nuffield Design & Technology Projects.

Teaching STEM in the Secondary School

Helping teachers meet the challenge

Frank Banks and David Barlex

Routledge
Taylor & Francis Group

LONDON AND NEW YORK

First published 2014
by Routledge
2 Park Square, Milton Park, Abingdon, Oxon OX14 4RN

and by Routledge
711 Third Avenue, New York, NY 10017

Routledge is an imprint of the Taylor & Francis Group, an informa business

British Library Cataloguing in Publication Data
A catalogue record for this book is available from the British Library

Library of Congress Cataloging in Publication Data
Banks, Frank, 1953–
Teaching STEM in the secondary school : helping teachers meet the challenge / Frank Banks, David Barlex.
pages cm
Includes bibliographical references and index.
1. Science--Study and teaching (Secondary) 2. Technology--Study and teaching (Secondary) 3. Engineering--Study and teaching (Secondary) 4. Mathematics--Study and teaching (Secondary) I. Barlex, David. II. Title.
Q181.B26 20141
507.1'2--dc23
2013037913

ISBN: 978-0-415-67530-7 (hbk)
ISBN: 978-0-415-67531-4 (pbk)
ISBN: 978-0-203-80992-1 (ebk)

Typeset in Adobe Garamond Pro
by Saxon Graphics Ltd, Derby

Printed and bound in Great Britain by
TJ International Ltd, Padstow, Cornwall

Contents

Figures

Tables

Foreword

'STEM' has become an established term in education, but it has different meanings depending on whether you are inside or outside the school. To government and employers, it means an area of the school, college and university curriculum that is of great economic importance. All over the world, developed and developing countries see Science, Technology, Engineering and Mathematics education as fundamental to a successful industrial base. Prowess in STEM education is the new educational 'arms race', and governments are prepared to invest heavily in it. As Barack Obama said in his *Educate to Innovate* speech in 2009: 'Around the world, there is a hunger for knowledge, an insistence on excellence, a reverence for science and math [sic] and technology and learning. That used to be what we were about. That's what we're going to be about again.'

But inside schools and classrooms, 'STEM' can often have a subtly different meaning. The letters still stand for the same subjects, but now the emphasis is more on a group of subjects whose teaching can support and strengthen one another. In secondary schools, Science, Technology, Engineering and Mathematics are usually taught as separate subjects, with science and mathematics often getting the lion's share of the time and resources. Yet the advantages of linking and co-ordinating these subjects together are many, as this book shows. For a lot of students, technology and engineering provide the rationale for science and mathematics. The co-ordination of these four subjects leads to better engagement and motivation, and better teaching when they are arranged to support one another.

Yet the STEM subjects remain largely separate in secondary schools. There are understandable reasons for this: subject teaching expertise is important, and as you go up the school, the practicality of teaching these subjects in an integrated way becomes harder and harder. Yet, as this book shows, there are many ways that each subject can in turn draw on the others to motivation and rationalization.

Today, secondary schools in England are driven largely by assessment and accountability systems. The motivation to optimise performance in GCSE and other public exams is overwhelming, and this has had a serious effect on STEM teaching. In science, the drive towards ever better exam performance has had a negative effect on practical work, which has largely been shaped by the requirements of the assessment regime. In mathematics, pupils are being entered for GCSE before they are ready, and are even allowed to drop the subject once they have it in the bag. The new accountability arrangements for England are putting pressure on design & technology, once the most popular of all the optional GCSE subjects.

Yet parents want more from schools than examination performance alone. They want their daughters and sons to be inspired by their teachers, to develop skills of leadership and teamwork and to be employable when they move on from school. These qualities don't come from mere examination preparation: they need a style of teaching that aims to engage curiosity and inspire further study. Extended project work and problem-based learning can encourage enterprise, team working and engagement in ways that normal school lessons cannot. Enriching the curriculum through visits to industry and contacts with STEM ambassadors helps learners to see what awaits them in the world of work, and how to get there. STEM is about the world outside the school as well as inside the classroom, and the most effective schools take a whole-school approach to it.

All these themes, and more, are dealt with in this valuable book. Written by authors who have experience of all the elements of STEM, it is an important reassertion of the value of STEM within the school at a time when it has never been more important in the world outside.

John Holman, August 2013

Sir John Holman is Emeritus Professor of Chemistry at the University of York and advises the Wellcome Trust and Gatsby Foundation on education policy. He was National STEM Director for the English government between 2006 and 2010, and founded the National Science Learning Centre and the National STEM Centre.

Preface

At the start of our teaching careers the authors trained to be science teachers; Frank a physics teacher and David a chemistry teacher. As happened in those days we were soon required to teach all the sciences to pupils up to the age of 14. Whilst teaching in comprehensive schools, both of us then became interested in and enjoyed teaching technology too, and ultimately moved into higher education with responsibility for training technology teachers. David concentrated on curriculum development directing the Nuffield Design & Technology and Young Foresight Projects. Frank was in charge of both science and design & technology PGCE courses at The Open University. Both of us have an interest in the professional development of teachers.

Given our background and interests it is not surprising that we were intrigued by the rise of STEM as a potentially unifying concept across the related yet different disciplines of science, mathematics and technology which could be used to mutually enhance pupils' learning in these subjects. We saw that it was not easy for teachers to capitalise on the STEM potential despite successive initiatives and exhortations across many years for them to do so. Hence we have written this book to explore the advantages for teachers from mathematics, science and design & technology in "looking sideways" in their school's curriculum to see what is happening in the STEM subjects other than their own. We suggest that such a view will stimulate conversations that are the first and vital step in developing synergy in pupils' learning across the STEM subjects. We hope that we have been realistic in appreciating the difficulties in such work, yet have provided sufficient argument, guidance and examples to give those working in secondary schools the confidence to have those essential conversations and turn the emerging ideas in to action – action that will result in improved learning for pupils and more rewarding teaching for teachers.

Frank Banks and David Barlex
January 2014

Acknowledgements

We could not have written this book without the considerable help of the following colleagues to whom we are most grateful.

Dr Clare Lee from The Open University who provided the DEPTH mathematics diagram in Chapter 2. Peter Campbell who collaborated with the authors in developing the case study of in service activity with physics teachers in Chapter 3. Torben Steeg and Professor Celia Hoyles for giving interviews concerning the relationship between design & technology and science and mathematics in Chapter 4. Sue Pope who commented in detail on Chapter 5 and Rachel Rutland who suggested improvements for the use of mathematics in biology. Professor Matthew Harrison for his significant contribution on the place of engineering in the school curriculum in England in Chapter 7. Dr Wai Yi Feng for discussing with the authors her work on mathematics enhancement and enrichment activities in Chapter 8. Ronit Peretz, Ella Yonai, Vitor Soares Mann, and Marcos Berlatzky, delegates at the World ORT Hatter Technology Seminar on Integrated Approaches to STEM Education who contributed their thoughts to Chapter 11.

We are particularly grateful to Annamarie Kino and her colleagues at Routledge for their invaluable comments on draft chapters, and their sympathetic understanding of the changing times for STEM subjects, particularly in England, which we found challenging to pin down.

And finally we wish to acknowledge the Pullman Hotel on the Euston Road in London. The lobby of the hotel provides the essential comfort and coffee needed by collaborating authors when they meet to discuss their work.

1

What is STEM?

Introduction

Working with some upper primary school and lower secondary pupils recently I asked them to draw a picture of a 'Scientist' and a picture of an 'Engineer'. You can probably guess what the prevailing images were for the scientist: white, male, middle aged, balding, 'mad'-haired and white-coated – a bit like the character 'Doc' in *Back to the Future* or the crazy scientist in *Ben 10*. Although there were some pictures of women too, again all were in white coats and wore glasses. And the engineer? Depicted as male, wearing a hard hat and carrying a larger-than-life spanner. Whilst accepting that the very act of asking for pictures to be drawn might have led them to offer me a caricature of how scientist and engineers are commonly represented in the media, despite the impetus over the years to broaden the appeal of the physical sciences, particularly to girls, it is perhaps still surprising how firm such stereotypical images are fixed in the public imagination.

The STEM subjects – Science, Technology, Engineering and Mathematics – are kept separate in most national curriculum documents around the world but with common links at a range of levels, and with at least a nod to relevance in the 'real world' and to vocational usefulness. These links are structural too. For example, I recently looked up what is said online about the UK Parliament's Science and Technology Committee, wondering what it was and what it did. I found out that:

> The Science and Technology Committee exists to ensure that Government policy and decision-making are based on good scientific and engineering advice and evidence. … [It] can examine the activities of departments where they have implications for, or made use of, science, engineering, technology and research.
> (Science & Technology Commons Select Committee, 2013)

Guessing that this was not unique I wondered what the situation might be in the USA, which has an Office of Science and Technology:

Congress established the Office of Science and Technology Policy in 1976 with a broad mandate to advise the President and others within the Executive Office of the President on the effects of science and technology on domestic and international affairs.

(US Office of Science and Technology, 2013)

Finally, I looked at what happens in Australia. I discovered that:

The Department of Industry, Innovation, Climate Change, Science, Research and Tertiary Education helps shape Australia's future economy through skills, learning, discovery and innovation. […] we are working to accelerate productivity growth and secure Australia's prosperity in a competitive low carbon global economy.

(Australian Government, 2013)

Although they might not draw the same pictures of the scientist and engineers as the youngsters, it is clear that politicians too have some stereotypical views and often refer to 'Science and Technology' as an epistemological unit, more-or-less the same thing, a single activity inseparably linked. The aims and processes of science, however, are fundamentally different from those of technology and the links between them are not as formal as many people think. Maybe the confusion is because science is seen, erroneously, as necessarily always underpinning technology – providing the foundation to develop 'useful knowledge'. Disappointingly, the confusion is also present in the UK school curricula where, in perhaps rather crude and simple terms, science is often seen as 'theory', i.e., 'know *why*', and technology as practical, i.e., 'know *how*', and therefore in some way technology is dependent on science. We will consider curriculum links across STEM subjects in Chapter 2, but first we must clarify our understanding of why STEM has gained such interest in recent years and, in particular discuss 'science', 'technology' and maths, and how science knowledge and mathematical ability is 'exploited' in technology and vice versa; and how those link to and use mathematics. This chapter considers:

- the birth of STEM; when did we start thinking of this area of knowledge in linked capital letters?;
- some milestones in the development of STEM subjects in schools;
- the distinction between science knowledge and technology knowledge;
- the relationship between science and technology, mathematics and engineering using examples from history;
- common ground between science and technology;
- STEM as the lead subjects for considering affective knowledge and personal values;
- some key aspects of all STEM subjects: problem solving and systems thinking.

The birth of STEM

In February 2013 President Barack Obama gave his 'State of the Union' speech and said:

> Tonight, I'm announcing a new challenge, to redesign America's high schools so they better equip graduates for the demands of a high-tech economy. And we'll reward schools that develop new partnerships with colleges and employers, and create classes that focus on Science, Technology, Engineering and Math, the skills today's employers are looking for to fill the jobs that are there right now and will be there in the future.
>
> (White House, 2013)

Like many politicians over the years, Obama sees the STEM subjects as key to economic growth. As we have seen, many national committees see science-and-technology as the same thing, not only essential for vocational subjects, but actually the same indivisible subject. But what were the beginnings of the promoting of STEM in schools and in society? In 1944, an earlier US President wrote a letter to the Director of The Office of Scientific Research and Development. He made the point that, under a great secrecy, extraordinary developments had been made for the war effort and it was time to consider how similar progress could be promoted in peacetime. He wrote:

> What can be done, consistent with military security, and with the prior approval of the military authorities, to make known to the world as soon as possible the contributions which have been made during our war effort to scientific knowledge? The diffusion of such knowledge should help us stimulate new enterprises, provide jobs for our returning servicemen and other workers, and make possible great strides for the improvement of the national well-being [...] New frontiers of the mind are before us, and if they are pioneered with the same vision, boldness, and drive with which we have waged this war we can create a fuller and more fruitful employment and a fuller and more fruitful life.
>
> (Franklin D. Roosevelt, The White House,
> Washington DC 17 November 1944)

The post-war period was one where the STEM subjects were indeed to the fore as the US economy boomed with consumption of new cars and domestic white goods raising the standard of living to a level that few had experienced before. A slower post-war revival in Europe also promoted and encouraged an interest in STEM as means to follow the USA and 'stimulate new enterprises, provide jobs for our returning servicemen and other workers'. In Britain, the first commercial jet airliner and the first nuclear power station were held up as examples of British competence in 'Science and Engineering', again building on remarkable advances that had taken place during the war years. But in 1957, the capitalist west was to be shaken to the core by the launch of Sputnik. The shock was profound, particularly a sudden realisation that STEM education – so important for developing the industrial base and providing jobs – seemed to be lagging behind the Russians. The Space Race had begun and the starting pistol for STEM education had been fired.

How did we get here? Some important STEM education milestones

TABLE 1.1 The STEM milestones.

1957	Launch of Sputnik, the first artificial satellite	This was the starting pistol for the Space Race between the USSR and the USA. It caused shock in the West as 'Russia' went into the lead. What should be done about our lagging science and technology education? In the US, $1Billion was put into National Defense Education Act to promote science, mathematics and foreign language education.
1962	School Mathematic Project (SMP)	Although moves to change the mathematics taught to secondary (high) school students has its roots before the Second World War, the change to a discovery approach to learning mathematics accelerated when new school textbooks were published. Introducing ideas such as Set Theory and using number bases other than 10, this approach exposed all pupils to a wider appreciation of the wonder of mathematics. It was criticised by many as being too abstract and not a good grounding for science and engineering. There was a 'back-to-basics' backlash – including a need for more arithmetic for example – a decade later.
1966	Nuffield Science Teaching Project	Pupil and teacher guides were produced which encouraged an experiential approach to teaching of science through a range of new practical ideas and pupil experiments. This, coupled with an assessment regime that encouraged application of scientific ideas rather than simple recall of facts, was a revolution in child focused learning.
1969	First moon landing	Space Race that initiated so much STEM funding comes to a climax. Next decade sees education funding cut as rise in oil prices causes economic inflation across the West. Computers start to appear in schools. The computer on the Moon lander had less memory than a mobile phone had in 2013, and less processing power than a modern washing machine.
1980	Assessment of Performance Unit (APU)	Series of tests of 11, 13 and 15 year olds on their scientific understanding of topics such as electricity and the chemistry of metals – and their practical manipulation of apparatus to investigate their scientific thinking helped to inform changes to the curriculum. This led to a Secondary Science Curriculum Review (1980–1989).

(continued)

TABLE 1.1 (continued)

1980–1989	Children's Learning in Science Project (CLISP)	Directed by Ros Driver at Leeds University, CLISP was very influential in promoting a 'constructivist' view of learning in science. In a nutshell, pupils construct their understanding of the world around them and teachers should appreciate that:

- what is already in the learners mind matters;
- individuals construct their own meanings;
- the construction of meaning is a continuous and active process;
- learning may involve conceptual change;
- the construction of meaning does not always lead to belief;
- learners have final responsibility for their learning;
- some constructed meanings are shared.

1982	Singapore Math	In Singapore a new country-specific maths program with a focus on problem solving and on heuristic model drawing was introduced. Trends in International Mathematics and Science Study (TIMSS) in 2003 showed Singapore at the top of the world in 4th and 8th grade mathematics.
1983	Technical and Vocational Educational Initiative (TVEI)	TVEI was funded by the Department of Industry rather than the Department of Education and by the time of its eventual demise in 1997 almost £1 billion had been spent on it. There were two broad aims of TVEI; first to align the school curriculum more closely to the 'needs' of industry and commerce and rectify some of the knowledge, skill and particularly the 'attitude deficits' of school leavers. Through the funding, new topics like Microelectronics, Pneumatics and system approaches were introduced across science and technology.
1985	The Department of Education's 1985 'Science 5–16: A Statement of Policy'	'The essential characteristic of education in science is that it introduces pupils to the methods of science'. Also, the findings from the Assessment of Performance Unit (APU), about children's understanding of the concepts of science, led to the view that 'science should be an active process whereby learners construct and make sense of the world by constructing meaning for themselves'. The project followed on from the publication of 'Insight to Science' by Inner London Education Authority (ILEA) in 1978/1979. The 'Science in Process' materials were developed by a team of ILEA teachers and were trialled in schools.

(continued)

TABLE 1.1 (continued)

1988	The Great Educational Reform Act – Introduction of a prescribed National Curriculum in Science and Mathematics from ages 5–16 in England, Northern Ireland and Wales.	Core subjects were established for science and mathematics and technology (which included design & technology, and also information technology) was designated as a foundation subject. The difference between Core and Foundation subjects was never clear. The specification for science and maths was published in 1988 and technology in 1990.
1990–1999	The Science Processes and Concepts Exploration (SPACE) research project	The SPACE research was conducted at the University of Liverpool and King's College, London, with Wynne Harlen and Paul Black as joint directors. It investigated the science 'misconceptions' of primary (elementary) school pupils aged 5–11 in topics such as light, sound, forces and the Earth in space.
1990–1999	Nuffield Design & Technology Projects (Nuffield D&T)	Launched as technology became part of the national curriculum, Nuffield D&T was very influential. It recommended 'Resource Tasks' to address specific skills and knowledge to be used in larger 'Capability Tasks' and these were adopted into the revised curriculum structure (under different names).
1992	Publication of 'Technology in the National Curriculum – Getting It Right'	Commissioned by the Engineering Council and written by Alan Smithers and Pamela Robinson, this was a blistering critique of Technology in the National Curriculum – suggesting it was 'a mess' – led to a series of consultations, and changes to the attainment targets and programme of study, finally settling on design & technology and information technology as separate subjects.
2000	Young Foresight – an example of school – industry links for STEM	Young Foresight is a curriculum initiative giving pupils aged 14 the opportunity to work co-operatively to conceive products and services for the future in consultation with mentors from industry.
2002	Changes to the National Curriculum for England, Wales and Northern Ireland	Science and mathematics (and ICT in England, not Northern Ireland and Wales) still a compulsory subject to age 16. Design & technology, however, only compulsory to age 14 – but it must be offered as a subject in all schools.
2013	Publication of the revised National Curriculum for consultation	The revised National Curriculum will be statutory from September 2014, with the Programmes of Study for all subjects available to schools between September 2013 and Spring 2014.

What is the difference between science, technology/engineering?

> Technology is about creating artefacts and solving problems, while science is primarily about describing and explaining phenomena in the world.
>
> (Noström, 2011)

I think most would agree that young people seem to want answers to two types of questions: they want to know firstly *how* something works and then *why* something is the way it is. The first type of question seeks knowledge of the 'knowing how' variety – how a thing works, how it is used, how it is possible to improve the function of something or the way something is done, or how to create something which has a new purpose. This is technological knowledge. It is the practical knowledge of application, i.e., 'know-how'. The second type of question seeks knowledge of the 'knowing why' variety – why the world is the way it is, primarily to help us understand the rules that confirm generally accepted agreement about what we know, and also to help us rationalise the experience of our senses. This type of knowledge is called scientific knowledge. Now that we have set out starkly the two types of knowledge, let us look more carefully at their subtleties. The press cliché is that we live in a 'technological age'. Some would say that we should all have an understanding of the workings of different objects and vehicles we use in our daily lives, yet most of us lead perfectly satisfactory lives on the basis of knowing how rather than knowing why. One can know *how* to drive a car without having much idea of *why* the engine and all its control systems do the job they do. Similarly, a motor mechanic (or a TV engineer and numerous other people in the 'services' industry) can mend engines without any knowledge of gas laws, combustion principles, materials properties, or other scientific knowledge of the 'knowing why' variety. The level of 'knowing why' needs to be appropriately matched to the needs for the 'knowing how' for them together be 'useful knowledge' for creating appropriate products.

Technology before science?

The subjects science and mathematics have been in the school curriculum for a long time, yet the subject of technology is a relative newcomer and engineering is rarely taught as a separate subject at secondary (High) school level. In many countries technology fights for survival as curriculum designers have perhaps tended to cling to the belief that science education provides a more appropriate preparation for pupils intending to follow careers in industry and that without a thorough understanding of scientific principles there can be little progress in the various fields of application. Engineering too has had a place in secondary schools but again it has to fight for a place in an increasingly 'academically' defined curriculum as it has been associated with vocational preparation. The role of the 'E' in STEM will be considered fully in Chapter 7.

The assumption that science knowledge always precedes technology knowledge can be challenged through some wide ranging examples. For example, how to refine copper has been known since ancient times, millennia before the concepts of oxidation and reduction were understood. Around 1795, the Paris confectioner, Appert, devised a method of preserving food by heating it (to kill bacteria) and sealing it in a container without delay. The idea caught on quickly, and a cannery using 'tins' was already functioning in Bermondsey in 1814 when Louis Pasteur proposed a 'Theory of Bacterial Action'. England became the 'steam workshop' of the world in the eighteenth century following the invention of the first commercial steam engine by Thomas Savery and Thomas Newcomen at the end of the seventeenth century. Their knowledge of how to design steam engines spread as 'know how' across Europe and to North America. Yet the concept that heat was a form of energy able to do work came later. Later still Sadi Carnot, an officer in the French Army, became preoccupied with the concept of heat engines but it was years before his findings influenced steam engine design. The science of thermodynamics followed from the intellectual challenge to understand the operation of better steam engines. The principal point is that technology is more than the application of fully understood scientific knowledge; a point acknowledge by the economist Nathan Rosenburg:

> It is knowledge of techniques, methods, and designs that work, and that work in certain ways and with certain consequences, even when we cannot explain exactly why. It is […] a form of knowledge which has generated a certain rate of economic progress for thousands of years. Indeed, if the human race had been confined to technologies that were understood in a scientific sense, it would have passed from the scene long ago.
>
> (Rosenburg, 1982, p. 143)

Technologists today use a host of ideas and 'rules-of-thumb' that are helpful but not scientifically sound. Examples include the idea of a centrifugal force, heat flow (like a fluid) and the notion that a vacuum 'sucks'. For example, heat flow in science is often conceptualised using the kinetic theory of molecular motion. This is of limited value in technology where the idea of heat flow, related to conductivity or even 'U values' and temperature difference, is usually much more useful in solving problems in practical situations. In order to use a particular idea for practical action, it is sometimes the case that a full scientific explanation is unnecessary and too abstract to be useful:

> [Reconstruction of knowledge] involves creating or inventing new 'concepts' which are more appropriate than the scientific ones to the practical task being worked upon. … Science frequently advances by the simplification of complex real-life situations; its beams in elementary physics are perfectly rigid; its levers rarely bend; balls rolling down inclined planes are truly spherical and unhampered

by air resistance and friction. Decontextualisation, the separation of general knowledge from particular experience, is one of its most successful strategies. Solving technological problems necessitates building back into the situation all the complications of 'real life', reversing the process of reductionism by recontextualising knowledge. What results may be applicable in a particular context or set of circumstances only.

(Layton, 1993, p. 59)

In technology, if the knowledge is 'useful' then it continues to be exploited until it is no longer of use. In science, a concept that is not 'correct' in that it does not match experimental results or related theory is discarded. However, the rejection of certain established scientific ideas such as phlogiston and the caloric theory of heat; and acceptance of energy as quanta took many years!

It is obviously true that new technologies have arisen from scientific discoveries. Microelectronics is founded on the 'blue skies' fundamental science of semiconductors and similar fundamental research has led to many developments, including, for example:

- improved knowledge of the intrinsic properties of materials such as lightweight alloys, carbon fibres and plastics;
- the development of new types of superconductor, the laser and another electronic devices;
- high yielding, disease-resistant crops through an improved understanding of the scientific basis of genetics.

There is a link between scientific discoveries and new or improved technologies and technology *can* stimulate new directions for science too. Space research is an example of this. Technological developments, for example rockets that can launch the Hubble Space Telescope and the Curiosity Mars Rover – extraordinary technological achievements in their own right – can promote new challenges for science by revealing new and unexpected features of the universe.

Common ground between science and technology learning?

As we have seen, science does not need to precede technology but technology can be stimulated by the findings of science. Indeed, the above extracts from government science and technology committees around the world illustrate that in response to today's economic demands there are policy pressures to structure scientific research with the specific purpose of stimulating technology, and hence a nation's wealth. Of course, the 'laws of nature' as formulated by science set particular constraints within which all technological activity has to take place. For example, the Second Law of Thermodynamics suggests that the building of a perpetual motion machine is futile despite inventors' persistent efforts to 'break' the Law! Other constraints may include economic, human skill and imagination, cultural influences, resource availability and so on. Furthermore, scientific discoveries can suggest new products such as lasers and nuclear magnetic resonance imaging in medicine. Conversely, as illustrated above, technology does make a contribution to science in several ways. Examples include providing the stimulus for science to explain why things work in the way they do. The contribution of technology is especially evident in the way scientific concepts are deployed in technological activities.

It is useful to make a distinction between concepts which are directly related to 'knowing how' (i.e., technological concepts as defined above) and concepts related to 'knowing why' (i.e., scientific concepts). It is very difficult to make hard and fast distinctions between these two types of concepts but consider the following examples. An electron is a concept, a fundamental atomic particle; science is able to describe its mass, charge and other properties. In these terms the concept of an electron has no obvious practical application and is an example of a 'knowing why' concept. On the other hand, a light switch is also a technological concept because it has been designed for the particular purpose of switching on and off a flow of electrons. It is a 'knowing how' concept.

To see how the concepts are deployed in teaching science and technology, take the concept of *insulation*, (a technological concept) which has relevance to understanding *conduction* (a scientific concept) of electricity and of heat. In the context of a science lesson, a teacher might involve children in exploring *electrical conduction* through simple experiments, for example, by using an ohmmeter to compare the resistance of a variety of materials or using a simple circuit and noting the effect on the brightness of a lamp when different materials are placed in series with the lamp. In a study of *heat conduction* pupils might be encouraged to plot temperature/time graphs that compare the rate of cooling of a beaker of hot water wrapped with different materials. Very often such a science activity would be placed within an 'everyday' context (see Figure 1.1). The aim, in a scientific sense, is to find out the property of the material. This would lead on to the idea that if there is a lot of trapped air, then that material is a good insulator as it stops conduction (as gases are poor conductors). However, as Patricia Murphy notes, some pupils (particularly girls) are distracted by this realistic 'technological' context. The important first step in this science lesson is to strip away the context to set up a comparison experiment between beakers lagged with different materials; yet some pupils will wish to stick with the real-life problem presented and instead make a little 'jacket'. After all, that is what was asked for! And to do this, they use the material that would best make a mountaineer's jacket, not some abstract experimental method. Rather than making the science lesson 'real', the context has provided a serious distraction. The science lesson has different learning objectives from a textile technology lesson. Typically the boys see that distinction and will 'play' the school lesson game, but often the girls do not.

This is an example how knowledge that is important for a science lesson is not the totality of what is useful for a technology lesson. In technology such an

Imagine you are stranded on a mountainside in cold, dry, windy weather. You can choose a jacket made from one of the fabrics in front of you.

This is what you have to find out:

> Which fabric would keep you warmer?

You can use any of the things in front of you. Choose whatever you need to answer the question.
You can use:

> a can instead of a person
> put water inside to make it more life-like
> make it a 'jacket' from the fabric
> use a hairdryer to make an imitation on wind (without the heater switched on, of course!)

Make a clear record of your results so that other people can understand exactly why you have decided which fabric would be best.

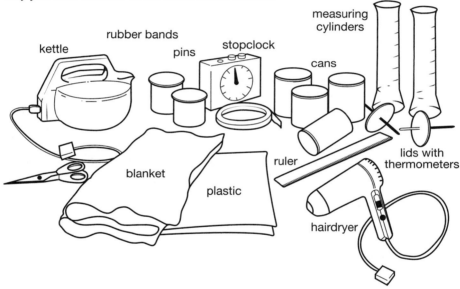

FIGURE 1.1 Investigating the 'best' materials for a mountaineer's jacket.

understanding of material properties would be an important factor to consider, but it would not be the only criterion. In addition, the pupils would need to consider non-scientific factors such as cost and availability, water resistance and toxicity, strength and flame-proofness, colour and density of the insulating materials that might be used. So, whereas scientific knowledge of heat conduction would contribute to the design process, a range of other factors could also influence the choice of insulating material such as its appropriateness to a given cultural context. Further, suppose scientific experiments in a country with few 'advanced' material resources show that the stripped and powdered bark of a local tree, or the cotton-like seed heads of a local plant would make a suitable low-cost heat insulating material. Why then should the technologists in that country use a hard-to-obtain and costly imported insulating material when the collection and preparation of this indigenous material also provides local employment? These wider considerations that are grounded in 'know-how' and the value systems of the people using the technology are an important aspect of technological design activities.

In summary, science often has a contribution to make when it comes to enhancing design & technology projects. However, teachers need to be clear about what that contribution may be, and teach it to pupils. It is also important to realise that in designing and making, scientific understanding is but one contributory factor among many competing concerns. Although scientific ideas *can* enhance projects, it is possible, in fact usual, for a pupil to conduct complex technological activity without first exploring and understanding all aspects of the science involved.

The contribution of 'M' in STEM?

So far, this chapter on 'What is STEM?' has focused on the way each of the 'STE' subjects interact one with another. As we have discussed already, this is particularly important as so many people talk about 'science-and-technology' as if it was one area of knowledge, or at least technology and engineering as always a user of science – the 'appliance of science' view. But what about the 'appliance of mathematics'?

In my early secondary school years (the 1960s!), I studied 'new math' which included such topics as the use of numbers systems other than 10, probability and statistics, set theory and manipulation of matrices. In many ways it was learning mathematics for the love of mathematics. It was part of the developments in the learning of mathematics that was gaining ground around the 'Anglo-Saxon' world, particularly the USA. It was argued that in traditional mathematics, numbers and equations were difficult and many lacked the necessary curiosity that is at the heart of maths, so they were replaced with more up-to-date elements that could be understood by all. So what was 'new' – and could you learn the 'new' without the basics of the 'old'? When challenged about why a topic such as set theory was important for all children to understand the argument was that it taught logic and, for example, Venn diagrams were the graphic representation of such logical thought. But some of the 'old maths', such as geometry, was excluded in the new curriculum and with it the logical build up from simple axioms that had served young mathematicians for thousands of years.

The criticism of the 'new math' approach was mainly two-fold. First, it was suggested that there was little coherence in the topics that were covered – it was a little bit of this and a little bit of that – which led to a certain learning of the abstract ideas by rote rather than gaining a full grasp of the underlying principles. Second, many teachers were working at the limits of their own understanding and some of the 'new math' was just that – *new* – and they struggled to understand it themselves. As is usual in many aspects of curriculum reform, there is a pendulum effect and the swing away from the old to the new has to happen for the curriculum to settle to a more middle line. However, we must first recognise that mathematics is a wonderful domain of learning in its own right and 'new math' brought that to prominence in school mathematics.

It hardly needs saying that an elegant solution to a problem or the construction of curves and geometrical shapes are things of beauty, both metaphorical and physical. But as we shall explore much more in later chapters, using mathematics enhances understanding in science and facilitates designing and making in technology and engineering. In Australia a paper produced by Engineers Australia said there is:

> need for the curriculum to encourage students to develop positive attitudes to mathematics and mathematical learning.
>
> (Engineers Australia, 2009, p.4)

I confess that at the time I was learning 'new math' I wondered 'what is the point of all this?' and was much happier when I studied applied mathematics in the upper school. However the 'new math' topics eventually did prove very useful. For example, in programming computers I have used both binary and hexadecimal numbering systems, I have applied statistics to explain molecular movement in gases, and I used matrices to help understand (some of!) Dirac's formulation of Quantum Mechanics. What seemed remote and abstract when I learnt it at the age of 14 was later practically useful.

This balance between an appreciation of the exploration of mathematics as a subject of intrinsic value and its usefulness as a tool to tackle problems and represent data in science, technology and engineering (and indeed across all subject domains) is central to any consideration of the learning of the subject. There are many examples where mathematics serves, in a utilitarian way, STE subjects. I have brainstormed a few here:

- The mathematics of error-correcting codes is applied to CD players, ATM machines, and cleaning up pictures from space probes such as Curiosity and Voyager II.
- Statistics are essential in medicine, for analysing data on epidemiology and on the safety of new drugs.
- Maths and logic is at the heart of computer software design.
- The physical sciences (chemistry, physics, oceanography, astronomy) require mathematics for the development of their theories.
- In biological and ecological systems, mathematics is used when studying the laws of population change, for example, to understand what might happen if badgers are culled in an attempt to reduce bovine tuberculosis.

At the school level, descriptions of equations of motion related to laws of motion can be algebraic or graphical. The use of performance characteristic graphs in technology can be used to make decisions – which electric motor and what batteries are best for my purpose? Simple calculations on strength and stiffness of component parts – will it break, how much will it bend/stretch if it is only this thick? Is not a set of common principles regarding introducing equations and graphs across the school STEM subjects, linked to these clear practical uses inside and outside school more likely to lead to 'a positive attitude to mathematics'?

What else do the STEM subjects contribute?

Affective knowledge and values

The STEM subjects cannot be divorced from other dimensions of human thinking and behaviour since the beliefs and values of individuals and communities are influenced by, and exert pressure on both science and technology themselves. In technological activities it is just as important to involve pupils in making value judgements about the *human*, or rather *humane*, dimensions of technology as it is to focus solely on technical details about the functioning of the technological product. In science, experiments involving animals and humans have ethical dimensions that are paramount. Given that the *purpose* of technology is to respond to certain sorts of need, pupils should be expected to find answers to questions such as:

- Whose needs are to be met?
- Who has identified the needs?
- Are proposals for a particular technological development acceptable to the individuals and communities who are to use or be influenced by the development?

In science, despite an assumption that answers can only be 'right or wrong', there is also a strong values dimension, especially in the design of experiments that affect living creatures or have an impact on the environment. Questions that should be asked include:

- How should a particular experiment be constructed – and what does it tell us about 'the nature of science'?
- What is the impact of the experiment? How does it affect people, animals and the environment generally?
- How are the scientific ideas communicated to others?

And, in mathematics, how statistics are gathered manipulated and displayed have a moral dimension too. The 'lies, damn lies and statistics' epithet has a grain of truth when newspaper articles include references to percentage falls and increases without a clear reference to the value of a base figure or graphs are shown not starting from zero or with misleading scale divisions. The very nature of mathematics as a subject domain of clarity and truth with 'just one answer' means one should be on guard to how data are analysed and presented.

Decisions about various scientific and technological *processes* are affected by a range of criteria, each of which depends on different kinds of values. For example, materials used may be in short supply or come from environmentally sensitive regions of the globe; new construction projects may disturb or destroy wildlife and so on. Evaluation of the *products* of technological activities is subject to decisions about fitness for purpose, the calculation of cost effectiveness, possible health hazards and so on. People's values affect every stage of the technological process from decisions taken about whether to embark on a particular innovation, through the process of development, to the acceptability of the subsequent product. The clarification of values is a responsibility of all those engaged in scientific and technological activities and it has a central role to play in the affective dimension of a pupil's education.

The different *social* meanings attached to science and technology are nowhere more evident than in the use of the terms like 'big science', 'high-tech' and 'intermediate technology'. The former is used to describe large-scale, capital-intensive projects such as atom-smashing machines or technologies like microelectronics which use a highly skilled workforce; and the latter is used to describe small-scale, labour-intensive technologies advocated for small communities that capitalise on local skills and resources which are at the community's disposal. It is of course quite possible that relatively high-technology electronics may be appropriate in small communities (e.g., those in remote areas) but this leads to issues about control of technology and economic power. These influences make the projects and applications considered in science and in design & technology rich in educational terms. The interpretation of what is needed, how it is to be done, how outcomes are measured, calculated and analysed and who is to benefit should be made explicit and debated in order to question the value judgements that underlie any assumptions about a course of action.

Problem solving

As you can see from the STEM milestones (see Table 1.1), problem solving is a key activity in all STEM subjects. 'Doing problems' is what many think of when they recall mathematics lessons. However, a worksheet that requires a pupil to practice a particular algorithm repeatedly is better described as mathematical exercises. As Francisco and Maher (2005) put it:

> Our perspective of problem solving recognizes the power of children's construction of their own personal knowledge under research conditions that emphasise minimal interventions in the students' mathematical activity and an invitation to students to explore patterns, make conjectures, test hypotheses, reflect on extensions and applications of learnt concepts, explain, and justify their reasoning and work collaboratively. Such a view regards mathematical learning and reasoning as integral parts of the process of problem solving.
>
> (Francisco and Maher, 2005)

Scott Chamberlin worked with a number of mathematics educators to establish the processes that children engaged in when problem solving in mathematics. The following were agreed as being present in true maths problem solving. Pupils:

- engage in cognition (they learn from the process);
- seek a solution to a mathematical situation for which they have no immediately accessible/obvious process or method;
- communicate ideas to peers;
- engage in iterative cycles;
- create a written record of their thinking;
- 'mathematise' a situation to solve it (it requires more than common sense);
- create assumptions and consider those assumptions in relation to the final solution;
- revise current knowledge to solve a problem;
- create new techniques to solve a problem;
- create mathematical models;
- define a mathematical goal or situation;
- seek a goal.

And the characteristics of a mathematics problem were agreed as follows:

- have realistic contexts;
- can be solved with more than one tool;
- can be solved with more than one approach;
- can be used to assess level of understanding;
- require the implementation of multiple algorithms for a successful solution;
- DO NOT lend themselves to automatic responses;
- promote flexibility in thinking;
- may be purely contrived mathematical problems;
- can be puzzles;
- can be games of logic.

Process has been a key part of the science curriculum too for many years and the government policy document 'Science 5–13' pre-dated any prescribed curriculum. It did not merely define what should be taught in terms of *content* such as electricity or plants, rather it emphasised the importance of a *process* approach. Science curriculum innovation in the middle to late 1980s saw a large number of new courses such as 'Warwick Process Science' and 'Science in Process' for secondary schools which focused not on science concepts but rather on processes such as observation, interpretation and classification. This mood was picked up in the developing primary science curriculum too. In the 1980s, the teaching profession generally welcomed a move away from what was considered as often merely the memorising of poorly understood facts, to a curriculum that might be more accessible to all pupils and which emphasised problem-solving approaches and skills applicable to other areas of life both in and outside school. The attention to 'doing' science – raising questions that could be answered by investigation – became the cornerstone of the developing investigation-driven, problem-solving approach especially for primary science. For example, the question 'What is the best carrier bag?' would be turned into an investigable question such as 'Which carrier bag carries the greatest weight?' To answer such a question, so-called 'dependent and independent' variables were identified. At the time, primary teachers were very concerned about the introduction of science into their day-to-day work, and the rhetoric from those advocating that science should indeed be part of the primary curriculum was that the teachers could 'learn with the pupils' as only the *process* was important, not the science facts or concepts that the teacher knew or did not know. Now, those intending to become primary teachers are required to hold a basic qualification in science as well as maths and English as a pre-requisite for their teacher-training course. Process was all-important and science content relegated as a side issue. In an almost content-free science curriculum 'good' pedagogy was that which promoted a questioning attitude amongst pupils and the means of answering such questions. What was important was knowing how to conduct practical work, in particular 'fair tests' to find things out. Doing of the practical work was most important, not getting the 'right' answer as such: the process is more important than the answer.

In time, the pendulum swing from content to process came into a more central balanced position. Murphy and Scanlon (1994) summarised it as follows:

> there emerged a consensus that scientific inquiry was not about following a set of rules or a hierarchy of processes but 'the practice of a craft – in deciding what to observe, in selecting which observations to pay attention to, in interpreting and discussing inferences and in drawing conclusions from and in drawing conclusions from experimental data' (from Millar, in Woolnough 1990). There was also considerable agreement evident in the various published discussions about the nature of scientific observation.
>
> (Murphy and Scanlon, 1994, p. 105)

The 1980s not only saw the introduction of primary science but a new emphasis in the initial and in-service education of teachers of a view of learning that recognised that pupils construct meaning by interacting with the environment around them. Rather than being 'empty vessels' into which new knowledge and understanding could be poured, teachers came to recognise that, for a fuller understanding, pupils themselves had to make sense of the world around them by seeing how their new experiences, along with the views of others, matched their own preconceived ideas and notions. However, teachers failed to take sufficient notice of what was involved when pupils attempted to construct new understandings and integrate these with their existing knowledge of the world. Ros Driver pointed out some problems with 'discovery' pedagogy for science:

> Discovery methods in science teaching put pupils in the role of investigator, giving them the opportunities to perform experiments and test ideas for themselves. What actually happens in classrooms when this approach is used? Although, of course, pupils' ideas are less sophisticated than those of practising scientists, some interesting parallels can be drawn. The work of Thomas Kuhn indicates that, once a scientific theory or paradigm becomes established, scientists as a community are slow to change their thinking. Pupils, like scientists, view the world through the spectacles of their own preconceptions, and many have difficulty in making the journey from their own intuitions to the ideas presented in science lessons.
>
> (Driver, 1983, p. ii)

A focus on the investigative problem-solving process rather than content might have been considered 'good practice' as suggested above, but questions for investigation eventually have to link to some real content when they are answered. A primary science question such as 'Can you make your plant grow sideways?' or 'What happens if you pinch the leaves off a young growing plant?' might be more concerned with the practical activity itself but they lead, for that particular group of pupils, to some understanding of tropism in plants. Before a national curriculum, secondary schools could not easily cope with the variety of experiences and so chose to ignore the fact that pupils might have already had some scientific experience in the primary school. Secondary school science teachers would simply 'start again'. Alternatively, secondary teachers would complain that primary teachers had stolen the 'best bits' of the theatre of lower secondary science such as the 'collapsing can' demonstration of air pressure, thereby 'spoiling' some of the excitement and spectacle of lower secondary science lessons. Some 30 years after the publication of 'Science 5–13', in-service work with secondary teachers still tries to tackle the lack of progress by pupils in the first few years of secondary school caused by a failure to fully recognise the now quite extensive and structured science understanding gained by pupils in the primary school.

Indeed, discussions that consider science and technology as vehicles for the teaching of problem solving sometimes become emotionally charged. Over the years, those proposing different technology curricula, the emphasis of processes in science and the dominance of STEM, in general, have used this argument as a principal way of advocating that STEM should have an enhanced status in the school curriculum, because a general ability to solve problems is central to satisfying human needs. Researchers suggest that learning is heavily influenced by the context in which it occurs. In particular, Professor Bob McCormick from The Open University suggests that this is to be expected if one takes a sociocultural view of learning, where knowledge is the result of the social interactions in which it occurs and is inseparable from them.

It is not always easy for pupils to transfer their abilities in a particular activity from one learning 'domain' to another. Technology teachers have assumed that if pupils are taught to investigate the factors influencing the design decisions for making one product, for example, a moisture sensor, then they will be able to transfer those techniques to consider the different design decisions for, say, developing a food product that meets certain dietary requirements. The evidence is that pupils do not easily transfer their understanding across these different contexts and require considerable support from their teacher to help them do so. Also, pupils may know what they want to do but not be able to realise their solution because they do not have the required knowledge or skills. More critically, when planning their work pupils may not consider certain approaches to a problem because they are ignorant of the existence of specific equipment or a particular technique which might help them. For these pupils 'problem solving' is doing little more than applying common sense.

There is a close association in a particular context between the conceptual knowledge associated with the particular problem and an understanding of what action needs to be done to tackle that problem (procedural knowledge). People think within the context in which they find themselves – 'situated-cognition' and when pupils are presented with problems in unfamiliar contexts they tend to use 'common sense' intuitive understanding as opposed to science concepts to tackle them.

So what is the best approach when teaching technology and engineering? Should pupils learn knowledge and skills in isolation that might prove useful later but for which they perceive little immediate value? Should pupils learn skills 'as needed' within projects when they appreciate the usefulness of what they are learning but without a coherent structure and without realising that there *was* something new that they should know, to transfer to future work? The best approach is probably to steer a middle line. A carefully planned selection of shorter projects or focused tasks emphasises particular skills and techniques, together with the longer, more open task which allows pupils to develop their capability by drawing on their accumulated experiences.

Systems thinking – black boxes

As has been emphasised a number of times, it is necessary for teachers to think carefully about the purpose of teaching a particular scientific concept for use in technology lessons and this will be considered in detail in Chapters 3 and 4. 'Systems thinking' is important in both biology and technology. Some examples of organs working together to perform a certain task include the digestive system, blood circulation system and nervous system. Such human systems are, of course present in other animals but in all cases they can be considered as a functional block that does a particular job – but with component parts. For the circulation system, components are the heart, blood and blood vessels, for the nervous system the brain, spinal cord and peripheral nerves. The approach to First Aid is also systemic, as is triage, the process of determining the priority of patients' treatments based on the severity of their condition, dealing with breathing and bleeding problems before taking action on broken bones. The design and use of systems is an example of the value of using 'know-how' rather than 'know-why' and these can be extended to activities in the classroom.

Let's take the example of electronic systems in technology. In technological activities pupils are expected to have a clear idea of what they want the electronics systems to do; it is a goal-oriented approach. Rather than focusing on any scientific understanding of the way in which the devices and circuits work, the emphasis is on the functional aspects of the electronic devices and circuits that the pupils are to use – considering each unit as a functional block. Pupils should be expected to ask questions such as:

- What do I want my electronics system to do?
- What operating conditions, e.g., power supply requirements, does it need to work?
- Will the device stand up to rigours of use in its intended environment?
- How much will it cost to make and run?
- What characteristics of this device are better for this design than other similar devices?
- Will it be safe and easy to use?
- Can the components needed be easily obtained?
- Will it be acceptable, culturally and economically, to the people in the community in which it is to be used?

To a technologist, meeting these functional and contextual criteria is as important, if not more important a consideration as knowing why the electronic devices used work in the way they do. The emphasis on *function* and *context* rather than *theory* and *fundamentals* may be misleading and seeming to lack opportunities for rigorous thought. However, the design and assembly of circuits and systems for specific purposes requires knowledge and understanding at the operational level. These operating precepts are just as demanding intellectually as the operating aetiology used by science to explain concepts such as electrical conductivity and potential. An example or two will make these points clearer.

An *electronics system* can be represented by three linked building blocks.

It is an assembly of functional electronic *building blocks* that are connected together to achieve a *particular purpose*, e.g., sounding an alarm when smoke is in the air. Examples of *input* building blocks include switches, e.g., mechanical and semiconductor types, microphones and light-dependent resistors. *Processor* building blocks include amplifiers, comparators, oscillators and counters. *Output* building blocks include light-emitting diodes, seven segment displays and loudspeakers and meters. Thus the *input* building block of a smoke detector would be a smoke sensor.

Its *processor* building block might comprise a comparator to switch on an audio frequency oscillator when the smoke level detected by the sensor has reached a pre-set danger point followed, perhaps, by an amplifier. The detector's *output* building block would be a small loudspeaker or piezoelectric device to generate an audio frequency sound when signals are received from the oscillator. Pupils quickly learn to associate a circuit board with a particular 'job'. For example, a 14-year-old pupil would easily solve the problem of making a 'rain alarm' by linking a moisture detector (*input*) to a buzzer (*output*) by using a transistor switch (*process*).

Such 'black boxes' can also be used to make more complex devices and to explain more complex systems too, such as the biological examples considered above. Design decisions are based on how the product is to be used and pupils are constrained by their specification criteria, not by a lack of understanding of why the circuit functions. Detailed knowledge at the component level is unnecessary. Let's assume that a pupil is going to design and make an anti-theft warning device to clip onto a bicycle that will produce an ear-splitting sound if the bicycle is about to be stolen, i.e., it is a portable device to be used by an individual. First and foremost, there needs to be a clear specification of what the system will do. Second, a consideration of the environment it will be used in, not just the physical environment (e.g., wet, dusty, hot, cold or dry) but the human environment too. So, the following questions need to be asked:

- Who will use it?
- What will it look like? Shape, colour, size and so on.
- How will it be used? For example, will it be fixed to the wheels, handlebars or spokes?
- How much will it to cost to make and to sell?
- Does the user need to have any technical skills to use it?

Only after these criteria are established through appropriate research is it possible for the pupil to select the functional building blocks that will enable a prototype system to be made which meets the criteria. There are several concepts which arise in this analysis of need. For example, in terms of *energy* there is a consideration of the power supply requirements. In terms of the *process*, a pupil will need to consider how the device can control the sound long enough and loud enough to alert attention. Will it have an automatic cut-out? What operating principle of the sensor which first detects the movement of the bicycle will be used? In terms of *materials*, cost, ruggedness, waterproofness and design of the casing for the unit and similar considerations for the components need to be tackled.

When it comes to the *manufacture* of the anti-theft bicycle alarm, however, the technical factors to be considered are more than simply selecting appropriate input, process and output devices, plugging them together and expecting the system to work. What is most often missed in designing electronic systems is the need to consider the requirements that enable each building block to respond to the signal it receives and send an appropriate signal to the building block that follows it. The concept being highlighted here is called *matching*. This is more complex, but at a basic level, pupils are able to use computer software that takes matching into account and will give the design for a printed circuit board combining the contributory functional blocks. So considering electronic devices in terms of input, process, and output blocks can simplify the learning of electronics. A technologist does not need to know about the detailed working of an integrated circuit, or even a transistor in terms of the physics involved, just how to *use* the circuit in a range of circumstances.

Before leaving systems thinking in technology, it is also worth thinking about using systems in a wider context and this often involves a consideration about where to put the 'system boundary'. A few years ago, I came across an interesting examination entry by a 16-year-old pupil which I later discussed with his teacher. The pupil had designed and made a 'panic alarm' in case he was attacked late at night. In a technical sense it was very well done, with proper consideration of the alarm's weight, power supply, loudness, ease of action, and so on. If anyone had attacked the pupil, everyone would know about it. I asked his teacher whether the pupil had considered the issue of *why* such an alarm was needed in his neighbourhood. The teacher looked puzzled by the question as he obviously thought it irrelevant; (in terms of the wider values exhibited by those in the pupil's locality) why such a panic alarm was needed was not part of the examination-marking scheme. However, I wondered if drawing the system boundary narrowly around the alarm itself was the best solution to the problem he faced? By not considering *why* he was afraid at night due to few late-night buses or limited and poor street lighting, his solution was, in some senses restricted. Maybe the 16-year-old pupil could not do much himself about the wider context of supplying free buses or better street lighting, for example. However, the narrow system boundary around the well-crafted and technically sound panic alarm provided only a partial solution to the pupil's problem and excluded any consideration of alternative approaches to crime reduction. A wider system view could consider not just burglar and panic alarms looking at the result of crime, but also engage with the possibility of changing the behaviour of the thieves – soft system thinking as well as hard system thinking.

Conclusion

STEM subjects have a number of common threads, such as problem solving, discovery approaches and direct applicability to everyday life. As we will see in later chapters, teachers can benefit their pupils if they 'look sideways' to take advantage of teaching and learning in related STEM subjects. But there are clear differences too. If technology is merely seen as applied science, then technology educators miss the point about the subject for which they are responsible. Technology is founded in human need to change the environment, science in understanding the whys and wherefores of the world around and mathematics is a service to both and an exciting and intriguing aspect of human endeavour in its own right. The 'know-*why*' of science is a fundamentally different goal from the 'know-*how*' of technology. Science and mathematics knowledge and understanding will often contribute to project work in schools, but it is necessary to keep in mind the sometimes-limited extent of such knowledge which is actually required. The contribution of science needs to be set against the other dominant factors such as *sustainability, aesthetics* and *appropriateness*. As Plant notes:

> It is also important to recognise the different STEM subjects have a part to play in stimulating technological activities. First, by revealing new frontiers to spur technological inventiveness. Second, by using the vocabulary of science for providing convincing explanations of the behaviour of technological devices. Third, in the provision of tools to develop convincing explanations of the behaviour of technological devices. Lastly, in the provision of resources for the constraints on technological processes.
>
> (Plant, 1994, p. 29)

History has shown that no one subject is more important than any other in STEM, sometimes science follows technology and mathematics is often key to help improve our understanding of both. The outcomes of STEM subjects are steeped in the culture and social values of the society that uses them. It is these often neglected value-laden aspects of teaching and learning across all STEM subjects that highlights the distinctive role for engineering and technology in enhancing human behaviour.

Background reading and references

Archer, L. B. (1973) *The Need for Design Education*. Paper presented to DES conference N850, Horncastle. Mimeo. London: Royal College of Art.

Australian Government (2013) Australian Department of Industry, Innovation, Climate Change, Science, Research and Tertiary Education. Available at: www.innovation.gov. au/pages/default.aspx (accessed 30 June 2013).

Barak, M. (2007) 'Problem-solving in Technology Education: The Role of Strategies, Schemes & Heuristics'. In D. Barlex (ed.) *Design and Technology for the Next Generation* (pp. 154–69). Whitchurch, UK: Cliffe & Company.

Bronowski, J. (1973) *The Ascent of Man*. London: BBC Publications.

Chamberlin, S. A. (2008) 'What is Problem Solving in the Mathematics Classroom?', *Philosophy of Mathematics Education Journal, 23*, 1–25.

Driver, R. (1983) *The Pupil as Scientist?* New York: Taylor & Francis.

Eggleston, J. (1992) *Teaching Design and Technology*. Buckingham, UK: Open University Press.

Engineers Australia (2009) *Response – National Science and Mathematics Curriculum Framing Papers*. Barton ACT: Engineers Australia.

Francisco, J. F. and Maher, C. A. (2005) 'Conditions for Promoting Reasoning in Problem Solving: Insights from a Longitudinal Study', *Journal of Mathematical Behavior, 24*, 361–72.

Hennessy, S. and McCormick, R. (2002) 'The General Problem-solving Process in Technology Education. Myth or Reality'. In G. Owen-Jackson (ed.) *Teaching Design and Technology in Secondary Schools* (pp. 109–23). London: Routledge/Falmer.

House of Commons (2013) Science and Technology Commons Select Committee. Available at: www.parliament.uk/science/ (accessed 30 June 2013).

Lave, J. (1988) *Cognition in Practice*. Cambridge, MA: Cambridge University Press.

Layton, D. (1993) *Technology's Challenge to Science Education*. Buckinghamshire: Open University Press.

Mawson, B. (2003) 'Beyond "The Design Process": An Alternative Pedagogy for Technology Education'. *Intentional Journal of Technology & Design Education*, 13(2), 117–28.

McCormick, R. (2006). 'Technology and Knowledge'. In J. Dakers (ed.) *Defining Technological Literacy* (pp. 31–47). New York: Palgrave.

Murphy, P. (2007) 'Gender & Pedagogy'. In D. Barlex (ed.) *Design and Technology for the Next Generation* (pp. 236–61). Whitchurch, UK: Cliffe & Company.

Murphy, P. and Scanlon, E. (1994) 'Perceptions of Process and Content in the Science Curriculum'. In J. Bourne (ed.) *Thinking Through Primary Practice*. London: Routledge.

Nostrõm, P. (2011) '"Engineers" Non-scientific Models in Technology Education', *Intentional Journal of Technology & Design Education*, (On-Line First) DOI 10.1007/s10798-011-9184-2.

Plant, M. (1994) *How Is Science Useful to Technology?* Course Booklet for E886. Milton Keynes, UK: The Open University.

Roosevelt, F. D. (1944) Personal letter in response to 'A Report to the President by Vannevar Bush', Director of the Office of Scientific Research and Development. Available at: www.nsf.gov/about/history/nsf50/vbush1945_roosevelt_letter.jsp (accessed 21 November 2013).

Rosenberg, N. (1982) *Inside the Black Box: Technology and Economics*. Cambridge: Cambridge University Press.

Schumacher, E. E. (1973) *Small is Beautiful*. New York: Harper and Row.

US Office of Science and Technology (2013) Available at: www.whitehouse.gov/administration/eop/ostp/about (accessed 30 June 2013).

White House (2013) *The 2013 State of the Union*. Available at: www.whitehouse.gov/state-of-the-union-2013 (accessed 28 February 2013).

2

A curriculum for STEM – 'looking sideways'

Introduction

As long ago as 1996 Karen Zuga said 'Communities of technology and science educators have been passing as two ships pass silently in the night without speaking to each other about their relationships' (Zuga, 1996). As we have already discussed in Chapter 1, most people would agree that there is a significant and symbiotic relationship between Science, Technology, Engineering and Mathematics but how is it possible for us to best exploit that relationship in our teaching for the benefit of pupils?

There has never been a better time to consider new ways of constructing a relevant curriculum and the associated assessment regime. Around the world, particularly in developing countries, it is recognised that building enough schools of the right quality for the vast numbers of young people is a necessary first step, but if the curriculum offered is considered irrelevant by them or their parents, then school attendance will be patchy and drop-out rates will be huge. In resource-rich countries, schools are pressed for ever-improved outcomes, and there is a realisation that a tightly regulated academic curriculum does not serve the needs of all pupils and the over-prescription of what 'should' be taught can stifle creativity in teaching. Those who desire to make teachers 'accountable' for their classroom work and to improve standards now believe that giving schools more freedom will encourage new ways of levering improvement rather than simply imposing greater and greater external control by government.

In Scandinavia as in the UK (particularly England) the detail of national curriculum documents has diminished over the years, and in England in 2013 although what *is* prescribed is becoming more specific, almost half of state schools are designated Academies or Free Schools and so it is now possible for them to create their own curricula rather than adopting the one prescribed by government. Some have been shocked by this new lack of external regulation on what is taught, and yet it has only been since 1988 that such a national 'one-size-fits-all' view of what should be taught in schools, articulated as a set of different subjects each with their own individual specification of what pupils should attain, has been set out.

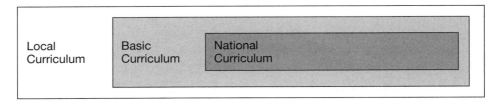

FIGURE 2.1 The school curriculum.

In many countries, then, there is a developing view that any state specification of the curriculum should be restricted, both in the number of subjects that are required to be taught and in the extent of prescription of those subjects.

Figure 2.1 sets out a model that many countries adopt either explicitly through local or national legislation, or implicitly in the way that teachers are provided with guide books and pupils are provided with resources such as a national textbook. First, there is a 'national curriculum', which is specified in some detail by external people at national or state level outside the school. It is what society at a broad level requires that all its citizens should 'know, understand and be able to do'.

Most schools also adopt a local curriculum based on topics that parents would like to see added to subjects their children study at school. Usually negotiated with the school board of governors or other local community representatives, these school-based curricula are very often a means to promote or perpetuate local cultural identities such as aspects of the art, dance or poetry of a particular tradition, or lessons in a community language.

In many countries the idea of a basic curriculum is dominant; one that is required and should be offered but not specified in detail by external prescription and, perhaps, not required to be studied by all pupils. For example, this might be an agreed approach to religious education, a requirement to offer careers education or experience of learning in the workplace.

A 'Cubic Curriculum'

Some years ago, Ted Wragg, a professor of education at the University of Exeter in the UK, proposed what he called a 'Cubic Curriculum'. What he really said was, 'Actually, it isn't a cube. It's a multi-dimensional hyperspace, but "The Multi-dimensional Hyperspace Curriculum" does not exactly have a ring to it.' It is based on a vision of a future curriculum wider than subjects alone, important though they are, and founded on some linked propositions:

■ Education must incorporate a vision of the future.
■ There are escalating demands on citizens due to what has been called 'spiralling credentialism' – examination grades are needed for more and more jobs.

- Children's learning must be inspired by several influences. *How* something is learned is as important as *what* is learned.
- It is essential to see the curriculum as much more than a mere collection of subjects and syllabuses.

In other words, a pupil's experience in school – their 'experienced curriculum', that part that is *designed* to be experienced rather than other aspects of the so-called 'hidden curriculum' – embraces subjects, cross-curricular themes and issues that affect development (like language and thought) and different forms of learning such as 'telling' and 'observing'. Most important here is a need to plan such a curriculum. Staff at all levels, from strategic planning by senior management to the day-by-day planning by the newly qualified teacher, need to embrace what a curriculum means for them and the implications it has for improving pupil learning.

So around the world, and particularly in the STEM subjects, there is an opportunity and an urgency to think of the school curriculum in new ways: to develop new, relevant content and to explore new organisation patterns.

What approaches to a STEM curriculum might suit your school?

As a way of exploring curriculum links between Science, Technology, Engineering and Mathematics, I will set out what I call the 'Specified Curriculum', the 'Enacted Curriculum' and the 'Experienced Curriculum'. I use the term 'curriculum' widely to comprise most of what children learn in school, including, under 'Experienced Curriculum', the values and behaviours that schools hope to inculcate such as respect for others or the acceptance of authority. As you read what follows, consider how the three dimensions of subjects, cross-curricular processes and different pupil learning experiences are being addressed.

In brief, by Specified, Enacted and Experience Curriculum, I mean:

- Specified Curriculum: The curriculum content (as found in official documents and local agreements, as shown in Figure 2.1);
- Enacted Curriculum: What teachers do, dependent on teacher knowledge (what teachers need to bring to bear to plan and implement their teaching);
- Experienced Curriculum: Pupil learning (how both of the above are interpreted and made sense of by pupils).

The Specified Curriculum

The following statements are from the final consultation draft of the national curriculum in England, published in July 2013, and I will use these merely as a case study to consider aspects of the STEM curriculum internationally and how they might interact with each other in a 'Cubic Curriculum' sense. They have been through a number of iterations and some descriptions of the originally proposed curriculum for England were hotly contested. Although now content, the design & technology subject community, for example, were initially very disappointed with the original proposals and stated:

> We believe that the draft programme of study for Design and Technology published on Thursday 7th February 2013 threatens the future of design education. It lacks academic or technical rigour, challenge or modernity and will fail to engage or inspire students.
>
> (DATA, 2013)

It is certainly the intention of the government to cut down the extent of the curriculum, and instead to be more specific in content and less specific in suggested pedagogy – and the government would not agree about 'lack of modernity'.

> We live in a rapidly changing world and we need a truly modern curriculum that provides schools and teachers with a baseline, a benchmark that will be meaningful to parents and the wider public but that does not fetter the ability of heads and teachers to innovate and adapt.
>
> (Gove, 2011)

The following statements from the July 2013 final consultation draft set out what the national curriculum designers see as the 'purpose' of each of the STEM subjects. The description of computing is particularly noteworthy as it signals a significant shift from the discredited 'Information and Communications Technology (ICT) (see Chapter 9).

The purpose of science: A high-quality science education provides the foundation for understanding the world through the specific disciplines of biology, chemistry and physics. Science has changed our lives and is vital to the world's future prosperity, and all pupils should be taught essential aspects of the knowledge, methods, processes and uses of science. Through building up a body of key foundational knowledge and concepts, pupils should be encouraged to recognise the power of rational explanation and develop a sense of excitement and curiosity about natural phenomena. They should be encouraged to understand how science can be used to explain what is occurring, predict how things will behave, and analyse causes.

The purpose of design & technology: Design & technology is an inspiring, rigorous and practical subject. Using creativity and imagination, pupils design and make products that solve real and relevant problems with a variety of contexts, considering their own and others' needs, wants and values. They acquire a broad range of subject knowledge and draw on disciplines such as mathematics, science, engineering, computing and art. Pupils learn how to take risks, becoming resourceful, innovative, enterprising and capable citizens. Through the evaluation of past and present design & technology, they develop a critical understanding of its impact on daily life and the wider world. High-quality design & technology education makes an essential contribution to the creativity, culture, wealth and well being of the nation.

The purpose of computing: A high-quality computing education equips pupils to understand and change the world through logical thinking and creativity, including links with mathematics, science, and design & technology. The core of computing is computer science, in which pupils are taught the principles of information and computation, and how digital systems work. Computing equips pupils to use information technology to create programs, systems and a range of media. It also ensures that pupils become digitally literate – able to use, and express themselves and develop their ideas through information and communication technology – at a level suitable for the future workplace and as active participants in a digital world.

The purpose of mathematics: Mathematics is a creative and highly inter-connected discipline that has been developed over centuries, providing the solution to some of history's most intriguing problems. It is essential to everyday life, critical to science, technology and engineering, and necessary in most forms of employment. A high-quality mathematics education therefore provides a foundation for understanding the world, the ability to reason mathematically, an appreciation of the beauty and power of mathematics, and a sense of enjoyment and curiosity about the subject.

These four statements lay out the rationale for the designation of these separate subjects as areas of study during the ages of 5 to 14 years. In Chapter 1, we considered some of the differences between the STEM subjects and also some of the common themes such as problem solving and systems thinking. Let us now look across the STEM subjects in terms of common requirements. In Table 2.1 some brief extracts from the proposed STEM subjects are set out to show where some common themes exist. It is particularly noticeable in the mathematics column that it refers across to exemplification through science. Similarly, in design & technology there are explicit links to the use of computing; and computing suggests examples to 'monitor and control physical systems' and this is important for both science and design & technology. The Specified Curriculum emphasises the possible curriculum links.

TABLE 2.1 Extracts from the proposed National Curriculum for 11-14 year old pupils in England.

Science	Mathematics	Computing	Technology
Measurement ■ use and derive simple equations ■ undertake basic data analysis **Current electricity** ■ potential difference, measured in volts, battery and bulb ratings; resistance as the ratio of potential difference (p.d.) to current measured in ohms	**Algebra: using equations and functions** ■ use formulae by substitution to calculate the value of a variable, including for scientific formulae ■ begin to model simple contextual and subject-based problems algebraically ■ use linear and quadratic graphs to estimate values of y for given values of x and vice versa and approximate solutions of simultaneous equations ■ use given graphs of a variety of functions, including piece-wise linear, exponential and reciprocal graphs, to approximate solutions to contextual problems	■ design, use and evaluate computational abstractions that model the state and behaviour of real-world problems and physical systems ■ explain how data of various types can be represented and manipulated in the form of binary digits including numbers, text, sounds and pictures, and be able to carry out some such manipulations by hand ■ use logical reasoning to evaluate the performance trade-offs of using alternative algorithms to solve the same problem ■ use procedures to write modular programs; for each procedure, be able to explain how it works and how to test it ■ understand the hardware and software components that make up networked computer systems, how they interact, and how they affect cost and performance ■ understand how computers can monitor and control physical systems	Through a variety of creative and practical activities, pupils should be taught the knowledge, understanding and skills needed to engage in an iterative process of designing and making ■ select from and use specialist tools, techniques, processes, equipment and machinery precisely, including computer-aided manufacture ■ select from and use a wider, more complex range of materials, components and ingredients, taking into account their properties

- undertake creative projects that involve selecting, using, and combining multiple applications, preferably across a range of devices, including to achieve challenging goals, including collecting and analysing data and meeting the needs of known users
- create, reuse, revise and repurpose digital information and content with attention to design, intellectual property and audience
- understand simple Boolean logic (such as AND, OR and NOT) and its use in determining which parts of a program are executed; use Boolean logic and wildcards in search or database queries

- use a variety of approaches, such as biomimicry and user-centred design, to generate creative ideas and avoid stereotypical responses
- develop and communicate design ideas using annotated sketches, detailed plans, 3-D and mathematical modelling, oral and digital presentations and computer- based tools

(continued)

Ratio, proportion and rate of change
- use ratio and scale factor notation and methods involving conversion, mixing, measuring, scaling, comparing quantities and concentrations
- use multiplicative reasoning where two quantities have a fixed product or fixed ratio represented graphically and algebraically
- solve problems with constant rates of change involving distance and speed

Describing motion
- the representation of a journey on a distance-time graph

Chemical reactions
- chemical reactions as the rearrangement of atoms
- representing chemical reactions using formulae and using equations, including state symbols
- combustion, thermal decomposition, oxidation and displacement reactions

TABLE 2.1 (continued)

Science	Mathematics	Computing	Technology
Describing motion ■ speed and the quantitative relationship between average speed, distance and time (speed = distance ÷ time)	**Geometry and measures** ■ use compound units such as speed, unit pricing and density to solve problems		
Relationships in an ecosystem ■ niches and the role of variation in enabling closely related living things to survive in the same ecosystem.	**Statistics** ■ describe simple mathematical relationships between two variables in observational and experimental contexts ■ identify appropriate questions, data collection, presentation, analysis and interpretation to conduct exploratory data analysis, including in science and geography	■ use data structures such as tables or arrays	■ understand developments in design & technology, its impact on individuals, society and the environment, and the responsibilities of designers, engineers and technologists
Inheritance, chromosomes, DNA and genes ■ the variation between individuals of different species ■ the variation between individuals within a species being continuous or discontinuous, to include measurement and graphical representation of variation			

The Enacted Curriculum

How can we enable pupils to see the links between the specified STEM curriculum and how can we help teachers to consider the curriculum that they enact in practice? To explore the nature of the 'enacted' curriculum in this volume, we will draw on work we have done with teachers across a number of countries. A key lesson to be learned from the rapid revisions of the Specified Curriculum of science, technology and mathematics over the last 20 years is that it is very difficult to impose a curriculum on teachers, be it from central government or from within a school management structure. A top-down method of seeking to construct a curriculum in close detail without working with teachers and those involved in pre-service and in-service teacher education, which would develop a common understanding of purpose, leads to a mismatch between the teachers' own views about their subject and what is specified to be taught. Teachers have personal views about what their subject is about and, although they wish their pupils to do well in externally set examinations, when the Specified Curriculum moves independently of their deeply-held views, teachers feel obliged to revert to 'teaching to the tests.' In doing so, they lose some of the fire and passion for their subject. It is therefore imperative that teachers are involved in curriculum development and that tests accurately reflect the intentions of the curriculum designers.

Sharing teachers' professional knowledge

In our observation of teaching it is evident that the success or failure of lessons organised by teachers was often linked, not only to their college-based subject knowledge and their choice of teaching strategies but also to their appreciation of how their subject is transformed into a school subject. Figure 2.2 is useful for STEM teachers as it allows them to compare what they know in terms of key subject knowledge and appropriate pedagogy and what they feel is important in teaching. The types of knowledge to consider are:

- **Subject content knowledge:** Teachers' subject matter knowledge influences how they teach, and teachers who know more about a subject will be more interesting and adventurous in their methods and, consequently, more effective. Teachers with only a limited knowledge of a subject may avoid teaching difficult or complex aspects and teach in a manner which avoids pupil participation and questioning and which fails to draw upon children's experience.
- **Pedagogical knowledge:** At the heart of teaching is the notion of forms of representation and, to a significant degree, teaching entails knowing about and understanding ways of representing and formulating subject matter so that it can be understood by children. This in turn requires teachers to have a sophisticated understanding of a subject and its interaction with other subjects. Knowledge of subject content is necessary to enable the teacher to evaluate

textbooks, computer software and other teaching aids and mediums of instruction. This is the *materia medica* or *pharmacopoeia*, as Shulman puts it, from which teachers draw their equipment that present or exemplify particular content.

■ **School knowledge:** To these types of teacher knowledge, I would add 'school knowledge'. By altering a subject to make it accessible to learners, a distinctive type of knowledge is formulated in its own right – 'school mathematics' or 'school technology'. In the same way that school science is different to science conducted outside the school laboratory, so school design & technology is different from technology as practised in the world outside the school.

One might initially see 'school knowledge' as an intermediary between subject knowledge (knowledge of technology as practised by different types of technologists, for example) and pedagogical knowledge as used by teachers ('the most powerful analogies, illustrations, examples, explanations and demonstrations'). However, such a viewpoint underplays the dynamic relationship between the categories of knowledge implied. For example, a teacher's subject knowledge is enhanced by his or her own pedagogy in practice and supported by the use of and familiarity with the resources which form part of their school knowledge. Which teacher has not confessed to only really understanding a topic when they were required to teach it to others! It is the active intersection of subject knowledge, school knowledge and pedagogical knowledge that brings teachers' professional knowledge into being.

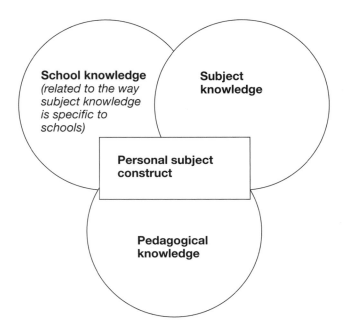

FIGURE 2.2 Framework of teacher professional knowledge.

At the heart of this dynamic process are the 'personal constructs' of teachers and pupils, a complex amalgam of past knowledge, experiences of learning; a personal view of what constitutes 'good' teaching and belief in the purposes of the subject. This all underpins a teacher's professional knowledge. This is true for all teachers. A student teacher has to question his or her personal beliefs about their subject as they work out a rationale for their classroom behaviour. We have discussed this diagram with a number of professionals in the UK and in other parts of the world such as Australia, Bangladesh, Canada, Finland, the Netherlands, New Zealand, Spain, South Africa and Sweden. These professionals all taught different subjects: science, mathematics and technology, and often English too. Also included were student teachers, teacher educators and researchers. Across this spectrum of teacher professional expertise the reaction to the model has been remarkably similar: the different aspects of teacher knowledge are recognised by all these groups as being meaningful. Teachers, in particular, are excited by the three types of knowledge and value the model as a way of easily articulating what they know and are able to do.

The model can be interpreted at different levels. Some see it as a tool for categorising personal understanding. Others see it as being useful for planning in-service development for a group of teachers. But a tool such as this is more than just a means to an end. In fact, the means is more important than the end as it enables STEM teachers to engage in what they do or 'enact' as they work with their STEM curriculum. In practice, discussions about what should be included in the circles in the diagram and the relationship between the circles helps teachers to reflect on practice more than any completed picture ever could. The process of thinking, initiated by the diagram, is more important than the diagram itself. Similarly, a completed diagram such as Figure 2.3 by Dr Clare Lee, a mathematics teacher, can engender considerable debate and further reflection on practice in explicit terms.

Looking sideways

In some of the following chapters we will look in some detail about how the different STEM subjects can support each other if teachers spend a little time 'looking sideways' at what is being taught in the other subjects – and when! However, what then happens is down to the approach that the school's subject departments wish to take. I will discuss three possibilities of working across the STEM subjects, a coordinated approach, a collaborative approach and an integrated approach, which is implemented in few parts of the world.

A coordinated approach

Which science teacher, especially someone teaching physics, has not asked the question, 'Have you done this is maths yet?' to a class scratching their collective heads trying to manipulate an equation. The silo nature of the traditional subjects has militated against proper coordination of the subjects for mutual benefit. In a

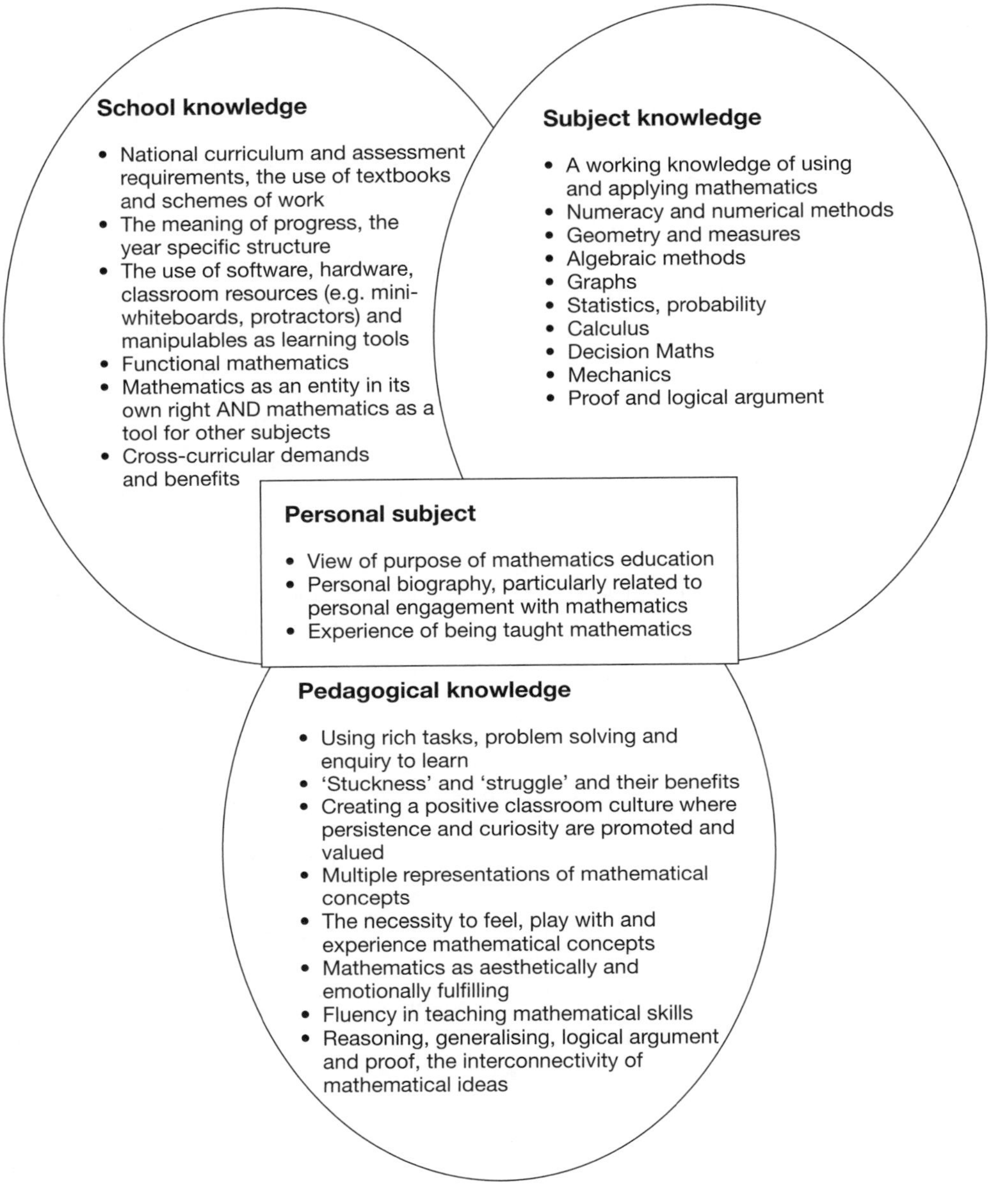

School knowledge

- National curriculum and assessment requirements, the use of textbooks and schemes of work
- The meaning of progress, the year specific structure
- The use of software, hardware, classroom resources (e.g. mini-whiteboards, protractors) and manipulables as learning tools
- Functional mathematics
- Mathematics as an entity in its own right AND mathematics as a tool for other subjects
- Cross-curricular demands and benefits

Subject knowledge

- A working knowledge of using and applying mathematics
- Numeracy and numerical methods
- Geometry and measures
- Algebraic methods
- Graphs
- Statistics, probability
- Calculus
- Decision Maths
- Mechanics
- Proof and logical argument

Personal subject

- View of purpose of mathematics education
- Personal biography, particularly related to personal engagement with mathematics
- Experience of being taught mathematics

Pedagogical knowledge

- Using rich tasks, problem solving and enquiry to learn
- 'Stuckness' and 'struggle' and their benefits
- Creating a positive classroom culture where persistence and curiosity are promoted and valued
- Multiple representations of mathematical concepts
- The necessity to feel, play with and experience mathematical concepts
- Mathematics as aesthetically and emotionally fulfilling
- Fluency in teaching mathematical skills
- Reasoning, generalising, logical argument and proof, the interconnectivity of mathematical ideas

FIGURE 2.3 A completed framework of teacher professional knowledge for a mathematics teacher.

properly coordinated approach, teachers in each STEM subject become familiar with the work carried out in the others and plan their curricula so that the timing of topics within each subject is sensitive to each other's needs; and taught in a way that supports the pupils' developing understanding rather than one that causes confusion. For example, if proficiency with the use of measuring in millimetres and collating data from respondents has been covered in lower school mathematics lessons this would be beneficial to technology lessons, and if the principles of electricity have been explained in technology using similar analogies and terminology to those used in science lessons, developing ideas are reinforced. Table 2.1 sets out the different topics that could be taught to mutual advantage. Some of the more obvious links are shown in Table 2.2.

TABLE 2.2 Topics that could be taught to mutual advantage.

Science	Mathematics	Computing	Technology
■ use and derive simple equations ■ resistance as the ratio of potential difference (p.d.) to current measured in ohms	■ use formulae by substitution to calculate the value of a variable, including for scientific formulae ■ begin to model simple contextual and subject-based problems algebraically	■ explain how data of various types can be represented and manipulated in the form of binary digits including numbers, text, sounds and pictures, and be able to carry out such manipulations by hand ■ use logical reasoning to evaluate the performance trade-offs of using alternative algorithms to solve the same problem	■ understand how more advanced mechanical systems used in their products enable changes in movement and force ■ understand how more advanced electrical and electronic systems can be powered and used in their products ■ apply computing and use electronics to embed intelligence in products that respond to inputs, and control outputs, using programmable components

A collaborative approach

Teachers in each subject plan their curricula, usually together, so that some activities within each subject are designed to support pupil learning of related ideas. In Scotland there has been much development of teaching resources for the new 'curriculum for excellence' and, as part of a STEM initiative, Learning and Teaching Scotland (LTS) has developed an interdisciplinary unit of work concerned with renewable energy (LTS, 2013). This study of renewable energy is introduced by a short video in which a prominent populariser of science and technology interviews young professional engineers who are working in the renewable energy industry in Scotland. Pupils then undergo four 'learning journeys' (also presented by video). The first journey, 'From fossil fuels to wind', meets some of the science requirements of the new curriculum. The second, 'Wind, wave and tidal', meets some of the technology requirements of the new curriculum. The third, 'Calculating the wind', meets some of the mathematics requirements of the new curriculum. In the fourth learning journey, 'This island is going renewable', pupils are challenged with making the case for the use of renewable energy on a small island community. In this challenge, the pupils will need to use their learning from the first three learning journeys, and also develop skills in using maps and geographical information systems to gather, interpret and present data relating to location of renewable technologies. This large challenge is divided into three smaller challenges.

- **Challenge 1:** An important part of any energy plan for a community includes consideration of energy consumption and ways to reduce this. Advise one of the following user groups about the use of energy to support their lifestyle/business:
  - An elderly couple who are retired and live in a small cottage.
  - A family consisting of a mother, father and two teenage children, living in a three bedroom detached house. The mother works at the local school, the father works at the slate mine and the children attend the local school.
  - A family consisting of a mother and father and a baby aged six months, the mother is a full-time mum, and the father works in the timber mill.
  - The local post office/community shop.
  - The head teacher of the school, which has 250 pupils.

- **Challenge 2:** Based on your findings on individual user groups from Challenge 1, work out the approximate energy usage for the whole island.
  - Could all the energy needs of the island be provided by wind, tides or waves? As a team, decide the kind of information you will need to know about renewable technologies to help you answer this question.
  - How will you analyse this information?
  - What criteria will you use for comparing the different possible renewable technologies?
  - Which other factors will you need to consider?

- **Challenge 3:** Create an exhibition stand displaying the findings of your investigations of the feasibility of using renewable energy on the island to help inform the islanders about the issues around energy such as:
  - Energy usage and consumption

- Options for generating energy from renewable sources
- Best locations for particular technologies
- A scaled model of the island to demonstrate the potential impact that the technologies could have on the landscape
- You could include examples or photographs of the working models you have been making in class, charts, diagrams, written explanations, PowerPoint presentations, leaflets, annotated maps, and so forth.

Although the approach to interdisciplinary work here is not dissimilar to that of the Nuffield Key Stage 3 STEM Futures project, there are significant differences. The challenge is set by the teacher and not negotiated with the class, the pupils' response to the challenge is clearly structured and there is not the explicit focus on developing closed loop solutions, although to some extent this is implicit in the challenge.

Futures case study

The STEM *Futures* resource is composed of a series of 'pods'. Each pod is a series of lessons organised around a particular sustainability theme. Typically, a pod contains an overview, teacher notes, pupil tasks, video clips, animations and a pupil presentation. The activities in each pod are ideally conducted in order, to scaffold the concept development.

Pod 1: Introduction

Pupils are introduced to the idea that many current human problems relate to food, energy and materials. They look at a brief history of civilization, to emphasise that humanity's quest for resources is nothing new. Advances in technology have increased the depletion rate of fossil fuels and other materials. Pupils engage with the idea that our linear take → make → dump culture is not sustainable. We need to learn some 'closed loop' lessons from nature where all waste is recycled through natural.

Pod 2: Waste

Pupils start by classifying debris on a beach according to whether it will decay or not. Pupils analyse product life cycles and generate questions about natural closed loop systems. They consider how cradle-to-cradle design could help provide closed loop systems for human activities.

Pod 3: Cars

Pupils consider conventional car engine design and review new green alternatives. They collect evidence for pollution in their local area and analyse the data. Pupils interpret graphs showing past and predicted oil consumption.

They use reports and data to assess the impact of legislation on traffic pollution. Pupils produce and present suggestions for alternative closed loop approaches to local transport.

Pod 4: Climate change

Pupils investigate the key components of the carbon cycle. They analyse evidence relating CO_2 to climate change. Pupils compare the carbon footprint of different activities and different societies. They use closed loop thinking to consider new ways of reducing CO_2 in the atmosphere. Finally they present the case for the construction of a local wind farm.

Pods 5: Pupil project

Pupils use the learning skills they have acquired in earlier pods to carry out a piece of project work. Pupils identify a problem or question relating to sustainability, and use STEM knowledge and understanding to present a closed loop solution. Their project involves research, analysing, evaluating and synthesising information, and communicating possible solutions creatively through a variety of media.

Here are some of the main topics covered in *Futures*:

Science
Carbon, nitrogen and water cycle
Photosynthesis and respiration
Energy from combustion Renewable energy
Global warming
Pollution
Properties of materials

Design & technology
Materials
Product life cycle
Car design
Sustainable products
Sustainable systems
Renewable energy

Is an integration of STEM subjects possible?

There are two ways of considering the integration of the STEM subjects. One is getting synchronous inputs from a range of staff for an off-timetable event or project. Here, all the staff support the activities through team-teaching and pupils turn to a member of staff for advice and support when they are available. The second is a full integration of the STEM subjects so that one teacher follows a themed project across a number of lessons, as is often the case in primary schools. If this is followed at the secondary level this assumes a lot of expertise is available in the one teacher, and is most often seen around the world through the formation of a single subject called 'science and technology'. It should be remembered that, for example, science and design & technology so significantly different from one another that to subsume them under a 'science and technology' label is both illogical and highly dangerous to the education of pupils. The Israeli approach to the relationship between science and technology is based on collaboration between science and technology teachers focusing on problem solving in a social context. The curriculum developers at ORT (a non-governmental Jewish education organisation) established a didactic model for collaboration between the disciplines, known as the STSS (Society-Technology-Science-Society) model. This is shown in Figure 2.4. This model serves as both a conceptual and a curriculum framework for dealing with social and environmental issues (e.g., 'The Noise Around us'). The STSS Model is underpinned by four elements:

- problem solving;
- the use of social, scientific and technological knowledge for problem solving and decision making;
- the view that science and technology are two distinct but interacting disciplines;
- the gap between the needs of society and reality; this gap is the 'driving force' for development in both science and technology.

Although there are considerable advantages to linking science and technology in the way described in the STSS model, there are a number of difficulties in implementing the model in schools. The two major impediments are:

- the lack of appropriate curriculum materials;
- this model is predicated upon integration of a topic between teachers from both subjects, and this is not easy to achieve.

At the implementation level, integrated teaching in the STSS model is currently more wishful thinking than reality. The reasons for this are the differences between science and technology teachers (including status, academic background), the lack of a collaborative component within the teacher training programmes, and organisational difficulties within schools.

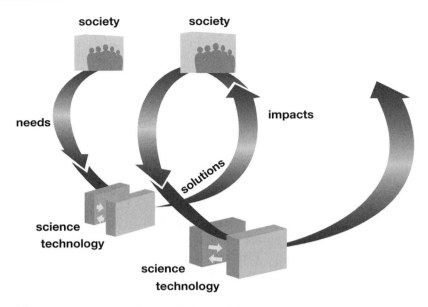

FIGURE 2.4 Society-Technology-Science-Society model.

The Experienced Curriculum

On initial teacher education courses it is common to ask the student teacher to do a 'pupil trail' and follow one or two pupils as they move from class to class and from teacher to teacher (as is common in the UK). The novice teacher often expresses surprise at the way the same pupil reacts very differently to the different teachers and the different environments such as a workshop, laboratory or classroom. Another way of looking at this – and I recommend everyone to do this once a year, whatever the stage of their career as a teacher – is seeing the curriculum actually experienced by the pupil.

From our research, and that of Professor Bob McCormick and other colleagues at The Open University, there is considerable evidence that problem solving – a key aspect of all STEM subjects – is often conducted in a sort of 'ritual' way in school classrooms (see Banks, 2009; McCormick and Davidson, 1996; McCormick, Murphy and Davidson, 1994). As it has the potential to bring together aspects of science and mathematics through design & technology, let us follow a small case study of a teacher of 12–13-year-old students working on an electronic badge project based on a 'face' with LEDs for eyes (these cases are taken from Banks and McCormick, 2006 and based on classroom research undertaken by McCormick).

The teacher deliberately has not emphasised the underlying processes; it was not one of his main aims, and he seemed to view designing as a logical approach rather than a process that involved sub-processes to be taught and learnt. He said:

although I'd like them to understand and use the design process and I think it's quite a nice framework for them to fit things on to, I don't think there's a great need to be dogmatic about it and say you must learn it...the nature of projects leads them through the design process despite the teacher's bit, going through it with them in front of the class...

(Teacher 1, Banks and McCormick, 2006)

The particular view that a teacher takes of the process being taught affects the way tasks are structured, the kinds of interventions that are made by the teacher, and the assessment of students' work. Not all of these will be consistent with each other, or with the view espoused by a teacher, but collectively they will have a profound effect on the students' perceptions and activities. But, whatever view is taken of the design process, there is a tendency to see it as an algorithm to be applied in a variety of situations. The teacher involved in the electronic badge project began by presenting the 'Situation':

A theme park has opened in [place] and it wants to advertise itself. It plans to sell cheap lapel badges based on cartoon characters in the park. To make these badges more interesting, a basic electronic circuit will make something happen on the badge.

(Teacher 1, Banks and McCormick, 2006)

This was set within the general title of 'Festivals', but the links to the 'Situation' were not discussed, and from then on no further reference was made to festivals. The teacher continued in the session by asking the students to draw up a spider diagram of 'Considerations' (a specification of the lesson plan), tasks which all the students seemed familiar with. He did not, however, elaborate on the 'Situation' or the 'Design brief', nor invite students to discuss them in the context of the planned project. Three students were followed, 'Bill', 'Tanvir' and 'Rose', who produced different design briefs that illustrated how they interpreted the 'Situation'. Bill and Tanvir interpreted it as a 'button is pressed to light up the eyes', whereas Rose makes no such inference: 'to design and make a clock badge'. Their initial ideas of their personal 'briefs' lingered and influenced future tasks; for example, Rose continued to talk about a 'clock face' for several lessons and abandoned the idea only when she realised that the electronics would not be like that of a watch. She also imagines that the battery would resemble that in a watch and was almost incredulous when the teacher showed a comparatively large conventional dry 9-volt battery that she (rightly) considered too heavy for a lapel badge. The teacher's discussion with Rose about this issue indicated that, unlike Rose, he had not entered into the 'Situation' and 'Design brief' in a meaningful way, but only ritualistically – his ultimate answer to the problem was to 'have a strong pin for the badge', a response Rose felt very dissatisfied with!

Next the teacher gave several tasks relating to drawing the faces for the badge, which implicitly reflected the sub-processes of 'generating ideas', 'developing a chosen idea' and 'planning the making'. However, this was again done in a ritualistic way as the following indicates. At the end of the first session students were asked, for homework, to create four cartoon faces as potential designs for the badge. No parameters were given other than that all four should fit into the design sheet and that students should be 'creative'. As with the 'Situation', 'Design brief' and 'Considerations', this step of producing four designs appeared to be a standard one and, again, was accepted without question by the students. However, in the next session students were asked to re-draw the faces so that they touch the sides of a fixed drawn square (70 × 70 mm). The reason for this was not made clear until a later session. Evidence from the students' folders indicates that students had to modify their designs in order to fit these new demands. For example, Rose had originally drawn a thin 'carrot' character, which she had to distort to make it fat enough for it to touch the sides of the square. The fact that the creation of several designs is sometimes perceived by students to be merely a ritual is seen in Rose's comments to the teacher implying she had in fact already made a final choice while she is still completing the four 'possible outcomes' drawings.

In looking at STEM teaching in the classroom we discovered some of the strategies that students actually adopted in response to the various ways the teachers viewed and enacted the problem-solving process. These strategies certainly do not resemble the 'algorithms' or 'ways of problem solving' that are so often taught. The first strategy we characterised as *problem solving through dealing with the 'classroom culture'*. This occurs when students try to 'work out' the rules the teacher sets in the classroom, and play by those rules. This example of students seeking out this culture is contrasted in the experience of two girls, 'Kathy' and 'Alice', producing a mobile. Alice wanted to do something that 'clinks' when the wind blows, and so had an idea of using metal. So, given a restricted choice of material, she chose to cut thick mild steel in the form of disks about two inches diameter. Because she played by the rules of the classroom, Alice's mobile took a long time to make given the difficulty of working with mild steel and she ended up with very sore hands; her endeavour resulted in a very inappropriate way of creating the effect she wanted. (But she did learn quite a lot about mild steel, as it turned out.) Kathy had designed a mobile comprising the moon and planets, and wanted some kind of glinting material. When presented with the choice of material, Kathy in contrast to Alice looked elsewhere and saw some aluminium (not available to the class) and asked to use this. The teacher agreed, and she cut this easily with tin snips. Kathy took this approach many times throughout the project. She broke the rules of the classroom, knowing what she could and couldn't get away with. She experienced different kinds of issues and problems from Alice, but she was avoiding many technological problems that Alice faced.

The second strategy is *problem solving as giving and finding a solution*. This can be illustrated in a case study of a project involving a moisture sensor. The teacher in this study defined the task in terms of making a box in which to put the electronics (the transistor circuit, the bulb or the little speaker, switch, etc.). This had to be appropriate to the situation of detecting moisture or lack of it. He taught them to cut the material (styrene) in straight lines with a steel ruler and a knife because when he said 'box', he had in mind a rectangular box. He also gave them a jig so that they could put the two edges together at right angles and run the solvent along to stick the two together. But some students wanted curved shaped boxes, which gave some of them at least three emergent problems. First they had to cut a curved shape, and students asked each other and the teacher how to cut the shape as the steel ruler method wouldn't work at first (the solution was to cut it slowly). Second, a curved profile on one part of the box required one side to bend to follow the profile, but the styrene they were given was too thick. The students asked the teacher who simply gave them a thinner gauge of styrene, without any discussion. Third, students did not know how to support or hold the thinner styrene in place to apply the solvent, and so again asked the teacher. This time the teacher had to think and was obviously trying to solve the problem too, but again he gave the *results* of his thinking as a ready-made solution to the students and did not involve them in his problem-solving process. The students only received the solution and none were involved in the problem solving. Continually 'giving solutions' becomes a culture of the classroom at the expense of a 'problem-solving' culture.

The above case study indicates just how pivotal the teacher is in enabling pupils to engage in genuine problem solving. The behaviour of the teacher in the study is a litany of what NOT to do if the intention is to give pupils the possibility of generating and developing their own ideas and dealing with the problems that emerge as they pursue their intentions.

The final strategy is the *student collaboration model*. In both science and technology students are usually set individual projects, so they may be working alongside each other on a table or a bench, and they can co-operate because they are doing similar things. In this first form of collaboration, projects are not identical but similar enough for students to be able to help each other and share tasks. The second form of collaboration involves students in dividing up the task: 'You do this bit, I'll do that bit.' 'You're good at that and I'm good at this.' Some of the learning is lost in this approach. But at least it is a way of collaborating, because they have to put the two bits together at some stage, and that has an element of good collaborative problem solving. The final form of collaboration occurs when students have a shared task, and they can talk about it. This means the design of the task must *require* the students to collaborate. Designed correctly tasks should require solutions to a problem to be considered by all students through discussion and decision making. This is the approach adopted by Young Foresight, which is briefly described in Chapter 10.

Conclusion

Let's draw together what I consider are the crucial points of this chapter and of the three ways of viewing the curriculum: Specified, Enacted and Experienced. Classrooms are social environments and the curriculum leads directly to what is enacted by teachers and what is experienced by pupils.

The Specified Curriculum:

- It is very difficult to control the intended learning of students by an elaborate specification in law of what students should know.
- In most parts of the world the Specified Curriculum as a legal document is being downplayed and schools are freer to construct their own curriculum. However, if teachers themselves are not part of the discussion on what STEM in school should be, they will 'teach to the test' to cover themselves leading to teaching strategies that have, for example, elements of 'ritual'. There will be a clash between their personal view of their subject and that specified by others and classroom practice will go through a period of extremes until some commonly-shared beliefs of what constitutes 'good' teaching emerge.

The Enacted Curriculum:

- In an effort to direct the learning outcomes for all pupils and make the tasks manageable in the classroom, teachers tend to closely direct the activity of pupils.
- If teachers 'look sideways' pupil learning can be enhanced. For example, technology teachers have much to teach science teachers on the handling of processes and science teachers have much to teach technology teachers about the problems associated with acquiring conceptual knowledge.

The Experienced Curriculum:

- Through constraints of time and resources, teachers transfer their subject into a form of 'School knowledge' and students play the game of discovering what that is. Some students never quite understand the rules of the game and the relevance of the subject becomes lost to them; others pick up incidental aspects because teachers have either not made clear what is salient or their classroom culture produces effects at odds with their rhetoric.
- The way that students engage in problem solving in D&T and in science and in mathematics depends on the view of designing and of investigating held by the teacher.

An overwhelming conclusion, however, would be that good practice in STEM classrooms is not shared well across and between schools. As new equipment produces yet more teaching opportunities we need to find out more about how their impact on the curriculum affects the student experience. STEM offers some very exciting opportunities.

Background reading and references

Banks, F. (2009) 'Research on Teaching and Learning in Technology Education'. In A. Jones and M. de Vries (eds) *International Handbook of Research and Development in Technology Education* (pp. 373–90). Rotterdam, The Netherlands: Sense Publishers.

Banks, F. and McCormick, R. (2006) 'A Case Study of the Relationship Between Science and Technology: England 1984–2004'. In M. de Vries and R. Custer (eds) *International Handbook of Technology Education* (pp. 285–312). Rotterdam, The Netherlands: Sense Publishers.

DATA (2013) 'We Must Fight to Replace this Regressive D&T Curriculum'. Warwickshire: Design and Technology Association (DATA). Available at: https://data.org.uk/news/we-must-fight-to-replace-this-regressive-dt-curriculum/ (accessed 25 November 2013).

Gove, M. (2011) Speech to Twyford Church of England High School, January.

Hennessy, S. and Murphy, P. F. (1999) 'The Potential for Collaborative Problem Solving in D&T', *International Journal of Technology and Design Education, 9(1),* 1–6.

LTS (2013) STEM Central, Learning and Teaching Scotland. Available at: www.ltscotland. org.uk/stemcentral/contexts/index.asp (accessed 10 February 2014).

McCormick, R. and Murphy, P. (1994) 'Learning the Processes in Technology.' Paper presented at the British Educational Research Association Annual Conference, September. Oxford: Oxford University.

McCormick, R., Murphy, P. and Davidson, M. (1994) 'Design and Technology as Revelation and Ritual'. In J. S. Smith (ed.) *IDATER 94 – International Conference on Design and Technology Educational Research and Curriculum Development* (pp. 38–42). Loughborough: University of Loughborough.

McCormick, R. and Davidson, M. (1996) 'Problem Solving and the Tyranny of Product Outcomes', *Journal of Design and Technology Education, 1(3),* 230–41.

Murphy, P., Lunn, S. A., McCormick, R., Davidson, M. and Jones, H. (2004) *EiS Final Evaluation Report. Evaluation of the Promotion of Electronics in Schools Regional Pilot: Final Report of the Evaluation.* Milton Keynes: Open University.

Murphy, P. and McCormick R. (1997) 'Problem Solving in Science and Technology Education', *Research in Science Education, 27(3),* 461–81.

Wellington, J. (1988) 'Process and Content in Physics Education', *Physics Education. 23(3),* 150–5.

Zuga, K. F. (1996) 'STS Promotes the Rejoining of Technology and Science' in R.E. Yager (ed.) *Science/Technology/Society as Reform in Science Education.* Albany, NY: State University of New York Press.

3

Teaching science in the light of STEM

The nature and purpose of science education

In 2010, Wynne Harlen and a group of distinguished colleagues described ten principles of science education and, within these, identified three aims for science education:

■ Understanding of a set of 'big ideas' in science which include ideas *of* science and ideas *about* science and its role in society.
■ Acquiring scientific capabilities concerned with gathering and using evidence.
■ Developing scientific attitudes.

These 'big ideas' are shown in Table 3.1. It is worth noting that one of the ideas *about* science acknowledges that the knowledge produced by science is used in some technologies to create products to serve human ends. This knowledge can, of course, be found in the ideas *of* science and immediately provides some justification for developing a curriculum relationship between science and design & technology.

TABLE 3.1 Fourteen big ideas in science.

Ideas of *science*
1 All material in the Universe is made of very small particles.
2 Objects can affect other objects at a distance.
3 Changing the movement of an object requires a net force to be acting on it.
4 The total amount of energy in the Universe is always the same but energy can be transformed when things change or are made to happen.
5 The composition of the Earth and its atmosphere and the processes occurring within them shape the Earth's surface and its climate.
6 The solar system is a very small part of one of millions of galaxies in the Universe.
7 Organisms are organised on a cellular basis.

(continued)

TABLE 3.1 (continued)

8 Organisms require a supply of energy and materials for which they are often dependent on or in competition with other organisms.

9 Genetic information is passed down from one generation of organisms to another.

10 The diversity of organisms, living and extinct, is the result of evolution.

Ideas about *science*

11 Science assumes that for every effect there is one or more causes.

12 Scientific explanations, theories and models are those that best fit the facts known at a particular time.

13 The knowledge produced by science is used in some technologies to create products to serve human ends.

14 Applications of science often have ethical, social, economic and political implications.

Taken from Harlen (2010)

In his presidential address to the Association for Science Education in January 2012, Robin Millar made a compelling case for 'science for all'. Parts of his address were relevant to the idea of teaching science in the light of pupils' learning in design & technology. He quoted Jon Ogborn who signals that the economic argument, educating the next generation of scientists, has little worth in justifying science for all.

> A central fact about science is that it is actually done by a very small fraction of the population. The total of all scientists and engineers with graduate level qualifications is only a few percent of the whole population of an industrialized country. Thus the primary goal of a good science education cannot be to train this minority who will actually do science.
>
> (Ogborn, 2004, p. 70)

However, the voice from government, in the report of the Science and Learning Expert Group (2010) indicates that this minority will play a crucial role in the future of the UK:

> Global development means that the competition and market for the products of science, engineering and technology are greater than ever before. It is a truism to state that the future of the UK depends critically on the education of future generations. Science, Technology, Engineering and Mathematics (STEM) must be at the forefront of education in order for the UK to address some of the most important challenges facing society.
>
> (Science and Learning Expert Group, 2010)

Those concerned about the place of STEM in the curriculum have voiced concern about how the science curriculum appeals to pupils. The review by Sir Gareth Roberts 'SET for success' noted:

> widespread concern that science is taught in a way that does not appeal to many pupils and that the curriculum places too much emphasis on rote learning rather than relating theory to situations relevant to the pupil.
>
> (Roberts, 2002)

This provides a hint that relating science learning to the wider world in which it is applied could pay dividends.

However, there is a problem with much science understanding. It is counter-intuitive but a common-sense approach will almost certainly lead to ideas that aren't scientific. Learners have to contend with what Lewis Wolpert has called 'the unnatural nature of science'. This is compounded by the way in which pupils might respond personally to the nature of science, termed the 'affective challenge' by James Donnelly:

> Scientific knowledge offers a materialistic worldview which, in its substance, is devoid of humane reference, whatever might be said of its practices and its implications. Science is profoundly successful, on its own terms, and scientific knowledge profoundly authoritative. In consequence, creating scope for the individuality of pupils to come into play is difficult...these characteristics of science challenge pupils affectively and cognitively...It might even be said that they are somewhat at odds with the tenor of modern cultural life.
>
> (Donnelly, 2003, p. 19)

Robin Millar finds a telling quote from a student that supports this position. In science, 'there's no room to put anything of *you* into it'. Again there is the suggestion that enabling pupils to relate science learning to aspects of learning 'outside science' might pay dividends.

Science and design & technology in the light of STEM

David Layton, an acknowledged expert of in both science and design & technology education, played a key role in the conception of design & technology in the National Curriculum in England. He acknowledged the difficulty faced by science education. Writing as long ago as 1975: 'At the school level...the acquisition of scientific knowledge is inescapably tinged with dogmatism'. But 20 years later he used the following metaphorical question to explore the relationship between science and technology, 'Should science be seen as a cathedral, a quarry or a company store?' This has significant implications for the curriculum relationship between science and design & technology. In the 'cathedral' of science, the purpose of the endeavour is to explore and explain natural phenomena without much consideration of possible application or exploitation. The goal is understanding – 'worshiping science for its own sake'. This is a purist position. Of course, in reality there is a dynamic relationship between science and technology in which there is a spectrum of responses – from pure/fundamental science, driven by curiosity and speculation about the natural world without the thought of possible applications; through strategic science, yielding a reservoir of knowledge, out of which the as yet unidentified winning products and processes will occur; to applied science, related to a specific project and tied closely to a timetable with a practical outcome often specified by a client. Technologists, Layton argues, can rarely specify in advance what items in the cathedral will be most useful and so they treat it more as a 'quarry' to be visited and revisited, less as a place to marvel at the beauty of creation than to search out for items that might be of use. Note that in the middle ground Layton suggests the idea of the 'company store' – spaces where strategic investigations predominate. We would identify such spaces as research and development centres where, to quote Layton, 'the products of the cathedral are reorganised and remodelled to make them more accessible to practical users rather than worshippers'. So perhaps the science teacher wishing to teach in the light of pupils' learning in design & technology will need to view the knowledge, skill and understanding she teaches not only as a place of wonder and awe but also as a region into which her pupils can make forays of exploration for a variety of design & technological purposes – a space to be raided for that most precious of commodities – ideas that work.

Science and mathematics in the light of STEM

So far, this discussion has concentrated on the possible significance of a curriculum relationship between science and design & technology. We must now consider the relationship between mathematics and science. There is general agreement that mathematical thinking provides the ability to identify and describe patterns in a wide range of phenomena. Clearly, this ability will prove useful in science, particularly in the move from qualitative to quantitative thinking. Consideration of, for example, speed, velocity and acceleration, only becomes worthwhile and potentially useful once such phenomena can be described algebraically and the 'describing' formula can be used to justify, for example, speed limits with regard to road safety. Here again we have an example that takes the 'dogmatism' of science required for particular and precise definition and can be linked to the wider world and the personal interests and welfare of pupils. Such work could be extended in a variety of ways that make use of mathematics, including the derivation and interpretation of graphs to describe the motion of driven vehicles and the collation and interpretation of road safety statistics.

We have seen that the views of significant members of the science education community concerning the implementation of one science curriculum 'for all' have revealed how the very nature of science can cause tension. We have noted that there is the possibility of resolving this tension to some extent by relating science learning to its application in the wider world through developing curriculum relationships with mathematics and design & technology. However, it is important to consider the status of those engaged in this relationship. We discuss this issue in the following section.

A relationship among equals?

There is little doubt that science and mathematics are privileged subjects in terms of their curriculum status. Mathematics has long been regarded as an essential element in the education of all pupils. It has significant cultural status having been developed over centuries and providing the solution to some of history's most intractable problems. Jonathan Osborne, in his address at the 50-year celebration of the Nuffield Foundation, reminded the audience that this was not always the case for science education. At the end of the nineteenth century and beginning of the twentieth century some thought that the 'proper' education for an elite was deeply rooted in the Classics and humanities. This view was that science and technology were a necessary evil and that they did not offer proper training for the mind and that science had nothing to say about the human condition. It was believed that 'ordinary' people need only be educated in the three Rs. A particularly well known rebuttal of this anti-science education position came in 1959 from C. P. Snow, who argued that anyone who did not know and understand the implications of the Second Law Of Thermodynamics could hardly be considered educated. And now some 60 years later, science along with mathematics has an apparently unassailable opposition in the curriculum. But what of design & technology – a relative newcomer to the curriculum existing in England as a defined entity within the national curriculum only since 1990? Both Jonathan Osborne and Robin Millar are clear that science education has definite instructional goals. There are singular answers to particular questions. Millar (2012) sums this up well when he writes 'There is no merit in helping a learner to construct an idiosyncratic personal theory of matter or of motion (to take two examples) – it is the kinetic particle model and Newton's Laws that we want then to understand and be able to use' (p. 23).

Similarly, in mathematics teaching the educative goal is to some extent to impart agreed mathematical truths and procedures to enable mathematical thinking. This indicates a very real difference from design & technology where the values of both the designer and end user are integral to the process. Of course, there are clearly identified matters to be taught and learned in design & technology; properties of materials, ways to manipulate and join materials, ways to enable control and systems thinking for which there is an agreed understanding – but this is only half the story. Pupils then use this learning to develop products and systems to meet needs, wants and opportunities and it is perfectly possible, and indeed desirable, that the outcomes of this development produced by different pupils vary widely from one another. The extent to which particular developments meet needs, wants and opportunities is a matter of judgment and it is possible for quite different responses to be worthwhile. Hence design & technology does not suffer from the 'dogmatism' identified by David Layton. John Holman and Michael Reiss were very clear in their report to the Royal Society, 'S-T-E-M Working Together for Schools and Colleges', that it was important that any form of curriculum collaboration between science, mathematics and design & technology respected the legitimate differences between the subjects as well capitalising on areas of common interest. A difference of particular importance is the legitimacy of individual interpretations and responses in design & technology compared with the almost exact opposite in mathematics and science.

In the previous section we considered how difficulties in pursuing science for all caused by the nature of science itself might be resolved to some extent by forging curriculum relationships with design & technology and mathematics. In this section we have noted that within these relationships it is essential that legitimate differences between the subjects are both recognised and valued. In the following section we will provide examples of how science activities can be related to pupil learning in design & technology and mathematics, taking these issues into account.

Examples of teaching science in the light of STEM

It is important to illustrate that all areas of science can benefit from teaching in the light of learning in design & technology and mathematics. Hence the following examples cover the breadth of science. They take into account the importance of recognising and valuing legitimate differences in the subjects involved.

Example 1: The magnetic effects of electric currents

Teaching the magnetic effects of electric currents

Imagine a sequence of lessons concerned with teaching the effects of an electric current. You, as the teacher, could use iron filings and button compasses to show that as a direct electric current flows through a straight wire it generates a circular magnetic field around that wire. You could then challenge the pupils to explore what sorts of magnetic fields are formed when a coil of wire is used. With some guidance the pupils should be able to find out that the circular fields combine to give a field like that of a bar magnet. You could then challenge pupils to investigate the reverse possibilities with the question 'what effect does a magnetic field have on the electricity in a wire?' With some scaffolding their investigations you could show that a moving magnetic field causes an electric current to flow in a wire. You could place this learning in the 'cathedral' of science indicating that these breakthroughs was made by the great Danish scientist Hans Oersted and the great English scientist Michael Faraday in the first half of the nineteenth century.

In the early days of scientific investigation the prize sought was understanding with little thought of application. What we would now call 'blue sky research'. Yet the results of this understanding led to the development of solenoids, electric motors and dynamos. But it took over 50 years before these discoveries about the relationship between electricity and magnetism led to a powerful and useful electric motor. This is a clear example of Wynne Harlen's ideas *of* science – objects can affect other objects at a distance – and ideas *about* science – for every effect there is one or more causes and the knowledge produced by science is used in some technologies to create products to serve human ends. At this stage it would be worth reminding the class of the electric motors that they use in their design & technology lessons – small direct current motors containing permanent magnets. It would also be worth showing the class the internal structure of such a motor and giving them the opportunity to construct a simple electric motor for themselves (Gupta, 2014). Through these activities the pupils will begin to appreciate how the 'cathedral' can become the 'quarry' that can be mined for ideas of practical application. In this case, the understanding of the phenomena of electromagnetism being exploited to develop the electric motor.

Now it is worth the pupils considering how they might use their understanding of magnetism and electromagnetism in their design & technology lessons. The Design and Technology Association have developed visual materials that allow teachers and pupils to explore open starting points for their designing and making. These enable a class to explore a range of possible options without starting with a pre-defined product. Six starting points have been identified – playtime, keeping in touch, keeping secure, staying safe, thinking machines and other worlds. For example, let's say that a design & technology teacher is exploring playtime with the class. She could suggest that whatever is designed uses electromagnetism and or magnetism. This would provide a technical focus for the activity without overly limiting the variety of toys that the pupils might choose to develop. The simple electric motor the pupils have already constructed could be a starting point for some pupils. It is not powerful but does spin very quickly and could be made the basis for a wide range of amusing and intriguing visual effects. Here, we have an example which illustrates the moves from the 'non-negotiable precision' required by science to the flexible interpretation necessary in design & technology. A science teacher could deal with the teaching of electromagnetism through demonstration only, communicating explanations to be learned. By requiring pupils to carry out investigations and simple making, the activity moves to a place where pupils have to construct their own understanding. Using the understanding and the artefact, both 'constructed' by the pupils, in a designing and making task moves the pupils into situations where speculation is crucial – 'What if I do this? 'Can I do this?' 'Will this work' 'What about this?' The pupils are treating their science knowledge and understanding as a resource to be exploited, pushing it to the limits in their quest to produce an engaging toy. This almost playful pushing to the limits will in some cases require pupils to reformulate and increase their understanding.

With all electrical items powered by batteries there are opportunities to consider battery life. This requires the use of calculations which use data about the current that flows when the item is used. In this case of simple electric motor driven toys, some pupils will be able to measure current consumption and use this to calculate how long particular batteries or arrangements of batteries might last. This is not a trivial task and for pupils aged 11–14 this would almost certainly be seen as extension work for those who had shown an aptitude to using mathematics. Conversations between all the subject specialist teachers are important here to ensure that the relevant science concepts are used appropriately, that the mathematical manipulations are sound and that the circuits under consideration are appropriate.

Example 2: Floating and sinking

The work of Archimedes in the second century BC is perhaps one of the first historical examples of scientific activity that can be seen to occupy David Layton's 'company store'. Archimedes was set the task of determining whether a crown made for King Hiero had been made from pure gold as supplied by the king or whether silver had been added by the goldsmith. Using the principle of buoyancy – the loss of weight when an object is immersed in water – Archimedes was able to show that the goldsmith was dishonest and had adulterated the pure gold with silver.

Teaching buoyancy

Young pupils are introduced to the idea of buoyancy in the primary school by means of classifying materials as floaters or sinkers. This leads to the idea that some materials are more dense than others. It is not until they become older that they are asked to explain the mechanism that causes some materials to float and others sink. Here, they are required to consider the forces acting on the material and conduct experiments in which they weigh materials in air and immersed in water and compare the apparent loss of weight on immersion with the weight of the water displaced by the material. Ultimately, they come to a statement of Archimedes Principle: any object, wholly or partially immersed in a fluid, is buoyed up by a force equal to the weight of the fluid displaced by the object. This is a clear example of Wynne Harlen's ideas *about* science – for every effect there is one or more causes and scientific explanation best fitting the facts known at a particular time.

The science teacher can help pupils relate this principle to their everyday experiences of floating in the bath, the swimming pool or the sea. So given a table of the density of materials it becomes relatively easy to spot the pattern that if a material has a density greater than that of water (1g per cubic centimetre) then it will sink. It doesn't matter how much of the material is present – a single gram of lead will sink just as surely as a kilogram. The calculation of the density of different materials, involving weighing and the measurement or calculation of volume would be an appropriate mathematics activity and there is no reason why some of this investigation into why some materials sink and others float should not be carried out as a part of mathematics lessons as well as science lessons. Mathematics teachers appreciate the difficulty pupils experience in understanding compound measures and exploring density would provide a useful activity to support learning in this area.

Both the mathematics teacher and the science teacher can challenge pupils' understanding with the question, 'If iron and steel sink then how come ships made of iron and steel float?' Discussion can lead to the idea of shaping materials so that the shape can displace more than the volume of the material. This is easy to demonstrate in the design & technology workshop as follows. A disc of thin aluminium sheet when placed in water sinks. The disc can then be formed into a bowl by beating with a pear-shaped mallet in a dishing block and will then float when placed in water. This can be the starting point for a designing and making activity in design & technology in which pupils make water toys. These can include bath toys and small-scale replicas of yachts and powerboats. This links to Wynne Harlen's ideas *about* science – its use to create products. In all cases the way the toy floats will be dependent on both the material of the hull and the form of the hull. A hull made of solid wood will float very low in the water – it will be almost submerged. So in order to float in a realistic way the wood must not only be shaped to resemble a hull but also hollowed out to some extent. A hull made by vacuum forming thin sheet plastic over a hull-shaped solid block floats very high in the water, almost skimming along the surface. In this case additional weight needs to be added to reduce the buoyancy and achieve realistic floating. If the hull is to be made from sheet metal then it has to be formed from flat 'tin plate' into a hull shape. This is difficult to achieve without cutting the sheet into a net which is then folded up into a hull shape and soldered at the joins to prevent water leaking into the hull. The need to meet these making challenges in design & technology can be seen in the context of the learning about buoyancy that takes place in science lessons.

Example 3: Clean, accessible drinking water for all

'Chemistry for Tomorrow's World: A roadmap for the chemical science' produced by the Royal Society of Chemistry identifies 10 challenges for the chemical sciences. One of these is drinking water quality. Access to safe drinking water and adequate sanitation varies dramatically with geography and many regions already face severe scarcity. Current population forecasts suggest that an additional 784 million people worldwide will need to gain access to improved drinking water sources to meet the UN Millennium Development Goal target: to halve the proportion of people without sustainable access to safe drinking water and basic sanitation by 2015. The World Health Organization estimates that safe water could prevent 1.4 million child deaths from diarrhoea each year. Technology breakthroughs required include:

energy efficient desalination processes; energy efficient point of use purification, for example, disinfection processes and novel membrane technologies; developing low-cost portable technologies for analysing and treating contaminated groundwater that are effective and appropriate for use by local populations in the developing world, such as for testing arsenic-contaminated groundwater. There are strong links here with Wynne Harlen's ideas about science – the knowledge produced by science is used in some technologies to create products to serve human ends.

Teaching purification

For the science teacher, teaching about the simple purification techniques such as filtration and distillation is the starting point to developing the knowledge and understanding required to tackle this global problem. Situating the teaching of this elementary science in the context of this problem would indicate clearly the importance of science knowledge and understanding in tackling the large problems faced by the world.

There is a growing movement to encourage designers to tackle the problems encountered in the developing world. Books such as *Design for the other 90 per cent* (2008), *Design like you give a damn* (2006) and *Design Revolution* (2009) are written to inform the general public about the way design can be a powerful means to improving the situation and to provoke a response from the design community. There is no reason why this approach cannot be extended to pupils in schools through the design & technology curriculum and build on the work carried out in science. Pupils could be challenged to develop simple filtration devices that 'clean' cloudy water and simple distillation devices to desalinate salt water. Such devices need only be developed into preliminary working prototypes that indicate their effectiveness. The pupils could then compare their designs with the devices developed by professional designers to identify differences and similarities, note where the basic science separation techniques were used, and enhance their appreciation of user-centred design and the importance of designs that empower people to improve their situation.

This learning of science in the light of learning in design & technology can also be extended to include mathematics quite simply. Asking pupils in mathematics lessons to estimate the amount of water they and their families use each day and compare this to that available to those living in developing countries would be a valuable learning activity. It could also lead to pupils considering the water shortages that might take place in the UK and the way such shortages are dealt with. This would inevitably lead to the question 'Where does our water come from?' which would take the learning science in the light of STEM full circle back to the science curriculum and the water cycle.

Example 4: The properties and applications of metals

Teaching metals

Consider the topic of 'metals'. The classification of some elements as metals or non-metals was an important step towards understanding the behaviour of these elements in chemical reactions. Most chemistry teachers will teach about metals: what they are like (their properties); where they come from (natural resources); how we get them (reduction of metal ores); what they are used for and why (properties related to use).

The design & technology curriculum is concerned with teaching what metals are like (properties); what they can be used for (properties related to use); how we can manipulate them (making skills) to design and make products that people need and want. Clearly, there is an overlap in teaching intention here and there is the possibility of capitalising on this through a collaborative scheme of work in which the science teaching about metals is tackled in the light of the learning that is taking place in design & technology. It will of course be important to engage with pupils in their daily lives and a simple 'homework' investigation of where there is metal at home and what is it used for will reveal its ubiquity – door handles, coat hooks, door knockers, casings for white goods, interiors of washing machines, filaments of light bulbs, electrical wiring, cooking utensils, cutlery, plumbing pipe work, mobile phone cases, etc. Pupils' attention can also be directed to the underlying structural framework of most modern buildings plus the chassis, body shell and moving parts of most cars and railway lines and the trains that run on them. Such a homework exercise can be divided between science and design & technology. Of course, the bigger picture must also be considered i.e., the amount of production and its impact, the use and disposal of metal and the multifarious ways that metal is utilised in the made world. To find and use data about this requires some understanding of statistics and the ability to question what such data means. Hence there is an interesting role for the mathematics teacher in this collaboration.

Chemistry teachers will teach about the reduction of metal ores through practical activities that are reliable and intriguing. In design & technology lessons the designing and making of simple body adornments is a relatively standard yet highly enjoyable exercise – copper rings, brooches, bangles, and bracelets are all possible. It could be possible to link the production of copper from its ores learned in a science lesson to the use made of copper in the manufacture of body adornment. One possible way is to start with the copper ore in a science 'lesson' and from this produce enough copper to be used in making copper rings and bangles. This is perhaps not amenable to the everyday timetable but as a STEM club activity, the production of copper from a small sack of green ore (malachite) by means of a home-made blast furnace would provide insight into industrial processes that produce the materials pupils use in their daily lives difficult to achieve in any other way.

Chemistry teachers may also teach about the electrolytic purification of crude copper that has been obtained by the reduction of copper ores. The electrolytic deposition of copper from a solution containing copper ions can also be used in design & technology lessons to decorate brass with designs made from copper. It is a relatively simple activity involving using the brass as the anode onto which copper will be deposited and masking areas of the brass so that electrolytic deposition takes place in the form of the desired decoration. Only a thin film of copper need be deposited to give a good effect. Once pupils have been taught about electrolysis in science it would be an interesting assessment of their learning to challenge them with decorating brass with copper as part of a sequence of design & technology lessons concerned with producing body adornment.

Example 5: Nutrition

Teaching digestion and respiration

Many science courses for pupils aged 11–14 years teach digestion and its relationship with respiration. The 'key idea' here is that in many foodstuffs the molecules are large, in the form of polymers, and that for these materials to become useful to the body the large molecules need to be broken down in order to be absorbed through the gut wall (small intestine) and enter the bloodstream. Once in the bloodstream they can be transported throughout the body. Often, but not always, the treatment of digestion is limited to the digestion of starch which breaks down to form glucose and that the glucose is then available as a source of energy to drive the chemical reactions on which the body depends and the use of muscles.

The formation of glucose from starch is often demonstrated through an experiment involving visking tubing, a semi-permeable membrane representing the gut wall. A starch solution is placed in some visking tubing sealed at one end and saliva is added. The tubing is lowered into water at body temperature. The pupils test for the presence of starch and glucose at regular intervals in small samples taken from within the visking tubing and the surrounding water. Care must be taken to avoid contamination between the solution inside the visking tubing and the surrounding water. Ideally, the test results should show the disappearance of starch from within the visking tubing and the appearance of glucose in the surrounding water. Students are given information about the size of starch molecules, glucose molecules and the perforations (holes) in the visking tubing and have to deduce the activity of the enzymes in the saliva in breaking down the large molecules of starch to much smaller molecules of glucose which can pass through the holes in the visking tubing which are too small to allow starch molecules to pass. This explanation is linked strongly to Wynne Harlen's idea *of* science – all material in the Universe is made of very small particles – but extended to include the idea that these very small particles can be of different sizes. It can be related to another of Wynne Harlen's ideas of science – organisms require a supply of energy and materials for which they are often dependent on or in competition with other organisms – by discussing with pupils where we might acquire starch in our diet in order to produce glucose.

It is at this point when the science teacher might consider reminding pupils of their work in food technology. Through discussion with stakeholders, Marion Rutland has identified the following conceptual framework as being essential for a modern food technology course:

1. Designing and making food products
2. Underpinned by an understanding of the science of food and cooking and nutrition
3. Incorporating an exploration of both existing, new and emerging food technologies
4. In the context of the sustainable development of food supplies locally, nationally and globally
5. Incorporating an appreciation of the roles of the consumer, the food industry and government agencies in influencing, monitoring, regulating and developing the food we eat.

Learning about digestion as described above links strongly to the second concept mentioned above (understanding of nutrition in particular) and also the fourth concept (concerning food supplies). So it should be relatively easy for the science teacher and the food technology teacher to collaborate around the teaching of digestion, where the food technology teacher continues the work of the science teacher but deals with sources of starch in various food stuffs, naturally occurring, processed and synthetic, and relates this to the labelling of food stuffs that now indicate their calorific value.

Calorific values are a cause of considerable conceptual confusion for pupils. Calorific values are derived by burning foods and measuring the heat produced. For many pupils the relation of this to the energy released during respiration of small molecules derived from such foods in our bodies is so counter intuitive that it seems to be completely mysterious. Pupils can of course calculate the heat released when potato crisps or breakfast cereals are burned but this is not a trivial task. This might take place in either the science or food technology classroom – perhaps even both. First, the material to be burned must be weighed. Then as it is burned the heat from the burning must be transferred to a measured amount of water. The temperature rise caused by the burning must be accurately measured. This temperature rise must be converted into the amount of calories that caused the temperature rise. This, plus the weight of material burned, must be used to calculate the heat released per gram. This involves a lot of calculations relying on sound arithmetic (or competent use of a calculator) and a strong understanding of ratio and proportion. So a conversation with the mathematics teacher would not be amiss here. Indeed the mathematics teacher might welcome the opportunity for pupils to be engaged in using mathematics for such a 'real world' purpose. The results obtained will probably not mirror those produced by professional food technologists and listed on food packaging. If the order of magnitude is similar then this is of great credit to the pupils. There are several sources of error over which they have little control given the equipment available in junior high schools. For example, some of the heat released will be absorbed by the atmosphere and some will be transferred to the container holding the water; measuring the temperature will be accurate only to one or two degrees; weighing the material to be burned will be accurate to only 0.1 gram. These inadequacies in experimental design can of course be discussed with the pupils in terms of Wynne Harlen's ideas *about* science – scientific explanations, theories and models are those that best fit the facts known at a particular time. Here the facts are being derived from experimental data and are used to support a scientific explanation of respiration of foodstuffs providing the body with energy. To achieve genuine understanding it is necessary to make the link between the measurement of calorific value of food by heat transfer and the energy made available to cells throughout the body through respiration of small molecules derived from the food by digestion which is expressed on food packaging. It is difficult to see how else this can be achieved other than by collaboration between the science, food technology and mathematics teachers. In food technology lessons pupils sometimes develop products for those with special dietary requirements and controlling calorie intake is often essential. Demystifying the energy content of various foodstuffs by enabling pupils to understand how such values are obtained gives an important scientific dimension to such activities.

Example 6: Genetic modification

Teaching genetics

Most school biology courses now describe and explain genetic modification (GM) and discuss possible costs and benefits of applying this knowledge to the development of genetically modified organisms particularly with regard to GM crops. Here we have examples of Wynne Harlen's ideas of science – genetic information is passed down from one generation of organisms to another and ideas about science – the knowledge produced by science is used in some technologies to create products to serve human ends and applications of science often have ethical, social, economic and political implications.

The production and use of GM crops is a topic that raises strong emotions. In 1999, the UK reaction against GM crops was so strong that supermarkets removed products containing or associated with GM crops from their shelves. The science writer Bernard Dixon provides an interesting account of the influences of many different stakeholders that led to this rejection citing, in particular, the circulation wars in the popular press leading to sensationalism which coupled with public ignorance led to an irrational fear of the new and emerging technology. The treatment in most science courses is now much more balanced giving voice to concerns by those who are apprehensive towards or against the use of GM crops, providing counter arguments and engaging pupils in discussion of the issues from different stakeholder perspectives. Such an approach is exemplified by the twenty-first century science biology course for pupils aged 14–16 years (Nuffield, York Twenty First Century Science, 2011). Hopefully, in the future such courses will lead to a general public who are better informed. However, as far as the UK is concerned the damage has been done and GM products are not available. Yet, the debate still continues so it is important for the science teacher to keep up to date with developments. For example, at the time of writing, the state of California is about to vote on Proposition 37 which would require the labelling of all foods containing GM ingredients and prohibit such foods from being marketed as 'natural'.

There appears to be little evidence that GM ingredients are intrinsically harmful to humans. GM can be used to develop pesticide resistance in crops, allowing farmers to use pesticides on such GM crops without harming the crops while preventing weeds from competing with the crops. But there is some evidence that this can lead to pests evolving resistance more rapidly. The situation is complex and proponents of GM argue that rather than preventing the use of GM, it should be extended to include a wider range of GM crops which could reduce the likelihood of resistance emerging by allowing farmers to switch the chemicals they use before pests evolve resistance. There are some, e.g., Greenpeace, who are philosophically opposed to the use of GM on the grounds that it is not natural and that natural plant breeding methods can and should be used. They have sited a developed strain of sweet potato that has four to six times the beta-carotene of an average sweet potato without recourse to genetic modification. Beta-carotene is a precursor to vitamin A in the body and important in preventing blindness in young children. A two-year project in Uganda involving 110,000 households demonstrated that eating the improved variety almost doubled the number of children who escaped vitamin A deficiency. This approach is in direct contrast to the Golden Rice project which has developed GM golden rice (golden in colour as opposed to the white) which contains significant amounts of beta-carotene. Ordinary rice contains no beta-carotene. The latest trials of golden rice using isotopic labelling indicated that just 100 to 150 grams of the rice – about half the children's daily intake – provided 60 per cent of the recommended daily intake of vitamin A. An editorial in the *New Scientist* magazine in 2012 called for multiple solutions to be adopted to combat preventable blindness; not just natural breeding, not just GM but both.

There are those who argue that natural breeding methods will be totally inadequate and it is only through significant investment and deployment of GM that the world food problem can be addressed. Mark Lynas, once a committed activist against GM, has now completely changed his position in response to consideration of planetary boundaries with particular regard to the nitrogen boundary. The natural mechanisms of the nitrogen cycle do not provide enough nitrogen in forms that can be used as fertiliser to support growing the food the world needs. The synthesis of ammonia and nitrates from nitrogen in the atmosphere has enabled the world to produce significant amounts of fertiliser that are used worldwide but at significant environmental cost. He argues that it will be essential to develop GM crops that are more efficient at utilising nitrogen thus reducing and even eliminating our dependency on synthetic fertilisers.

Where does all this leave the food technology teacher? Marion Rutland has argued that a modern food technology programme should involve a consideration of new and emerging food technologies and GM would seem an important example. Often in design & technology classes pupils are challenged with the question 'What would you use this or that technology for?' Clearly, if the technology in question is GM it is important that the food technology teacher is *au fait* with the learning that has taken place in science. Similarly, it is important that the science teacher who is teaching about GM knows that there is the possibility that pupils will be asked to consider its applications as a new and emerging technology in their food technology lessons. In considering GM in food technology, especially when speculating about possible uses, it is important that the speculation deals with what is feasible and that it is underpinned by current scientific understanding. Marion has also argued that in a modern food technology programme pupils should consider the sustainable development of food supplies locally, nationally and globally. Considering the role of GM crops would certainly enable pupils to engage with the global picture. And it is here that the use of mathematics will be significant in helping pupils understand the sheer scale of the GM problem: the projected growth in world population, the different foods needed to feed the increasing population, the extent of malnutrition in the world and resultant dietary related disease, the amount of fertiliser and pesticides that are needed to maintain the food production. The statistics used to track these issues and their interpretation to inform global food policy will provide a rich context for learning and using mathematics.

Example 7: Building your own laboratory equipment

Teaching experimental equipment

In attempts to modernise science curricula many teachers use data logging equipment. But such equipment is expensive and when finances are limited schools can only afford to purchase one or two of such items then their use is confined to demonstrations. Joshua Pearce, an associate professor at Michigan Tech in the US, has found a solution to this problem, one he applies to his own work in higher education and one that he feels is also appropriate for secondary (high) schools. Joshua advocates the use of a 3D printer to produce structural parts and the open source Arduino microcontroller to drive the 3D printer and provide data capture functionality. For schools in the UK the PICAXE microcontroller could be used to achieve the same result.

Joshua Pearce waxes lyrical about the benefits of using 3D printers in educational settings:

> The open-source microcontroller is key. The beauty of this tool is that it's very easy to learn. It makes it so simple to automate processes. Here's how it works. The Arduino chip – which retails for about $35 at RadioShack – can run any number of scientific instruments, among them a Geiger counter, an oscilloscope and a DNA sequencer. But it really shines when it operates 3D printers like the open-source RepRap. This microwave-sized contraption starts at about $500 and can actually make parts for itself. Once you have one RepRap, you can make an entire flock. My lab has five. 3D printers make stuff by laying down sub-millimetre-thick layers of plastic one after another in a specific pattern. This allows users to make devices to their own specifications, so they don't have to make do with what's available off the shelf. The Arduino controls the process, telling the printer to make anything from toy trains to a lab jack. Lab jacks raise and lower optical equipment and aren't radically different from the jacks that raise and lower your car, except that they are more precise. I received a quote for a $1,000 version, which inspired me to design my own. Using a RepRap, inexpensive plastic filament and a few nuts and bolts my students and I made one for under a buck. Then we posted the OpenSCAD code used to make the lab jack on Thingiverse, a web repository of designs where members of the 'maker community' can submit their designs for all kinds of objects and receive feedback. Immediately someone I'd never met said, 'This isn't going to work quite right, you need to do this'. We made a simple change, and now I have a lab jack that's superior to our original design. The Thingiverse community already has a whole line of open-source designs for over 30,000 'things', and everyday it's only getting better. Using open-source hardware has easily saved our research group thousands of dollars, and we are only getting warmed up. This will change the way things are done.
>
> (Pearce, 2012)

3D printers are becoming available to secondary schools in England and at the time of writing the Department for Education has initiated a small pilot study to explore their use in the design & technology curriculum. The use of microcontrollers, usually PICAXE, has become well established in some design & technology departments due to in-service training programmes that focus on the use of digital technologies. Hence, for a science teacher who wants her pupils to develop their own experiments there is the possibility of students using the learning in design & technology to devise and manufacture the necessary equipment. This would not be a trivial task. The science and design & technology teachers would need to discuss at some length the sorts of experiment that the pupils might wish to carry out, the equipment required and the programming of the microcontrollers necessary to enable sensors to collect the required data. In all probability the design & technology department would have computer assisted design (CAD) software that students could use to design structural parts and produce files that could be loaded directly into the 3D printer. This would eliminate the need to programme a microcontroller system to drive the 3D printer. In developing the structural parts for their experiment there is scope for considerable mathematical thinking that uses pupils' knowledge and understanding of both measurement and geometry. Achieving the correct size, shape and form for laboratory equipment such that the result can contain the electronics and required battery, allows access for battery replacement and microcontroller programming, connection of sensors is no mean feat. A three-way conversation between the science, design & technology and mathematics teachers would reveal the extent to which mathematics learning could be used to enhance and facilitate this task.

Action Programme 10 of the National STEM Programme in England was devoted to improving the quality of practical work in science. The body responsible for this aspect of the programme was SCORE (Science Community Representing Education). SCORE is a partnership between the Association for Science Education, the Biosciences Federation, the Institute of Biology, the Institute of Physics, the Royal Society, the Royal Society of Chemistry and the Science Council. SCORE acts under the auspices of the Royal Society. SCORE developed a framework for practical work in science and an accompanying professional development programme enabling teachers to discuss the framework and build it into their teaching. The framework identified a range of features present in high quality practical work including the following:

- Self-directed enquiry by individuals, or more commonly by groups, which promotes 'pupil ownership' of science and can be motivating and enjoyable.
- Investigations to encourage teamwork with members being given particular roles in the planning, implementing, interpreting and communication of the work.
- Extended enquiry or projects which encourage pupil autonomy and opportunities for decision making.
- Use of ICT for handing and presenting data and contemporary technical equipment to relate science techniques in school to modern practice.

Developing your own laboratory equipment in the way advocated by Joshua Pearce would meet the features identified by SCORE in high quality practical work and provides an inspirational example of teaching science in the light of STEM.

As we have seen from the examples above it is possible to teach some science topics in the light of STEM but one of the challenges is for teachers to be given an introduction to the possibilities. The following case study shows how physics teachers were able to respond positively once given this introduction.

Continuing professional development for physics teachers – a case study

In an attempt to address the issue of CPD, I worked with Peter Campbell in providing a professional development session for physics teachers concerning links between physics and design & technology. Peter is a highly experienced physics teacher and curriculum developer. In 2009, he was the course tutor for a 40-day physics in-service training course, part of the 'Science Additional Specialisms Programme' that helps practising chemistry and biology teachers to become effective physics teachers. As part of this course, one session posed the question, 'Is it worth physics teachers and design & technology teachers having a conversation about what they teach and how, with a view to improving pupils' learning experiences?' The half-day session began with a presentation clarifying the difference between science and technology and the place of design in technology. It also set the scene for considering the interaction between physics and design & technology in the secondary school curriculum. After the introduction the teachers tackled a range of practical activities. The activities were divided into two sets. The first set involved exploring phenomena, taking the position that a technology is a phenomenon that is captured and put to use. The second set involved considering how artefacts might be improved through re-design. The activities are summarised in Table 3.2. Peter answered a range of questions in response to the session and the activities.

In response to the question, 'Why might it be important for physics education to interact with design & technology education?' Peter answered:

Physics is not an isolated discipline. It is important to make connections with other subjects explicit while teaching physics, because this can stimulate new interests for pupils or enhance their existing interests. Without help, few pupils manage to see such connections. Connecting physics to other curriculum subjects helps keep the physics curriculum broad. A school physics curriculum that focuses too narrowly on general principles and mathematical models will deter most pupils from engaging. Very few pupils, if any, will emulate Paul Dirac in a quest for the abstract. Those who leave school to continue their physics education, as aspiring engineers or physicists, do move progressively towards this goal. As well as being important for pupils, it is also important for the physics teacher to make connections with other subjects. The viewpoint of other subjects can give fresh insight into a physics topic. For example, understanding the mechanical properties of materials in physics is enhanced by engaging with design & technology perspectives such as manufacturing processes, cost, and availability.

In response to the question, 'In general, what do you think the experience gave the non-specialist physics teachers?' Peter commented:

The session exploring links to design & technology was the third in a series of 'eye-opening' sessions; music and art had been considered previously. Hence, to some extent the teachers were predisposed to consider connections in a favourable light. The principles used to formulate the nature of the activities were an important feature of the experience. In the world of pure science, research projects typically involve collecting huge data sets which are painstakingly analysed to draw conclusions (e.g., the COBE mission team's study of cosmic background radiation critically scrutinised their data for two years before finally publishing it in 1992). By contrast, these activities concentrated on either a) investigating a phenomenon to inform the design of an artefact that utilises the phenomenon or b) investigating an artefact to gain understanding to improve or modify the performance of the artefact.

TABLE 3.2 Practical activities to explore the relationship between physics and design & technology.

Exploring a phenomenon

1	Exploring the Peltier effect
2	Exploring the behaviour of a small paper helicopter
3	Considering the properties of sheet material
4	Observing rolling cylinders
5	Investigating magnifying glasses

Engaging with designing

6	Investigating paper crumple zones
7	Investigating a turning toy
8	Investigating a musical instrument
9	Investigating a wind energy conversion system
10	Investigating LEDs, lamps, super capacitors and rechargeable batteries

Peter's comments on the individual activities were as follows:

■ Exploring the Peltier effect: 'For most of the teachers, this was a new phenomenon which they found intriguing. The fact that the device they used is available from a well-known supplier, at low cost, made the activity a practical possibility in their classroom. Taken together these two factors led to a high level of engagement.'

■ Exploring the behaviour of a small paper helicopter: 'This was not a new activity for the teachers and it initially appeared deceptively simple. However, making observations and taking measurements proved a challenge. It required repeated observations, the use of scatter graphs to make sense of the observations and video capture with slowed-down playback to observe details of the phenomenon. This data collection challenge led to a high level of engagement.'

- Considering the properties of sheet material: 'This required the teachers to explore the potential of corrugated card as a structural medium. The activity unfortunately failed to engage the teachers. In retrospect, this was probably because the starter activity involved reading a case study about card furniture rather than practical engagement with structural forms. An exploration of flat pack to 3D structure might have been a more appropriate starting point.'

- Observing rolling cylinders: 'This required teachers to explore the behaviour of cylinders on a ramp, partially filled with liquids of different viscosities (water and glycerine) or different solids of different granularity (lead shot, ball bearings). For most of the teachers this was a new phenomenon, so engaging that they were only able to concentrate on explaining the phenomenon (which they found extremely challenging) and thus ignored possible applications. In retrospect, the introduction of some "real world" examples such as rolling barrels of beer during delivery to public houses might help move consideration from phenomenon to application.'

- Investigating magnifying glasses: 'This required teachers to explore a range of lenses to identify those features responsible for magnification. Most of the teachers could see that this had potential but were disappointed with the experience due to the very limited range of lenses available. To improve this would require some effort to source lenses not normally available in science departments.'

- Investigating paper crumple zones: 'This was not a new activity for some of the teachers but they still found it useful because new possibilities for quantifying the impact were made available. Also it provided an opportunity to discuss different approaches each of them had previously used. Going beyond a formal treatment and using practical contexts such as road safety can engage pupils in thinking about collisions generally.'

- Investigating a turning toy: 'This activity provided the opportunity for a very open-ended investigation that motivated questions and learning about movement. The use of an investigation to support learning instead of being used for assessment was new for many of the teachers and as such provoked interest.'

- Investigating a musical instrument: 'In this activity the teachers investigated the musical notes produced by vibrating cantilevers. The use of the oscilloscope to "see" the notes produced was novel but easily carried out due to their familiarity with the device. This is an example where physics can connect with more than one other subject, in this case music and design & technology.'

- Investigating a wind energy conversion system: 'Most teachers were familiar with this activity as the equipment was from a well-known curriculum project. The challenge was to get good data from the apparatus and to some extent this was marginalised by the over-structured approach of the support materials.'

- Investigating LEDs, lamps, super capacitors and rechargeable batteries: 'This was a failure because the apparatus we provided made circuit wiring a formidable challenge and the task was too wide-ranging. In the future, limiting the activity to investigating super capacitors would allow an approach similar to that of the Peltier effect.'

To gather the teachers' views on the session and to explore whether the overall experience was likely to lead to a change in practice the teachers completed a short questionnaire shown in Table 3.3:

TABLE 3.3 Teachers' questionnaire

Last term you took part in a range of activities designed to explore possible relationships between the teaching of physics and design & technology. It would be very useful if you could answer the following three questions:

1   Did you enjoy the session? (Very much 1, 2, 3, 4, 5 Not at all)
     Please give reasons for your answer.

2   Did you find the session useful? (Very much 1, 2, 3, 4, 5 Not at all)
     Please give reasons for your answer.

3   In what ways has the session impacted on your practice?
     Please give examples.

Returned questionnaires revealed that the overwhelming majority enjoyed the session (11 answers at 1; 11 answers at 2; one answer at 4) and a large majority found the session useful (nine answers at 1; nine answers at 2; five answers at 3). In terms of impact on practice, however, the picture is mixed. Eleven indicated no change to practice with one indicating that previous attempts to establish links between science and design & technology had been resisted by design & technology, hence he was still reluctant to open discussions on the topic. The remainder, just over half, did indicate possible changes to practice. One teacher indicated that she planned to build the activities into an existing after school STEM club and another indicated that he would use some of the activities to start such a club at his school. Three teachers indicated that they had begun talks across the science and design & technology departments with a view to planning collaboration in general, collaborating during a STEM week which would include joint science, design & technology days. Two more teachers indicated that they were considering the introduction of integrated curricula that involved both science and design & technology. Two indicated the intention to change some of their physics practical sessions starting with 'artefact' investigations as opposed to the usual experiments to establish principles. One teacher indicated that he would start to build links by adding extension questions to science tasks which deliberately required pupils to make links between science and design & technology learning. One teacher indicated that he had established links which required pupils to build illustrative models of science learning as part of the design & technology curriculum, in his case 3D models of nuclear power stations. One teacher was rewriting the Year 7 schemes of work such that pupils would investigate properties in physics lessons and use the results to make decisions when designing and making a product in design & technology.

Given the limited success of some of the activities as revealed by Peter Campbell's comments and the small amount of time taken to explore the potential for links between physics and design & technology it is encouraging that such a large proportion of the teachers were prepared to make changes to their practice. Clearly, some next steps are required to show the effectiveness of such changes and establish such activities as permanent features within the curriculum in which science is taught in the light of learning that takes place in design & technology.

What might other continuing professional development sessions consider?

Imagine that you were asked to organise a similar session for other specialist science teachers. What might you include? If the session were for chemistry teachers it would be an interesting opportunity to focus on the role of chemistry in personal hygiene and appearance. A starting point could include looking at a range of cosmetic products – shampoos and conditioners, soaps, simple cosmetics such as lipstick, eye shadow and mascara and perhaps perfumes and aftershave lotion. The development of packaging for a variety of products has become a standard design & technology task in those courses that specialise in so-called 'graphic products'. Imagine the possibilities for linked learning if the products to be packaged had been previously explored in chemistry lessons with a view to understanding their composition and how they are made and how they work. There is the possibility of devising experiments to explore the performance of commercially available products in the light of advertising claims and information on the packaging. In some cases, e.g., lipstick, mascara and perfume it might be possible for the pupils to make the product which they then package. It would be important for the chemistry teachers to carry out the activities themselves, just as the physics teachers did in the case study above, and consider their feasibility. The results of such work might manifest themselves in collapsed timetable days organised by chemistry and design & technology teachers working together.

If the session were for biology teachers what might be considered? Systems thinking is used significantly in both biology and design & technology. The precise language used by biology teachers is likely be different from that used by design & technology teachers although they are describing identical concepts. The time at which the concepts are introduced may vary between the subjects and the features of progression may also differ. Here is an area that clearly merits some discussion. Biology is often concerned with the interplay of form and function, and designers often use living things to inspire and inform their designs. Here again is an area that it would be useful for biology teachers to discuss with design & technology teachers. Due to the nature and funding of the physics teacher course previously discussed it was not possible to invite design & technology teachers to attend but the presence of teachers from both biology and design & technology would almost inevitably lead to greater collaboration and changes in practice.

Now imagine a session in which biology, chemistry and physics teachers come together to discuss the way some of their older students use mathematics in their science lessons. The biology teacher might want some consideration of statistics so that his students could better understand the work of ecologists and also plan their own investigations into local biodiversity. The chemistry teacher might be keen for her students to become *au fait* with the idea of logarithms in order to become proficient at pH calculations. The physics teacher might be keen for his students to develop an understanding of calculus in order to explore rates of change in a variety of phenomena. For example, a group of good mathematics teachers could hold court to requests in the form of a questions and answers panel and suggest in their answers the sorts of collaborations that could be used to enable the teaching of science in the light of students' learning in mathematics.

As we have seen from the examples given in this chapter and the use of continuing professional development it is possible to enhance the teaching of science by taking into account pupils learning in design & technology and mathematics and teaching science in the light of STEM. In the following section we revisit the issue raised in the previous section, 'A relationship among equals?' There is a short discussion on the importance of giving equal weight to the perspectives offered by science, mathematics and design & technology within any relationship between the subjects.

Maintaining the integrity of learning in the interacting subjects

Each of the examples of teaching science in the light of STEM can be justified in terms of meeting an aspect of Wynne Harlen's ideas *of* science and *about* science. Hence, although the science teaching has been undertaken in the light of learning that has already or might take place in mathematics and design & technology it has not been compromised. The design & technology activities that were described in this chapter, as in all of the examples, link science learning to either design & making activities or to designing activities to which there are multifarious, as opposed to single correct answers. Hence, the particularly significant difference between science and design & technology has been respected and preserved. And in each example, science understanding has informed designing and making such that the utility of the science is exemplified without the science teaching becoming distorted. The nature of the mathematics activities is varied and includes simple measurement and estimation, the use of both arithmetic and algebraic calculations, the use of nets, understanding compound measures, using ratio and proportion and the interpretation of statistical data concerned with real world activity. All of these activities relate to topics that are prominent in most mathematics courses for pupils aged 11–16 years today. The mathematical perspective provided through making these links informs both science and design & technology and in some cases provides a mathematical window onto significant global problems. Hence, as with science, the utility of the mathematics is exemplified without mathematics teaching becoming distorted.

Conclusion

This chapter raises many questions. Does the nature of science really make it that difficult to teach because it is essentially 'outside students' individuality'? Is there room for a personal response to science within science for young people at school? One approach is to rely on creative pedagogy. The use of a blast furnace to create copper may appear intrinsically boring but if the response to learning about this and showing understanding is through creative writing then maybe it could actually be much more interesting. Asked to respond in such a manner we know of one student who wrote a short parody of a James Bond movie. 'My name is Bon, Car Bon. When things get hot I don't sweat, I just get stronger. That devil iron is no match for me when it comes to a contest over oxygen!' Of course many teachers do use creative pedagogy but the thrust of this chapter is that there is another very powerful weapon in teachers' armoury that can be used to combat some students' disillusion with science and to enhance the science curriculum for all. That is, science teaching should be carried out in the light of STEM where links with design & technology enable students to 'raid' science for useful ideas and links with mathematics can reveal the elegance of relationships within phenomena that can be described in no other way. We hope that the examples of teaching science in the light of STEM we developed here have shown what is possible. You might find some implausible or inappropriate for your particular situation; that is almost inevitable given the different circumstances in which schools and teachers find themselves.

Our hope is that you will be able to look at your own curriculum and see where you might teach science in the light of STEM to the advantage of your students. We firmly believe that professional development is an essential means for you to explore how you might teach science in the light of STEM. The experience of exploring practical activities and tricky concepts with a view to teaching science in the light of STEM is an important first step. Good ideas will come from the conversations you have with your colleagues.

Finally, we have had to wrestle with the issue of curriculum status. This is a particularly sensitive issue for design & technology in England at the moment with a government expert panel suggesting that the subject has 'weak epistemological roots' compared to other subjects more established in the curriculum. We believe that it is imperative to acknowledge the integrity of *each* subject, respect their ways of knowing and understanding and appreciate their different learning intentions.

Vera John Steiner has written about the dignified interdependence that underpins creative collaboration. We fully support her position with regard to the highly creative and collaborative endeavour of teaching science in the light of STEM. Hence, in teaching science in the light of STEM our advice is not to neglect the importance of regular conversations with colleagues from design & technology and mathematics.

Background reading and references

Architecture for Humanity (2006) *Design Like You Give a Damn: Architectural Reponses to Humanitarian Crises*. San Francisco: Architecture for Humanity.

Donnelly, J. (2003) 'A Loss of Faith in Science Education?', *Education in Science*, 203, 18–19.

Gupta, A. (2014) Instructions for assembling electric motors from everyday items. Available at: www.arvindguptatoys.com/toys/motor.html (accessed 10 February 2014).

Harlen, W. (2010) *Principles and Big Ideas of Science Education*. Hatfield: Association for Science Education.

John-Steiner, V. (2000) *Collaborative Creativity*. Oxford: Oxford University Press.

Layton, D. (1975) *Science for the People*. London: Allen and Unwin.

Layton, D. (1993) *Technology's Challenge to Science Education*. Buckingham: The Open University.[1]

Lynas, M. (2011) *The God Species: How the Planet Can Survive the Age of Humans*. London: Fourth Estate.

Millar, R. (2012) Association for Science Education Presidential Address 2012. Rethinking Science Education: Meeting the Challenge of 'Science for All', *School Science Review*, June, 93, 345, 21–30.

National Science Learning Centre (2008) *The STEM Framework National Science Learning Centre*, York.

New Scientist (2012) 'Nutrient-boosted Golden Rice Should Be Embraced', August. Available at: www.newscientist.com/article/mg21528783.000-nutrientboosted-golden-rice-should-be-embraced.html (accessed 10 February 2014).

Nuffield/York (2011) *Twenty First Century Science: GCSE Biology Workbook*. Oxford: Oxford University Press.

Ogborn, J. (2004) 'Science and Technology: What to Teach?' In M. Michelini (ed.) *Quality Development in Teacher Education and Training* (pp. 69–84), Udine: Forum.

Osborne, J. (2012) 'Sustaining the Spirit of Nuffield?' Presentation given at an event to celebrate the 50th anniversary of the Nuffield Foundation's work in curriculum development. Available at: www.nuffieldfoundation.org/sites/default/files/files/Jonathan_Osborne_speech_8_May_2012.pdf (accessed 6 October 2012).

Pearce, J. (2012) Do It Yourself and Save: Open-source Revolution is Driving Down the Cost of Doing Science. Available at: http://phys.org/news/2012-09-open-source-revolution-science.html (accessed 6 October 2012).

Pilloton, E. and Chochinov, A. (2009) *Design Revolution: 100 Products That Are Changing People's Lives*. London: Thames and Hudson.

Roberts, G. (2002) *SET for Success The Supply of People with Science, Technology, Engineering and Mathematics Skills*. London: HMSO. Available at: http://webarchive.nationalarchives.

gov.uk/+/http:/www.hm-treasury.gov.uk/d/robertsreview_introch1.pdf (accessed 26 November 2013).

Royal Society (2007) *S-T-E-M Working Together for Schools and Colleges* (unpublished).

Rutland, M. (2011) 'Food Technology in Secondary Schools in England: Views on its Place in a Technologically Advanced Nation in Kay Stables'. In C. Benson, M. de Vries (eds) *Perspectives on Learning in Design & Technology Education Proceedings of the PATT 25*: CRIPT 8 Conference 2011, 349–56. London: Goldsmiths University of London.

Science and Learning Expert Group (2010) *Science and Mathematics Secondary Education for the 21st Century*. London: Department for Business, Innovation & Skills.

SCORE Improving Practical Work in Science. (2013) Available at: www.gettingpractical. org.uk/m3-3.php (accessed 10 February 2014). Science Community Representing Education (SCORE) is convened by the Royal Society. The other founding partners are the Institute of Physics, the Royal Society of Chemistry, the Institute of Biology, the Biosciences Federation, the Science Council and the Association for Science Education.

Smith, C. (2008) *Design for the Other 90 Per Cent*. New York: Smithsonian Cooper-Hewitt National Design Museum.

Snow, C. P. (1959) *The Two Cultures and the Scientific Revolution*, Cambridge: Cambridge University Press.

Wolpert, L. (1992) *The Unnatural Nature of Science*. London: Faber.

Note

1   In this seminal book David Layton argues that science education has now to serve the needs of technology education and act as a resource for the development of technological capability. This new role has implications for traditional science lessons as they will need to be reworked if the learning is to be useful in practical situations and related to design parameters.

4

Teaching design & technology in the light of STEM

The nature and purpose of design & technology

There is little doubt that humanity has behaved technologically since the emergence of the species from Africa. Underpinning this was the development and use of tools. It is a moot point as to whether tools enabled the development of language or vice versa but the powerful combination of tool use and language has defined the development of human civilizations ever since. Jacob Bronowski explained this in terms of human's ability to envisage what might be.

> Man is a singular creature. He has a set of gifts, which make him unique among animals; so that, unlike them, he is not a figure in the landscape – he is a shaper of the landscape.

> (Bronowski, 1973, p. 19)

Bronowski captured the nature of this accomplishment in three brilliant sentences.

> The hand is the cutting edge of the mind. Civilisation is not a collection of finished artefacts; it is an elaboration of processes. In the end, the march of man is the refinement of the hand in action.

> (Bronowski, 1973, p. 116)

For those devising the National Curriculum for England in 1988 it was important to include a subject that reflected this unique feature of human achievement. David Layton echoed this in an interim report (Department for Education and Science and Welsh Office (1988)) to the government of the time as follows:

> What is it that pupils learn from design & technological activity which can be learned in no other way? In its most general form the answer to this question is in terms of capability to operate effectively and creatively in the made world. The goal is increased 'competences in the indeterminate zones of practice'.

> (Layton, 1993, p. 3)

In the early days of the National Curriculum the above statement was puzzling to many teachers, and in Chapter 2 we noted some of the changes that took place in the statutory requirements for the subject as it evolved from its inception to its current form. Put briefly, the subject evolved in a direction that valued procedural competence which was taught through the activity of designing and making at the expense of defining a clearly articulated body of knowledge to support this activity. This position has led to a significant criticism of the subject and its place in the revision of the National Curriculum, taking place at the time of writing.

The current Minister of Education in England, Michael Gove, has decided that it is crucial to identify the essential knowledge that children need in order to progress and develop their understanding. He sees this understanding as being categorized under four headings: facts, concepts, principles and fundamental operations (Department for Education, 2011). The expert panel tasked with identifying this 'essential knowledge' has had difficulty with design & technology, indicating that in their view it lacked the disciplinary coherence associated with other more established subjects in the school curriculum. This was compounded by an exchange between Andy Mitchell, Assistant Chief Executive of the Design and Technology Association and Michael Gove in 2011 in which the Minister challenged the Design and Technology Association (DATA) to show that design & technology could be a rigorous subject within the school curriculum. Recent research by John Williams and John Lockley (2012) explored the views of early career science and technology teachers as to what might be considered 'enduring ideas' within the subjects they taught. Interestingly, this research revealed that whilst the science teachers had little difficulty in identifying such ideas, this was not the case for the technology teachers. The authors noted that this may be in part due to the extensive place of procedural knowledge in technology but also that technology has no commonly agreed epistemology. Hence in the current political climate it is important that design & technology defines itself in ways that take into account these ministerial requirements. We believe that a useful approach to this problem would be to adopt that used by Wynn Harlen and her colleagues for science education. They identified important ideas *of* science and important idea *about* science. What would we list as ideas 'of' and 'about' design & technology? Ideas *of* design & technology might include:

- Knowledge of materials: sources, properties, footprint, longevity.
- Knowledge of manufacturing, by: subtraction, addition, forming, construction.
- Knowledge of functionality: powering, controlling, structuring.
- Knowledge of design, methods for: identifying peoples' needs and wants; identifying market opportunities; generating and developing design ideas; evaluating design ideas.
- Knowledge of critique, for: justice, stewardship.

Ideas *about* design & technology might include:

- Through design & technology people develop technologies and products to intervene in the natural and made worlds.
- Design & technology uses knowledge, skill and understanding from a wide range of sources especially but not exclusively science and mathematics.
- There are always many possible and valid solutions to technological and product development challenges some of which will meet these challenges better than others.
- The worth of technologies and products developed by people is a matter of judgement.
- Technologies and products always have unintended consequences beyond intended benefit which cannot be predicted by those who develop them.

How would these ideas play out in the way the subject will be taught? If we continue to look at the work of our colleagues in science we see that their prevailing pedagogy is based on constructivist thinking encapsulated by Rosalind Driver's seminal work *The pupil as scientist* (1983). By analogy we might want a pedagogy based around the 'pupil as technologist', an idea already espoused by Richard Kimbell and David Perry in *Design and technology in a knowledge economy* (2001). Clearly such pedagogy would include design & making activities but might also include activities in which pupils make without designing, design without making and explore the relationship between technology and society. But in the immediate future, especially in England, it will be important to show how these activities teach ideas of design & technology, and ideas about design & technology.

Design & technology and science

In 2011, to gain insight into the links between design & technology and science I interviewed Torben Steeg. Steeg is a freelance consultant in education, and is widely regarded as a national expert in the teaching of electronics, systems and control and modern manufacturing. He also has a strong background in science education having spent the early part of his teaching career as a physics teacher. Initially, Steeg identified the 'usual suspects' of science topics that might be useful in design & technology: electricity, energy, materials and structures, forces and motion, food and nutrition. But then he noted that it is more important (essentially because pupils could refer to these topics themselves if necessary, although this would be demanding for some pupils) to establish an understanding of scientific method, or, even better, inculcate scientific thinking i.e. the ability to approach a question in design & technology with a desire for empirical evidence; the attitude of 'let's find out'. Steeg thought this would be a great asset. Pupils should also learn when such an approach is and is not appropriate for design & technology – and that equally, science teachers might also want them to be able to do this. In deciding technical matters, such as defining the cross sectional area of a material to give the required strength and stiffness, it is obvious that empirical investigations and the application of material science concepts are likely to be useful and are hence appropriate. In contrast, deciding on the overall appearance of a product such that it is 'cool' or has what product designers Dick Powell and Richard Seymour term visceral appeal: 'you want it before you know what it is' does not rely on a scientific approach.

Steeg then noted that science teachers often use examples of applications to illustrate scientific principles. This revealed an interesting difference in the approach of the science and design & technology teachers. The science teachers might use the example of a drawing pin to illustrate pressure, instructing the pupils to hold the pin between thumb and forefinger and squeeze – but not too tightly – and then ask them to explain what they felt. The design & technology teacher might ask the pupils to take 'user trips' with a variety of drawing pins – different lengths of pin, different surface area of head, different types of head, pushed into different surfaces – and explore how easy it is to use different types of pin and speculate why there are different types. Although the physics of the drawing pin as a pressure multiplier underlies both activities the science teacher is using the drawing pin to help pupils understand the nature of pressure whereas the design & technology teacher is using the drawing pin to help pupils understand users. In fact this design & technology activity could, inherently, require no explicit discussion of pressure as force/area.

Steeg then considered the understanding of electricity in the design of masks that light up in the dark. There would clearly be a case for considering what pupils might have learned in science about simple circuits. If the lit-up elements are in series then the number of elements that can be used is quite small, but if they are arranged in parallel then a far greater number can be used. If the pupils were required to explain the behaviour of their circuit and its limitations then science learning would be useful here. If the pupils are required to consider battery life i.e. work out how long the mask can be used for on a single battery then the need for technical understanding increases. Whether this requires an increase in scientific understanding is an interesting question. If the explanation of the circuit is couched in terms of current flow then the explanation will revolve around the statement 'the higher the current flow, the less time the battery will last'. Hence Steeg was inclined to measure current and use the fact that most batteries provide an mAh value; this reduces the science understanding demand significantly as there is no need to consider voltage or power. This indicates that it might unnecessarily complicate matters to require pupils to understand all the science behind the performance characteristics of the components they are using. This led Steeg to consider the use of chooser charts. An example is shown in Figure 4.1. These are charts which describe the performance characteristics of components or materials or the usefulness of particular techniques. Their aim is to provide pupils with the information they need to make informed design decisions either unaided or with minimal support from their teacher. An able pupil can use such charts to make decisions, which he or she can then justify to the teacher. For a less able pupil the teacher can ask questions,

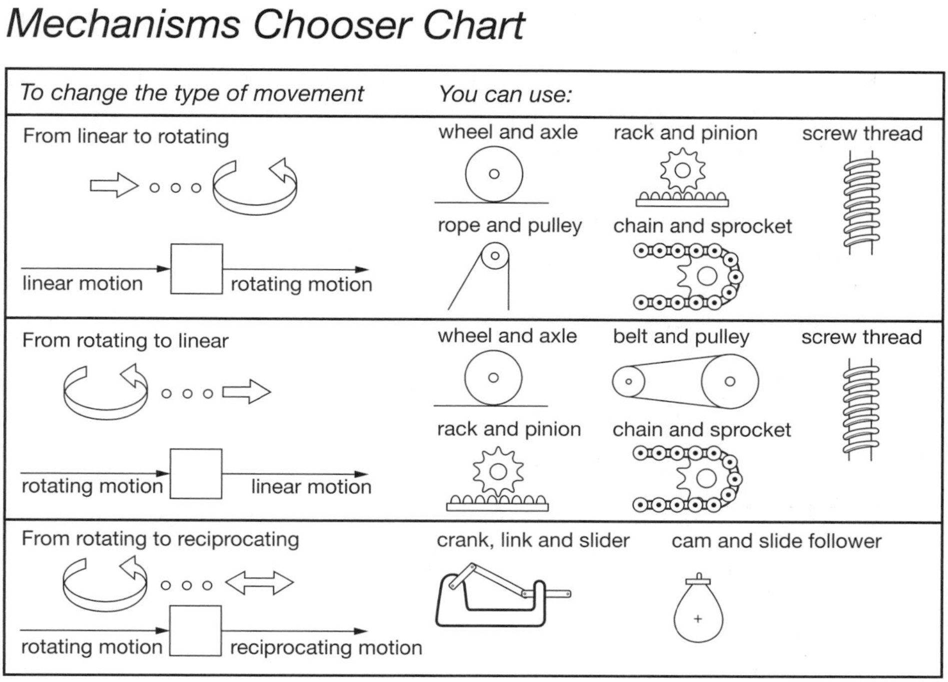
Mechanisms Chooser Chart
To change the type of movement
You can use:
From linear to rotating
linear motion
rotating motion
wheel and axle
rack and pinion
screw thread
rope and pulley
chain and sprocket
From rotating to linear
rotating motion
linear motion
wheel and axle
belt and pulley
screw thread
rack and pinion
chain and sprocket
From rotating to reciprocating
rotating motion
reciprocating motion
crank, link and slider
cam and slide follower

FIGURE 4.1 Part of a chooser chart from the Nuffield Design & Technology Projects.

engaging the pupil with the content of the chart and leading the pupil to make their own decisions. Of course, the best way to use such a chart involves annotating the chart with possible choices by drawing circles, adding ticks or crosses and notes. Steeg was clear that chooser charts aren't a substitute for all knowledge – pupils will need to know something to make sense of chart content and be able to use it appropriately. A key question is 'When will science knowledge be needed?' And this is exactly where being comfortable with using scientific thinking could come in useful as indicated by Steeg.

Design & technology and mathematics

To gain insight into the links between design & technology and mathematics I interviewed Celia Hoyles in 2009. Hoyles has been professor of mathematics education at the Institute of Education, University of London since 1984 and was the UK Government's Chief Adviser for Mathematics between December 2004 and November 2007. She is Director of the National Centre for Excellence in the Teaching of Mathematics. Hoyles explained that much of the mathematics curriculum for pupils aged 11–14 years is about discerning and expressing structure, pattern and relationships which include exploring data and appreciating and describing trends. Within this latter activity, there are important concepts that need to be understood if pupils are to be successful: for example, understanding the scale used on axes, the nature of the units used, the gradient of straight line graphs and how all these might relate to compound units, rates of change and effects over time. Understanding probability and its relationship with assessing risk is also an important area to be explored. Hoyles identified sustainability as an area of increasing importance across the curriculum. This manifests itself with a concern for dealing with resource depletion (the world is running out of natural resources) and global warming (the impact of increasing carbon dioxide emissions on climate change). Inaction is not an option and despair is counterproductive. So looking at relevant data using mathematical understanding to gauge the scale and significance of the problem is important. Only then is it really worth giving our pupils the chance to think, just as a professional designer would, about how these problems might be solved. So a joint venture might be that mathematics teachers and design & technology teachers identify the sorts of data needed for a collaborative venture around sustainability. Such a project could provide a rich context for learning about data, its representation and interpretation in mathematics with the understanding of the data being used to explore designing for a sustainable future in design & technology. Since measuring is a fundamental part of both mathematics and design & technology Hoyles thought it would be an area of exploration likely to be of mutual benefit. The conversation moved quickly on from the hoary bone of contention 'measuring length in millimetres in design & technology versus centimetres in mathematics' to the more positive arena of collaborating over the designing and making of a measuring device of some kind, suitable perhaps for Year 9 pupils. She wondered about pupils designing and making a weighing machine to meet an identified need in school e.g., a weighing machine that can be used in the school prep room to weigh small animals. Here the nature of the artefact immediately suggests mathematical thinking: understanding the range of measurement, an appropriate scale, calibrating the device, understanding the need for, and demonstrating reliability as well as other considerations, such as ease of use and comfort/minimal distress for the animal being weighed. Developing such a device might involve calibrating the stretch characteristics of a range of elastic bands such that the device could operate over a wide range of loads. Hoyles thought this was an example that would be worth mathematics and design & technology teachers discussing.

The development of product design specifications at GCSE has led to the possibility of pupils moving outside individual materials areas and tackling mixed media projects. Disaster relief provides a context for such work with pupils designing and making a pack that can be dropped via parachute into an area of natural disaster that survivors could locate easily and then use to provide emergency food, shelter and clothing. Hoyles thought it would be interesting to speculate on where mathematics might be used to enhance the design decisions made by the pupils, in an authentic way: for example, in maximising the volume and insulation of the pack. However, Hoyles did raise a word of warning: it would be important not to impose constraints on the design & technology that rendered the task non-authentic. She thought it was very important to be aware that making the mathematics more visible might in some cases be counter productive for the design as it introduces constraints that are just too artificial.

Finally, Hoyles made this one point very strongly. An essential requirement is for mathematics teachers and design & technology teachers to work together is time: time for them to initially explore possible mutual benefits that might be achieved through collaborating around a carefully selected design, time to make the activity and time to actually tackle the 'design and make' assignment for themselves, checking if it works and ultimately experiencing the mutual enhancement of mathematics and design & technology learning. Then they can jointly plan the classroom experience and review it following teaching. If this activity is started towards the end of the academic year it may be possible for mathematics teachers design & technology teachers to work alongside one another in the classroom. Alternatively, student teachers may be able to work alongside specialist teachers in the complimentary discipline.

The views of Steeg and Hoyles clearly indicate the considerable benefits that are possible if design & technology is taught in the light of knowledge and understanding acquired by pupils in science and mathematics lessons. However, it is important to ensure that the learning in these subjects is not compromised by attempts to form a curriculum relationship between them. This issue is now discussed in terms of maintaining subject integrity.

Maintaining subject integrity

As indicated by both Torben Steeg and Celia Hoyles, in using pupils' learning in mathematics and science to enhance their learning in design & technology it is essential that the integrity of design & technology be maintained. It is all too easy for the learning intentions to become subverted so that the learning of mathematics or science dominates the proceedings. The simplistic and erroneous definition of technology as 'applied science' can easily lead to situations in which the application of science overrides all other considerations to the detraction of learning in design & technology. Brian Arthur's definition of technology as the 'exploitation of scientific phenomena' is to be preferred because it enables a much wider interpretation as exploitation encompasses far more than application. This reduces the possibility of important wider influences being ignored. This point is given further weight by David Layton who argued that the knowledge constructed by scientists in their quest for understanding of natural phenomena is not always available in a form which enables it to be used directly and effectively in design & technology tasks. Knowledge that has been conceptualised so that it is useful in providing explanation is not necessarily the knowledge needed to inform the taking of action, although both formulations of knowledge are concerned with the same domain. Indeed, there are examples in the history of science and technology in which the knowledge to take action preceded the knowledge needed for explanation. The classic example is the development of the steam engine by James Watt almost 50 years before the explanation of the underlying thermodynamics by Sadi Carnot in 1824. This is discussed in greater depth in Chapter 3, Teaching science in the light of STEM.

One way to maintain integrity is to plan on the basis of the utility-purpose model proposed by Janet Ainley and colleagues. They argue that it is possible to engage the utility of some subjects in pursuing the learning purposes of others. Hence it should be possible to capitalise on the utility of mathematics and science in pursuing the learning purposes of design & technology. If one considers that a fundamental purpose of design & technology is for pupils to learn how to make genuine design decisions then it is not difficult to see how such decisions can, and ought to be informed by learning in mathematics and science. It is important that such decisions are genuine and authentic design decisions and not simply technical decisions contrived to support learning in mathematics and science. Ainley and colleagues also argue that there is mutual benefit in this arrangement. In utilising mathematics and science pupils will become more adept at these subjects whilst at the same time enhancing their ability in design & technology.

In this section we have considered the benefits of teaching design & technology in the light of STEM and briefly discussed the importance of maintaining subject integrity. In the following section will provide examples of design & technology activities that build on the advice from Torben Steeg and Celia Hoyles and exemplify the utility-purpose approach developed by Janet Ainley and her colleagues.

Examples of teaching design & technology in the light of STEM

It is important that all areas of design & technology benefit from teaching in the light of learning in science and mathematics. Hence the following examples cover the breadth of design & technology. They take into account both the utility-purpose model and the views of Torben Steeg and Celia Hoyles.

Example 1: Trying to exploit a scientific phenomena in product design

Consider a unit of work in which pupils aged 14 are required to design and make a device that exploits a scientific phenomenon – echoing Brian Arthur's definition of technology. For example, the phenomenon to be exploited could be the Peltier effect. The Peltier effect is enshrined in a solid state device that when activated transfers heat from one side of the device to the other side against the temperature gradient. Although this phenomenon is outside the usual science curriculum for 14 year olds it is likely that pupils will find the sensation of a device that is 'cold on one side hot on the other side' highly intriguing. And such a new phenomenon provides the opportunity to investigate the extent to which it can be exploited – what do we have to do to get the cold side really cold and the hot side really hot, i.e. how do we maximise the effect? Here is an opportunity for a genuine investigation that will provide information useful to pupils in pursuing a design and make task.

This clearly mirrors the utility-purpose argument proposed by Ainley and colleagues. With appropriate collaboration it would be possible for the investigation to be carried out in pupils' science lessons and the results used in design & technology lessons. This would provide the science teacher with an investigation that is linked to a purpose wider than developing explanation and the opportunity to see how scientific the pupils could be in pursuing such an investigation. If it were not possible to carry out the investigation in a science lesson then pupils could carry out the investigation as part of their design & technology lessons, assuming the design & technology teacher felt confident enough and had the necessary scientific understanding to do this. However, it almost certainly would be a lost opportunity for pupils to see the potential for their learning in science to be related to their learning in design & technology. This idea has been developed into a unit of work by Philip Holton, a head of faculty at a school (pupils aged 11–19 years) in South East England and published by the Design and Technology Association. The demands of the task are considerable as demonstrated by the instructions shown in Figure 4.2.

It is noteworthy that understanding the physics of the Peltier device in terms of a scientific explanation is NOT required for this unit of work. Hence although the underlying science will not be taught until pupils are several years older it is possible for Year 9 pupils to engage with the performance characteristics of the device and that is the knowledge needed to be able to take action. In Holton's classroom pupils have designed and made a variety of cooling devices for different purposes that they

---

Peltier Cell project

In this project you are challenged with designing a unique concept product using Peltier Cell technology.

You will need to conduct research into the capabilities of a Peltier Cell; understand current and patented uses of the technology; before undergoing creative designing of conceptual uses for the cell.

You will need to model your best idea to a level where it can be tested; evaluate your concept; and finish by creating a patent document which describes the unique idea you have developed.

FIGURE 4.2 Instructions for the Peltier Cell project.

consider worthwhile, including a device for cooling drinks and a device for maintaining an organ for transplant at the correct temperature during transportation. Holton's pupils are also introduced to some of the commercial applications for the Peltier effect through considering existing patents. Recently, there have been some very innovative proposals for new devices that use the Peltier effect. For example, a team from Tokyo University have been exploring the use of Peltier elements in thermal gaming, these include: *Thermodraw*, which sits an element beneath a screen that changes temperature based on the colours painted – an icy tundra will find the image cold to touch, Hawaii holiday photographs produce the opposite; *Thermogame* places the elements inside the controller, helping the player navigate fire and ice hazards. Awareness of such applications is likely to increase pupil interest.

This is an interesting opportunity for the science teacher to reinforce the idea that science is concerned with explanation involving the use of concepts by questioning the pupils about the working of their finished devices. If a pupil has added metal fins to the hot side of the device, questioning should reveal whether they can explain their function in terms of conduction and convection. There will also be opportunities to probe the extent to which pupils are distinguishing the concepts of heat and temperature. It is extremely worthwhile for the design & technology teacher to sit in on this questioning to give insight into the sorts of conceptual confusion that can arise and the way that the use of language in both design & technology and science lessons for such tricky ideas needs to be consistent. Note that this approach of developing a product that exploits a scientific phenomenon could provide a generic approach to teach design & technology in the light of STEM. Conversations with science colleagues to identify a range of such phenomena would indeed be worthwhile. This would also link strongly to Torben Steeg's point of utilising scientific thinking as an important feature of design & technology.

Example 2: Designing and making moving toys

Pupils aged 11–14 are often required to design and make simple moving toys. The movement is often provided by means of simple electric motors which produce very high no load speeds of rotation on the output shaft. Invariably this high speed of rotation is reduced by a transmission system. The simplest involves elastic band belt drives and pulley wheels. These are inexpensive to resource and forgiving in that they do not require a high level of accuracy to work well. The elastic bands stretch and can easily accommodate an error in locating the drive axle. Conversely, gearing systems have to be located precisely if the teeth in the gears are to mesh in a way that does not bind or slip. Compound gear trains clearly require more accuracy. Often pupils are provided with a set of wheels and a ready-made transmission system, items that the teacher knows will work, which to some extent guarantees a successful product. However, this approach denies pupils the opportunity to consider how fast they want their toy to move and what factors might affect this speed of travel. How fast the toy moves should to some extent be decided on the needs of the person who will play with the toy. If it will be played with indoors, in a small apartment for example, a slow speed would be preferable but if it will be played with outdoors, in a garden or school playground then a fast speed is required. Pupils can be introduced to the effect of wheel size on speed of movement by providing information as shown in Figure 4.3. Note that the chassis structure is deliberately simple. Pupils may already have carried out such constriction in primary (elementary) school. However, keeping the construction simple enables time to be spent on other features that contribute to the toy's performance.

Calculating the speed of each toy is not a trivial task. The speed of travel of the toy depends on both the size of the wheel and its speed of rotation. In the example below the toy with the slowest speed of rotation (Derek's toy) will travel the fastest because this speed of rotation in combination with the wheel size gives the greatest distance travelled per minute. There are many opportunities for interesting conversations between pupils working in pairs and between the teacher and the pupil about the factors that will affect the speed of travel. And such conversations can reveal any misunderstandings pupils might have about the concept of speed and be used to help pupils address such misunderstanding. Understanding speed is a precursor to understanding acceleration so the science teachers will be interested to know which pupils are having difficulty with the idea of speed. At the same time, the mathematics teacher will be pleased that pupils are gaining practical experience in dealing with compound measures.

It might be necessary to have discs of the different diameters available and so that pupils can experiment with rolling them the requisite number of revolutions to develop an accurate representation of how the different toys will move. From this experience they can decide which toy is the fastest and how to adapt a toy (such as Mary's) so that it becomes the fastest. Other pupils will be able to reach this decision by using annotated sketches. Some pupils might be able to reach the decision intuitively but it will be important to ask them to justify their decision. At the moment this is a theoretical exercise and it is essential to use the understanding achieved in deciding on the motor speed and wheel size for the toys they are designing and making. Usually teachers provide only one sort of motor and most suppliers provide data sheets which will give no load speeds in revolutions per minute. However, once under load, the rate of revolution decreases significantly.

We then need to find out just how fast the motor turns under load and the effect of different sized wheels being turned by the motor on the speed of the toy. Some empirical evidence is required here. Depending on the time and finances

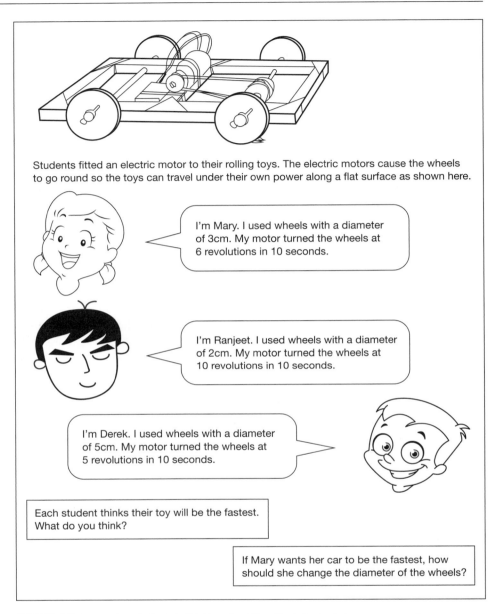

FIGURE 4.3 Introducing students to thinking about the effect of wheel size on movement.

available a teacher could provide a range of motors, pulleys and gears as well as different sized wheels. Some pupils could pause their investigations and use the results they have gathered so far to predict what might happen with different arrangements of motor, transmission system and wheels. This provides a great introduction to mathematical modelling. If the speed of the motor under load (obtained from the investigation) is known, the ratio of the transmission system (obtained from decisions about pulley or gear size and how they are arranged) and the diameter of the wheel (chosen from the range available) we can work out how fast the toy will go. Pupils can show their understanding of the model by responding to 'what will happen if' questions e.g., 'You know how fast your toy will travel but what if you make this pulley bigger, this wheel smaller?' The aim here is to help the pupils discern the patterns of behaviour in the arrangement of components and their understanding of the relationship between their behaviours to make design decisions that lead to a toy that is suitable for a particular user. This approach engages pupils with pattern recognition and the use of relationships, key parts of mathematics, as noted by Celia Hoyles, and vital for carrying out investigations. These are also key parts of science as noted by Torben Steeg. Taken together the utility of these activities inform the purpose of designing and making a moving toy.

Of course, the unexpected can still occur in terms of the toy's performance. The wheels might fail to grip the surface and slip, thereby reducing the toy's speed. Attempts to make the wheels look attractive, e.g., cutting large holes in them, might reduce their weight so that the motor can turn them faster than predicted increasing the toy's speed. Adding a larger battery to the toy may mean that it can be played with for longer, but it might also result in the toy being too heavy for the motor/transmission system to move. In such cases the limitations of the model of performance are revealed and this is an important learning point. And of course there is a range of other design decisions to be made, including: overall appearance (what sort of vehicle is the toy?); special effects (flashing lights, buzzers) and how these will be controlled; how the motor will be controlled (what sorts of switches and where are they placed); and how will all the different circuits be wired up to fit neatly into the toy ?

Example 3: Modelling wind turbines

Celia Hoyles indicated that using of mathematics could enhance the rigour with which sustainability issues were considered in the curriculum. As many design & technology schemes of work include a consideration of alternative energy sources there is the opportunity to engage with mathematics. The Science Enhancement Project (SEP) produces a useful wind power booklet to support practical activities using the SEP Wind Turbine and to help explain the science behind wind power. The SEP Wind Turbine is ready-assembled and can be used to carry out a wide range of experiments on wind power. In some design & technology schemes of work pupils can be required to make simple wind turbines from given components or design and make their own wind turbines. All of these activities enable pupils to develop an understanding of how the energy in the wind can be harnessed to produce either mechanical or electrical energy.

These activities can be extended to include consideration of wind turbines that might be used to produce significant amounts of energy, reduce carbon footprint and the use of fossil fuels. To gain a quantitative appreciation requires the use of mathematics and Learning and Teaching Scotland (LTS) have developed some interesting resources. These materials provide activities that enable pupils to develop their mathematics by considering important relationships such as:

- How is the area swept by the arm related to its length?
- How does wind speed relate to wind energy?
- How is wind energy related to power?

In all cases pupils are required to plot and interpret graphs so that they derive the relationship and ultimately the formulae that describe the relationship. These formulae are much more comprehensible as pupils have experienced deriving them from data. They are then required to use the formulae to explore the performance of different wind turbines at different wind speeds.

Here is an interesting arena for collaboration between design & technology and mathematics. The exploration of relationships involving the use of tables, graphs and background knowledge of direct proportion is extremely useful mathematics learning. Teaching about wind energy in design & technology allows this mathematics learning to be considered in an authentic context supported by a range of practical activities. The mathematics allows the pupils to begin to consider the feasibility of wind energy as a source of power and so enables the engaging practical activities to be extended to include an exploration of technology and society. Without mathematics, this topic lacks the rigour that will enable pupils to sensibly consider the energy supply issues facing society. The utility of mathematics in making important decisions comes to the fore. Of course there are issues other than the mathematics of wind and of wind turbines. The situation is complex. Where the turbines are situated and their impact on natural beauty and local wildlife are important factors that need to be considered. The availability and variability of wind on any chosen site need to be taken into account. The cost of setting up and maintaining the wind turbines versus the price for which the electricity generated can be sold has to enable both business and industry to make a profit. The government will be involved in providing incentives to business and industry but unless there is sufficient energy available in the wind that can be extracted by wind turbines then these wider considerations are irrelevant. This approach echoes strongly Celia Hoyle's point that using mathematics to explore data (in this case data about the wind) enables pupils to think in a 'designerly' way about how problems concerning sustainability might be solved. This approach would also benefit strongly from meeting Hoyles' plea that mathematics and design & technology teachers spend time together exploring the activities so that they are comfortable with each others' learning requirements and can see how to support them in their own lessons. The resulting plan of action might require the mathematics of wind energy to be considered in mathematics lessons either before or at the same time as the introductory practical activities in design & technology so that the wider discussions about using wind energy in particular situations can be informed by this mathematical understanding. If this were not possible and it was decided that the design & technology teacher would teach the mathematics of wind energy within the design & technology lessons then it would be very important for her to liaise strongly with the mathematics department on how best to approach this.

There are of course many links with science possible in teaching about wind energy in design & technology and investigations of the performance of small wind turbines pupils have constructed from given parts or designed and made provide many opportunities. For example, measuring the mechanical power of the output shaft by timing how long it takes to lift a mass through a metre is a very direct way. Alternatively, the output shaft can drive a small electric motor that acts as a generator to light up LEDs. The greater the number of LEDs lit the better the performance of the turbine. Within these activities there are opportunities for pupils to use the concepts of energy, force, work and power and to talk about their meaning. As with the conversations about heat and temperature in the Peltier effect project, discussion with pupils will reveal both understanding and misconception. Hence if possible it would be useful for the science teacher to discuss their investigations with pupils in ways that require pupils to use relevant concepts correctly. Here we have an inverse use of the usual suspects identified by Torben Steeg – their use in design & technology being scrutinised by the science teacher to reveal possible misconceptions.

Example 4: Lighting design

In many design & technology courses pupils aged 14–16 years are required to design and make simple lighting devices. Such tasks provide interesting opportunities to explore the way the technologies we use in daily life change over time and may change in the future. A comparison between filament lamps and light emitting diodes (LEDs) gives an interesting starting point for the way the provision of lighting is undergoing change. The way in which filament lamps work is relatively easy for pupils to understand and it is not difficult for them to appreciate how inefficient such lamps are in that only a fraction of the energy consumed is used in providing light. Most of the energy is used in bringing the filament up to the temperature at which the filament begins to glow. And of course pupils can feel filament lamps becoming hot. LEDs on the other hand do not rely on a heating effect to produce light.

Clearly, there are strong links here with the 'usual suspects' identified by Torben Steeg. The physics of the semiconductor materials that produce light in LEDs is probably not taught in science courses to pupils under the age of 16 years but it is relatively straightforward for pupils to carry out an investigation comparing the energy consumption of small filament lamps and LEDs. At the time of writing filament lamps for domestic lighting are being phased out in the UK and being replaced by lower energy consumption fluorescent bulbs which, whilst saving energy, do present environmental problems with regard to disposal because of their mercury content. There is considerable research and development activity into the design of LEDs that would be suitable for domestic lighting. The Technology Review website produced by MIT (www.technologyreview.com) gives an overview of recent research and would provide pupils with readings indicating how such research might inform future lighting development. Hence although the major part of a unit of work on lighting would be the designing and making of an LED-based light for, say, task or mood lighting it is possible to support this with science-based investigations into filament lamps and LEDs and an exploration of current research into the development of LED lighting for domestic use. An interesting extension activity would be for pupils to find out about the research work of electronics company Philips in developing lighting that uses bioluminescence. Here there is the opportunity for design & technology to link with the emerging field of biomimetics – adopting and adapting biological systems for use in technologies. It would be an interesting exercise for the pupils to compare the LED-based lights that they had produced with the lights being developed by Philips which use light-producing bacteria. This approach to lighting needs no wires, batteries or connection to an electricity grid. The energy comes from the bacteria's food source, which the researchers at Philips suggest could come from the sludge from a methane digester. The bio-light is part of a suite of products that feature in the Philips Microbial Home project.

In planning such a topic to exploit the links with science as indicated above it will be important to have conversations with the relevant science teachers. Of course, the physics teacher is likely to be interested in the filament lamp LED comparison and may be inclined to carry out the investigation as part of the pupils' physics course. If this were the case then it would be useful for the design & technology teacher to observe some of the lessons. She might also suggest that the pupils carry out additional investigations into the illumination provided by their light design proposals. Her guidance on this would be useful.

The biology teacher is likely to be interested in the bioluminescence part of the unit and may well be able to suggest practical activities in which pupils grow cultures of such bacteria. However, this is very specialist territory with particular health and safety issues so it would be wise for such activities to be taught by the biology teacher preferably in a science-teaching laboratory. The utility of scientific knowledge and understanding is clearly important in developing the investigations and this should be apparent to pupils as they pursue their lighting design and make tasks and explore the way the technologies we use for lighting have changed and may change in the future. This approach supports Brian Arthur's view that technology may be interpreted as the exploitation of scientific phenomena.

Example 5: Bread product development

In most food technology courses pupils will consider the production of bread as it is a staple food, comes in a variety of regional forms and has cultural significance for many communities. As it is consumed in such large quantities – in many societies people eat bread everyday – bread provides an interesting and accessible example of industrial production and distribution. In many schools, pupils will have experienced making bread already and there is no doubt that baking and then sampling freshly baked bread is a worthwhile experience, especially if the result is compared with commercially produced sliced and wrapped bread available from local supermarkets. Worthwhile as this experience may be it frequently misses the opportunity for pupils to understand *why* the bread making process is as it is, to understand the science behind it and to consider the nature of foams as a fundamental structure within foodstuffs generally.

The ingredients for bread are simple: flour, water, seasoning, sometimes a raising agent. The combination process is relatively straightforward and the baking process simple; hence it is relatively easy for pupils to devise experiments that enable them to investigate the role of various ingredients and processes and the influence they have on the nature of the final product. However, if all the pupils investigate the same variables the exercise is likely to take a long time. A more efficient approach and one that develops pupil's presentation and communication skills is to discuss the possible approaches with a class as a whole and then divide the class into groups so that each group carries out a different investigation. Each group is given the responsibility of presenting a poster describing their investigation and presenting their results to the class. The posters are put on display toward the end of the lesson and individual members of the class can visit each one and make a complete collection of results. It is through making sense of this wide range of results that the links between food technology and science are consolidated and the influence of different features on the final structure and appearance are demonstrated. Note also that in looking for relationships between the variables the pupils will be engaged in mathematical as well as scientific thinking.

Once the pupils have some sense of this they can be engaged with developing their own bread recipes to produce novel types of bread for particular occasions and different markets. In developing these recipes pupils should be able to justify their choice of ingredients with regard to their influence on the final product. Here we have a strong example of knowledge gained through scientific investigations informing pupil design decisions. A particular feature of food products is the wide range of sensory appeal they must achieve in order to be successful. Investigating this appeal with 'tasters' provides further possibilities of emphasising the scientific thinking argued for by Torben Steeg earlier in this chapter. Within food technology courses such investigations can take the form of a simple user trip in which testers comment generally about what they like about the product they are tasting. More focused testing is often formalised into ranking, preference and difference tests. Here there are opportunities to discuss with pupils why these tests are structured as they are and to reinforce their scientific nature.

It would be worth discussing all the above examples with both chemistry and biology teachers from two perspectives. First, it would be worth considering the extent to which the underlying concepts e.g., chemical reactions, the nature of gases and enzyme behaviour are already taught, and second, the possibilities of collaborating such that the teaching in food technology and science complement each other. An extension of the bread product development task described above is for pupils to consider their batch production. This immediately engages the pupils with the opportunity to use ratio and proportion, simple calculations and costing in developing a production specification for a particular sized batch. Such exercises can be linked to school fêtes so that the produce can be sold and the costs of the exercise recouped, and perhaps even a profit made. Discussion with mathematics teachers would be useful here to ensure that the approach to scaling up and costing was in line with the methods used in mathematics classes. There are interesting possibilities for considering the portion size and pricing of the bread in order to maximise profits. Exactly how mathematics, as opposed to intuition, might be used to decide on portion size and price forms the basis for an interesting conversation with the mathematics teacher and this could provide the basis for an investigation in the mathematics class, the results of which inform the batch production and sales of the bread products at the school fête. This example shows that making mathematics more visible is not counterproductive, as warned against by Hoyles, as it deals with issues that give the task more rather than less authenticity.

Example 6: Radio design

Designing a radio receiver circuit is beyond most school pupils but the experience of making a radio receiver that has been designed by someone else is a very worthwhile activity. Any teacher who has taught this will remember the expressions of surprise and delight on pupils' faces when they hear a local radio station on their own radio. There are several radio kits available from educational suppliers consisting of a printed circuit board, components and assembly plans to support this activity. There are different approaches to organising the assembly. Some teachers prefer to structure the activity on a step-by-step basis giving the class precise instructions for the identification and placement of each component. These teachers argue that this approach guarantees each pupil a working radio. Other teachers prefer to organise pupils in pairs, provide illustrated step-by-step assembly instruction and instruct each pair to produce two working radio circuits with each pupil in a pair being responsible for checking the other pupil's work. These teachers argue that this approach encourages the pupils to take more responsibility for their learning and enhances their collaboration and communication skills. Their position is that the few mistakes that cause circuits to malfunction can easily be identified and rectified, and the increased learning more than justifies this approach. In terms of design & technology learning, this making activity will enable pupils to learn how to identify a range of components, orientate components according to a layout diagram and soldering skills.

This learning can be extended to include a consideration of how the circuit actually works. This provides a useful opportunity to use a systems approach to describing circuits and to overlay the various components in the circuit onto the system blocks. In terms of links with science, this also provides the opportunity to consider the electromagnetic spectrum. This is an important and demanding idea that many pupils find difficult. Hence it will be important to liaise carefully with science teacher colleagues to ensure that the discussions in design & technology lessons about how the circuit works do not lead to conceptual confusion. Although it is possible for quite young pupils to assemble a working radio from given components, here it would probably be inappropriate to consider the electromagnetic spectrum. However, it can be used as a motivating starter activity to a design & technology electronics course for pupils aged 14–16 years and at this age it is likely that in their science courses, they will be learning about the electromagnetic spectrum (either in physics programmes or applied science programmes dealing with communication). Ideas about frequency and wavelength will almost certainly be considered. So it is possible that the science teacher could use the radios made by pupils in their design & technology lessons as a starting point for considering the electromagnetic spectrum.

It is likely that as part of their design & technology courses pupils will be required to produce a housing or enclosure for the radio circuit they have made. There are a variety of design decisions to be made in this activity and some of them can involve mathematics. For example, pupils will study nets in their mathematics lessons. Nets are two-dimensional shapes that can be folded to three-dimensional forms. These are sometimes studied in design & technology where they are called 'surface developments'. In mathematics, pupils may investigate the relationship between the surface area and enclosed volume and they may also link their study of nets to geometry, relating a variety of three-dimensional forms to the variety of nets from which they might be constructed. So it is possible that pupils will have at their disposal knowledge of a wide range of possible forms and associated nets to use for the radio enclosure. The net has to accommodate a variety of features and be large enough to accommodate the circuit and battery. These features include an on/off switch, a tuning dial and a volume dial and, if the radio is sufficiently complex, an AM/FM switch. All these features need to be arranged on the net to give user convenience and the overall appearance, which may include graphics, should have visual appeal. And, of course, the net should enable access for repair (e.g., wires coming loose) and maintenance (e.g., changing batteries). Hence designing a successful enclosure is not a trivial task. If the pupils can use CAD software to draw the required net with places to insert the various features then they can use their CAD files to drive a laser cutter to produce the required net from thin sheet material such as card or polypropylene, complete with creases to enable folding up around the circuit and battery to form the enclosure. The range and variety of enclosures formed will to some extent depend on pupils' initial knowledge of nets and it is here that conversations with their mathematics teachers can pay dividends. If the radio task can be timed to take place just after the pupils have studied nets then the mathematics teacher can contextualise the nets topic by using the radio enclosure design in the mathematics lessons. There is the possibility here of using Hoyles' example of considering the general case by which the volume for a particular enclosure can be maximised. This will enable the design & technology teacher to capitalise on the utility of the taught mathematics as pupils produce the enclosures. Even if such juxtaposition and contextualisation are not possible the design & technology teacher can still support pupils' designing tasks by helping them to remember what they have previously learned in mathematics and hence illustrate the usefulness of mathematics for design purposes.

Example 7: Protective textiles

In many design & technology courses concerning textiles pupils are required to design and make items concerned with protection. This provides the opportunity for pupils to consider the many different situations in which there is the need for protection that can be provided by the use of textiles. The following examples indicate the wide range of situations pupils might consider.

- Trawler fishermen keep warm and dry by wearing clothing made from waterproof fabric with welded seams and flaps over fastenings.
- Soldiers avoid being seen by the enemy by wearing clothing that is randomly coloured, causing the figure to merge in the background.
- Mechanics keep clean by wearing overalls made from densely woven fabric which does not allow grease or dirt to penetrate.
- American football players avoid being hurt by wearing padding that protects by absorbing impact.
- People keep warm in the snow by wearing coats made from thick fabric that traps air between clothes and coat to provide insulation.
- People out in the sun keep cool by wearing clothes made from thin fabric that allows perspiration to be absorbed and evaporate keeping the wearer cool.
- Cyclists maintain visibility by wearing brightly-coloured light-reflective fabric that enable them to be seen.

All these situations provide the potential for investigations into fabric performance and underlying these investigation is the important idea of 'properties'. This would capitalise on both of Steeg's categories of usefulness – a 'usual suspect' – properties of materials, and scientific thinking. Within the arena of textiles this is complex because the properties of fabrics depend on both the nature of the fibre and the structure of the fabric. To give the investigations purpose the pupils will need to consider the following or similar questions:

- What properties are important to achieve the protection required?
- Which fabrics or fabric combinations have these properties?
- What investigations can I carry out that will help decide which fabrics might be suitable?
- What other factors should I consider, e.g., cost, availability, or appearance?

Pupils will already have been introduced to the idea of materials having properties and how these are established by investigation, giving rise to tables of data describing such properties. It is possible for pupils to identify the fabrics that might be useful by using such tables. However, this requires a sophisticated understanding of the properties under consideration and initially it will almost certainly be necessary for pupils to devise and carry out simple investigations for themselves to understand the nature of relevant properties. Such investigations can be designed to give a rank order of materials with regard to a particular property, e.g., increasing ability to resist wear or to give values of properties in particular units, e.g., tensile strength of a fabric in kg/cm. Clearly, conversations with science teachers will be valuable here not least to ensure that the ideas concerning fair testing and measurement of properties that are taught in science lessons are utilised and built upon in the design & technology lessons. Science teachers might also use the investigations as part of their science teaching as in the Peltier device investigation described earlier in this chapter. As the pupils become familiar with a wide range of fabric properties through investigations, their ability to use information in tables of properties will increase and they will be able to justify their choice of fabric without necessarily carrying out investigations.

In those cases where pupils will design and make a textile item it is likely that the choice of fabric will be limited by cost. However, in some cases it would be appropriate for pupils to develop their ideas to a detailed design proposal only and stop short of actually making a finished article. In such cases a mock up in an inappropriate fabric, supported by details of the actual fabric to be used in the final article, would suffice. This would allow pupils to consider the use of very modern textiles unavailable to schools, Kevlar is an obvious example. Comparison of the properties of Kevlar compared with other textiles that might be used for protection purposes soon indicates how unusual and useful it is. However, without the preliminary understanding of the properties of materials, learning about Kevlar and considering possible uses will lack a 'wow' factor. It is not difficult to extend this approach to include pupils speculating about the uses of cutting-edge materials being developed by science-based research and development. Spider silk is such a material: five times stronger than steel, tougher than Kevlar and highly elastic, it is so potentially extremely useful – if only it could be manufactured. It has proved impossible to farm spiders in the same way as silk worms so scientists have been trying to get the best of both worlds – super-strong silk in industrial quantities – by transplanting genes from spiders into worms. Recent successful research represents a step towards the commercial production of a combination of silk and spider silk spun by silkworms. Currently, it is thought that the main applications for spider silk will be in the medical sector creating stronger sutures, implants and ligaments. But the GM spider silk could also be used as a 'greener' substitute for toughened plastics, which require a lot of energy to produce. Encouraging pupils to speculate about possible uses of genetically modified materials provides an interesting way of raising pupils' awareness of the way biomimicry and biological manufacturing are likely to become important in the future. Conversations with science teachers about how to relate this teaching in design & technology to the teaching of genetics in biology classes are an important part of ensuring that the utility-purpose argument developed by Ainley and colleagues is on a sound footing and can be extended to activities involving exploring technology and society.

After considering a wide range of examples of teaching design & technology in the light of STEM the following section revisits the issue of 'maintaining subject integrity' with a short discussion on the importance of ensuring that the learning in design & technology, mathematics and science isn't in anyway undermined by 'teaching in the light of STEM'.

Ensuring continuity of learning across the subjects

Having considered a wide range of examples in which design & technology can be taught with regard to links to pupils' learning in science and mathematics it is important to ask to what extent might this approach compromise the learning in the interacting subjects? It is vital that there is sufficient mutual benefit to the subjects involved to ensure that the not inconsiderable effort required for the interaction is worthwhile. Celia Hoyle's warning that the linking process should not impose constraints on design & technology that render the tasks non-authentic is key. And it is also important to ensure that the process of interacting does not confuse pupils by giving mixed messages about learning in the interacting subjects. In developing approaches to teaching design & technology with regard to pupils' learning in science and mathematics one must start with one or two activities and then build in evaluations to give some sense of the costs and benefits of the exercise. Ideally, the interaction between the subjects should enhance the learning across the interacting subjects. Hence the science and mathematics teachers should be able to see improvement in their pupils' learning as a result of the interaction. Similarly, the design & technology teacher should be able to see improved learning in design & technology through pupils' use of science and mathematics. Once a few successful 'teaching in the light of STEM' activities have taken place it will be easier to develop further effective examples.

Conclusion

So what are we to make of this chapter? If we define a knowledge base for design & technology will it become more acceptable as a subject suitable for a place in the national curriculum? Will such a definition cause the subject to become less concerned with procedural competence to such an extent that it loses the essence of its initial rationale, 'enabling competence in the indeterminate zone of practice'? Adopting pedagogy around designing and making would certainly make this less likely. Where does this leave teaching design & technology in the light of STEM? Torben Steeg and Celia Hoyles were in no doubt as to the advantages of pupils of being encouraged if not actually required to use their science and mathematics learning to enhance their learning in design & technology. And what of the danger of teaching design & technology in the light of STEM resulting in the legitimate learning requirements of design & technology becoming submerged and merely subservient to meeting the learning requirements of science and mathematics? The utility-purpose model proposed by Janet Ainley and colleagues goes some way to mitigating against this difficulty in that there is benefit to all the collaborating subjects only if design & technology can pursue its 'designerly purpose' which lies at the core of its learning requirements.

The examples of teaching design & technology in the light of STEM used in this chapter were developed in part to show that in taking such an approach the integrity of design & technology would not be compromised. We provided examples to illustrate that teaching design & technology in the light of STEM is not only possible but really worth exploring. If you can use our examples that is all to the good, but if you find them inappropriate for your situation it is our view that this should not be a barrier to developing your own examples that *are* appropriate. Indeed, we would urge you to develop your own ways to teach design & technology in the light of STEM. Of course, in tackling this task it will be important to avoid giving pupils mixed messages that will confuse rather than enhance their understanding. Developing a coherent appreciation of important ideas across the STEM subjects will only be achieved through on-going conversations between all those involved in the teaching. This will require time – something that the STEM Pathfinder Programme indicates that this was seen by teachers as the scarcest and most valuable resource needed for teaching collaboratively across the STEM subjects. So in teaching design & technology in the light of STEM our advice is don't neglect the importance of regular conversations with colleagues from science and mathematics.

Background reading and references

Ainley, J., Pratt, D. and Hansen, A. (2006) 'Connecting Engagement and Focus in Pedagogic Task Design', *British Educational Research Journal*, Volume 32, No 1, 23–38.[1]

Arthur, W. B. (2009) *The Nature of Technology*. London: Allen Lane.

Bronowski, J. (1973) *The Ascent of Man*. London: British Broadcasting Corporation.

Department for Education (2011) *The Framework for the National Curriculum: A Report by the Expert Panel for the National Curriculum Review*. London: DfE.

Department for Education and Science and Welsh Office (1988) *National Curriculum Design and Technology Working Group Interim Report*. London: HMSO.

Driver, R. (1983) *The Pupil as Scientist*. Milton Keynes: The Open University Press.

Holton, P. (2012) Peltier Project. Resources for Teaching the Peltier Project are available from the Design and Technology Association website: www.data.org.uk (accessed 8 January 2012). Applications of the Peltier effect in thermal gaming are available at: www.engadget.com/2011/11/30/peltier-elements-power-thermal-gaming-warm-backsides/ (accessed 8 January 2012).

Kimbell, R. and Perry, D. (2001) *Design and Technology in a Knowledge Economy*. London: Engineering Council.

Layton, D. (1993) *Technology's Challenge to Science Education*. Buckinghamshire: The Open University.[2]

LTS (2013) STEM Central, Learning and Teaching Scotland. The resources concerning the use of mathematics to explore wind energy are available at: www.ltscotland.org.uk/stemcentral/contexts/renewables/learningjourneys/calculatingthewind/supportingresources.asp (accessed 8 January 2012).[3]

Nuffield Design & Technology Chooser Charts. (1999) Available as free downloads at: www.nationalstemcentre.org.uk/elibrary/resource/107/ks3-chooser-charts (accessed 10 February 2014).

Philips Microbial Home Project (2012) Information is available at: www.design.philips.com/about/design/designportfolio/design_futures/design_probes/projects/microbial_home/index.page (accessed 8 January 2012).[4]

Science Enhancement Project Wind Power Booklet (2009) Available as a free download at: www.nationalstemcentre.org.uk/elibrary/collection/578/sep-energy-and-power (accessed 8 January 2012).

STEM Pathfinder Programme (2012) Details of the programme and its evaluation can be found at: www.nationalstemcentre.org.uk/elibrary/collection/304/stem-pathfinder-programme (accessed 20 November 2012).

Williams, P. J. and Lockley, J. (2012) 'An Analysis of PCK to Elaborate the Difference Between Scientific and Technological Knowledge'. In T. Ginner, J. Helstrom and M. Hulten (eds) 'Technology Education in the 21st Century: Proceedings of the PATT 26 Conference 2012', 468–77, Stockholm: Linkoping University.

Notes

1   In this paper the authors explore the dilemma between planning from objectives, which leads to unrewarding tasks and planning from tasks and thus high pupil engagement, but unfocused learning that is difficult to assess. They argue that planning

tasks on a utility-purpose basis can resolve this dilemma. This chapter provides examples of teaching science and mathematics that have utility for pursuing design & technology purposes.

2 In this seminal book Layton argues that science education has now to serve the needs of technology education and act as a resource for the development of technological capability. This new role has implications for traditional science lessons as they will need to be reworked if the learning is to be useful in practical situations and related to design parameters.

3 Learning and Teaching Scotland have developed a STEM Central website which contains a wide variety of resources which use the contexts of engineering activity to develop interdisciplinary approaches to teaching science, mathematics, technology and geography.

4 The Microbial Home is a proposal for an integrated cyclical ecosystem where each function's output is another's input. In this project the home has been viewed as a biological machine to filter, process and recycle what we conventionally think of as waste – sewage, effluent, garbage, waste water.

5

Teaching mathematics in the light of STEM

The 'Marmite' subject

In England there is an advertisement for a savoury spread called Marmite in which consumers responses are depicted as either 'love it' or 'hate it'. School mathematics is sometimes known as the 'Marmite' subject; pupils either love it or hate it. For those who hate mathematics, it is almost incomprehensible to them that someone could like it so much that they give their career over to being a professional mathematician. The popular image of the mathematician is not dissimilar to the popular image of the scientist mentioned in Chapter 1: male, elderly, unfashionable, untidy, withdrawn into world that only he, and I stress he, is interested in or understands and which he can't explain to others in everyday language. Yet, mathematics is the product of the human mind. Unfortunately, the mathematics we learn at school tells us little if anything of the mathematicians who produced it. Vera John Steiner and Reuben Hersh write compellingly about the 'life mathematical' enjoyed by those who commit to mathematics. They acknowledge that it is certainly not an easy life. It is full of intellectual struggle accompanied by a roller coaster of emotional highs and lows as ideas which seem promising turn out to be false and must be discarded in an ever more ruthless pursuit of truth. Among mathematicians there is fierce rivalry as well as intense friendship and loyalty, played out within a domain that few others can appreciate. However, Steiner and Hersh do acknowledge that for many the 'life mathematical in school' is a very different affair.

This phobia of mathematics is compounded in many western societies with an almost perverse pride in not being able to 'do' mathematics. Whereas those who cannot read go to great lengths to hide this failing, a large number of the population are more than happy to admit that they weren't good at mathematics at school. And those that did enjoy mathematics at school are more than likely to keep this accomplishment hidden from friends and colleagues. It seems only English has the popular expression 'too clever by half'. How does this situation arise? Steiner and Hersh have no doubt as to the answer. They write, 'People aren't born disliking math. They learn to dislike it at school!' This is not to decry the efforts of teachers but to acknowledge that the content of current mathematics courses in conjunction with their significance in high-stakes testing and examination success needed to gain access to college or university courses puts a very heavy burden on students who find the subject bemusing. This is not a particularly new insight. In 1902, Betrand Russell wrote:

> In the beginning of algebra, even the most intelligent child finds, as a rule, very great difficulty. The use of letters is a mystery, which seems to have no purpose except mystification. It's almost impossible, at first, not to think that every letter stands for some particular number, if only the teacher would reveal what number it stands for. The fact is, that in algebra the mind is first taught to consider general truths, truths which are not asserted to hold only this or that particular thing but of any one of a whole group of things. [...] Usually the method that has been adopted in arithmetic is continued: rules are set forth, with no adequate explanation of their grounds; the pupil learns to use the rules blindly, and presently, when he is able to obtain the answer that the teacher desires, he feels that he has mastered the difficulties of the subject. But of inner comprehension of the processes employed he has probably acquired almost nothing.
>
> (Russell, 1902, p. 60)

In fairness, we should acknowledge that Bertrand Russell's attempts at school teaching were not successful and the school he set up with Ludwig Wittgenstein was a complete failure. But we cannot deny that there is considerable concern over many young peoples' dislike of school mathematics and the resultant poor levels of attainment. We will now discuss this concern .

Causes for concern

Politicians need yardsticks with which to measure the educational achievements of their young citizens and compare them to that of young people in other countries. One such yardstick is the Programme for International Student Assessment (PISA). Since the year 2000, every three years, a randomly selected group of 15 year olds take tests in the key subjects: reading, mathematics and science, with focus given to one subject in each year of assessment. The students and their school principals also fill in questionnaires to provide information on the students' family backgrounds and the way their schools are run. Some countries and economies also choose to have parents fill in a questionnaire. PISA is unique because it develops tests which are not directly linked to school curricula and provides context through the background questionnaires which can help analysts interpret the results. The tests are designed to assess to what extent students near the end of compulsory education can apply their knowledge to real-life situations and be equipped for full participation in society. It is generally agreed that PISA data provides governments with a powerful tool to shape policy making.

The performance in mathematics in 2009 did not make encouraging reading for politicians in either the UK or the USA, with Shanghai-China, Singapore and Hong Kong-China in the top three positions. The United Kingdom came 28th with a score not statistically different from the OECD average and the USA came 31st with a score statistically significantly below the OECD average. President Obama was reported as being extremely disappointed by the results, vowing to improve US schools' performance. US Education Secretary Arne Duncan pulled no punches in his response, quoting President Obama, 'the nation that out-educates us today will out-compete us tomorrow' and acknowledging with brutal honesty that the PISA results 'show that a host of developed nations were out-educating the USA'. His view was that the big picture from PISA was one of educational stagnation at a time of fast-rising demand for highly-educated workers and that 'the mediocre performance of America's students is a problem we cannot afford to accept and cannot afford to ignore'. Michael Gove, the Minister for Education in England in 2011 was also a great admirer of the data generated by PISA, citing in a speech to the World Education Forum that the fall of student performance in mathematics from 8th to 28th in the past 10 years as a significant statistic that needed to be addressed by the coalition government. The theme is unrepentantly instrumental – education for economic success – but all the more difficult to achieve during a global recession. It is worth noting that the Trends in International Mathematics and Science Study (TIMSS) collects data concerned with the performance of students in primary (elementary) and secondary (junior high) schools. These tests are more closely aligned to the school curriculum and recently schools in England have shown improved performance. However, overall such tests give little comfort to politicians in England and the USA who are concerned at the disparity between the performance of young people in their countries compared to that of young people in other jurisdictions.

In England, the most recent Ofsted Report ('Mathematics Made to Measure', 2012) into the teaching of mathematics offers little comfort. As with all such reports the sample is limited. Inspectors visited 160 primary and 160 secondary schools and observed more than 470 primary and 1200 secondary mathematics lessons, but there is little reason to suspect that the findings are not typical of the wider picture. The report highlights the failure of much teaching to develop pupils' conceptual understanding alongside their fluent recall of knowledge, and a lack of confidence in problem solving indicating that too much teaching concentrated on the acquisition of disparate skills that might have enabled pupils to pass tests and examinations but did not equip them adequately for the next stage of education, work and life. The report emphasised the problems of a poor start which doubtless goes a long way to explain the 'hate it' as opposed to 'love it' response of many pupils:

> The 10% who do not reach the expected standard at age 7 doubles to 20% by age 11, and nearly doubles again by 16

(Ofsted, 2012, p. 4)

The report noted that this is compounded by the lack of curricular guidance and professional development in enhancing subject knowledge and effective pedagogy. In his introduction to the report, the Chief Inspector of Schools Sir Michael Wilshaw returns to the instrumental theme:

> Our failure to stretch some of our most able pupils threatens the future supply of well-qualified mathematicians, scientists and engineers.
>
> (Ofsted, 2012, p. 4)

Another report, 'A world class mathematics education for all our young people', developed by a task force chaired by Carol Vorderman and lead author Roger Porkess, paints a bleak picture of the disenchantment felt by many with regard to their mathematics experience and lack of success at schools:

> If you imagine those 300,000+ young people who have failed holding hands in a line, then that line of students would stretch the entire length of the M1 from London to Leeds. These are just this year's GCSE students who, after 11 years of being taught mathematics, have learnt to fear and hate the subject. And next year there will be another such line of students, and the year after, and so on.
>
> (Porkess et al., 2011, p. 4)

The report makes a wide range of recommendations for improving the situation, many of which have been welcomed by the current political administration and to some extent implemented, particularly those concerned with making teaching more attractive to mathematics graduates and raising the level of mathematics qualifications required by all those entering teaching whatever subject they might teach. The report also cites a publication by the Nuffield Foundation, 'Is the UK an outlier? An international comparison of upper secondary mathematics education'. The findings of this report are stark. In England, Wales and Northern Ireland fewer than one in five students study any mathematics after the age of 16 (Scotland does slightly better). In 18 of the 24 countries studied (mainly from the OECD) more than half of students in the age group study mathematics; in 14 of these, the participation rate is over 80%; and in eight of these every student studies mathematics. When it comes to the mathematics education of its upper secondary students the UK is out on a limb. The Vorderman-Porkess report indicates strongly that this situation should be addressed. It is important to note that Vorderman and Porkess do not in any way place blame on students, teachers or schools. They see these actors as victims of a system over which they have no control. Rather, the report identifies a lack of innovation in syllabuses; qualifications and provision, it argues, have been stifled by prevailing regulation and accountability procedures and pose a significant problem. This, the report suggests, has prevented the necessary developments to improve the experience of school mathematics such that it is rewarding and challenging without being daunting and such that it could provide qualifications of value which could also identify the suitability of young people for particular employment and further or higher education. Such developments could reveal the significance and potential of teaching mathematics in the light of STEM. Given the extent of these concerns it is important to consider how they are being addressed.

Responding to concern

The mathematical education community is not complacent and has responded vigorously and positively to the problems identified in the previous section. The report by the Advisory Committee on Mathematics Education (ACME) on the mathematical needs of learners is particularly insightful (ACME, 2011). The report is critical of the assessment regime that fosters 'teaching to the test' at the expense of developing a genuine understanding based on conceptual development. A particularly useful feature of the report is the development of a model for mapping a curriculum for learners' mathematical needs. To some extent the approach parallels that of Wynne Harlen and colleagues in identifying key ideas in science that we saw in Chapter 3. The approach relies on identifying BIG mathematical ideas associated with a particular domain and making suggestions how such ideas might be used in a particular contexts and practices. The model of progression involves starting with a wide range of early ideas, their reduction to a few key ideas, the development of new meanings which lead to a wider and richer set of later ideas. This framework is shown in Figure 5.1a. As proof of concept, two examples were worked through (1) the development of multiplicative thinking and (2) understanding of measurement. These are shown in Figures 5.1b and 5.1c respectively. Inspection of the framework

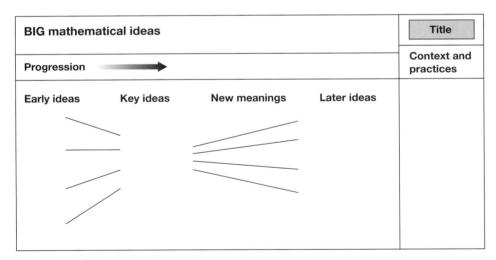

FIGURE 5.1a Framework for describing progression in the learning of BIG mathematical ideas.
Adapted from http://www.acme-uk.org/media/7627/acme_theme_b_final.pdf

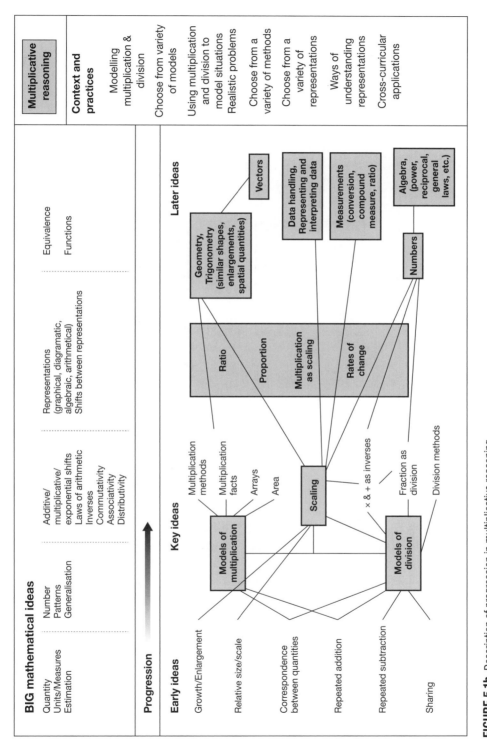

FIGURE 5.1b Description of progression in multiplicative reasoning

Adapted from http://www.acme-uk.org/media/7627/acme_theme_b_final.pdf

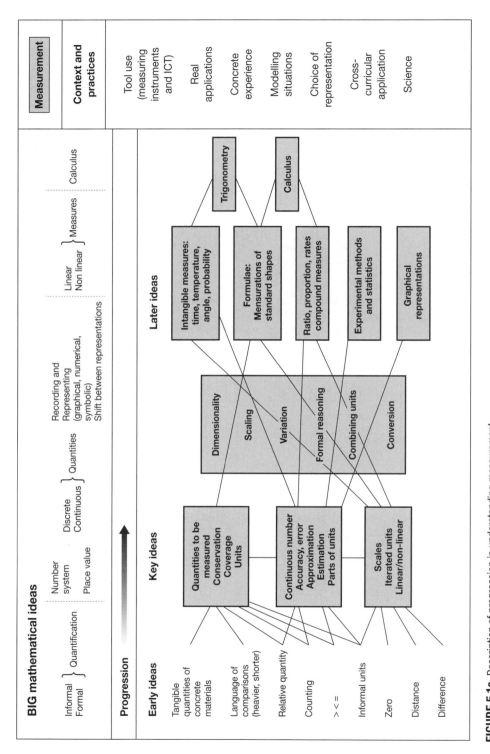

FIGURE 5.1c Description of progression in understanding measurement

Adapted from http://www.acme-uk.org/media/7627/acme_theme_b_final.pdf

and the examples indicate that they have the potential for providing particularly rich starting points for teaching mathematics in the light of STEM. Exploiting the dynamic relationship between the progressive development of ideas and their application as indicated in context and practices provides a flexible structure for ensuring that such cross-curricular endeavours will lead to the sort of in-depth conceptual understanding that is required to give both proficiency and intellectual satisfaction to students.

Building on good practice

Of course, there are schools in England in which mathematics is taught exceptionally well and an important strategy in improving the overall situation is to identify this practice and make it available to other schools. This was the rationale driving the case study approach of the National Centre for Excellence in the Teaching of Mathematics (NCETM). The report produced by the NCETM, 'Developing Mathematics in Secondary Schools' (2009) discussed five important issues: (1) what mathematics brings to the students and to the school; (2) recruitment; (3) retention; (4) continuing professional development; and (5) leadership and management. This chapter will concentrate on the first of these issues, what mathematics brings to students and schools. As far as the schools that taught mathematics well were concerned, the value of the subject lay well beyond public examination performance. They ensured that pupils appreciated the career value of mathematics. They used mathematics, particularly communicating mathematical ideas in class discussions to build students' self-confidence. They did not shy away from demanding a rigorous approach for all pupils whatever their level of achievement. They celebrated the enjoyment and love of mathematics as something for all. In addition, in some cases mathematics provided a language that pupils who were not adept at using spoken or written English could access and use fluently. And, particularly important from our STEM perspective, they valued the connection of mathematics with other subjects in the curriculum.

Linking research and teaching

The Targeted Initiative in Science and Mathematics Education (TISME) works with teachers to provide access to research-informed approaches to teaching. One particular project, Increasing Competence and Confidence in Algebra and Multiplicative Structures (ICCAMS), is of particular relevance to this chapter. Teachers who have taken part in this project have reported that the approach requires them to spend time enabling the pupils to have mathematical conversations and to 'listen in' on these conversations so that they are able to ask questions that provoke deeper thinking from the students such that they are more able to engage in conversations with peers. The word 'conversation' is significant here in that it implies both speaking *and* listening and also describes a learning environment in which talking and listening are important features. Given that taking tests in silence is one of the memories that haunt those who learned to dislike mathematics at school, the move to a 'conversational mathematics classroom' would seem a step in the right direction! The teachers confided that it was not easy to change practice from the traditional didactic model that had dominated their previous approaches but they were unanimous in their opinion that enabling conversations paid big dividends both in pupils' understanding of algebra and in their overall mathematical confidence. Pupils who are used to having mathematical conversations in mathematics might well be able to engage in such conversations in scientific and technological contexts. Hence such an approach might be conducive to teaching mathematics in the light of STEM – talking brings the learning of concepts and the exploration of new ideas into the open so that pupils can 'hear what they think'.

Developing new approaches to assessment

It is well known that employers and universities demand that school leavers are able to apply their mathematical knowledge to problem solving in varied and unfamiliar contexts. It is also acknowledged that most mathematics examinations have neglected this aspect and, in responding to the requirement for examination success, classroom teaching ignores this as well. Some attempts have been made to remedy the situation. In 2010, GCSE assessment for mathematics required the use of functional skills to respond to unstructured questions. There was an expectation that teachers might change their teaching to meet this requirement. More recently, Ian Jones of Loughborough University has been exploring the use of comparative judgement as a means of assessing pupils' mathematical problem-solving skills. His initial investigations reveal that comparative judgement has the potential to provide valid and reliable assessment of mathematical problem solving. In comparative judgement, the assessor compares two answers from different candidates and puts them in an order to show which candidate showed greater mathematical problem-solving ability. Given enough judgements across a large enough sample the results are valid and reliable and create an order of proficiency across the sample. Such an approach is a radical departure from traditional marking in which there is a marking scheme which gives particular marks for each aspect of each question on an examination paper. Where grade boundaries might be drawn is not decided by this method and the method does not give marks to each candidate – just their position in the sample. In assessing other mathematical qualities it is likely that more conventional approaches might be used. It is worth emphasising the concern over current assessment of mathematics. Roger Porkess (lead author of the aforementioned report 'A world class mathematics education for all our young people'), and colleagues have commented:

> Many really important aspects and ideas in mathematics cannot be assessed by exam only, for example, sampling and data collection in statistics, mathematical

modelling, numerical analysis, extended problem solving and appropriate use of computer software. Although these are written into the learning outcomes of many qualifications…the present regulations ensure that they are assessed… superficially.

(Porkess et al., 2011, p. 97)

Ian Jones and his colleagues envisage that a comparative judgement approach would enable the reliable assessment of an unstructured component that dealt with problem solving within a diverse range of assessment formats carefully chosen to appropriately assess the full range of valued competencies from technical fluency and conceptual understanding, through to problem-solving processes. Although there is still much to be done to establish the comparative judgement approach in mathematics assessment, its explicit use in assessing mathematical problem solving would encourage teachers to teach mathematical problem solving.

This aspect of mathematics would of course lend itself to teaching mathematics in the light of STEM as both science and design & technology are a rich source of problems for which mathematical problem solving provides useful insights.

The Khan Academy

Salman Khan has caused a considerable stir in the mathematics education community. A highly successful hedge fund manager, he has posted some 3,300 videos on YouTube many of which can be used to learn mathematics. The phenomenon is known as the Khan Academy. *Time* Magazine has reported the following statistics: 600 million exercises completed, some 2 million per day, 15,000 classrooms in which the Khan Academy is used in some form, 5 million unique users per month, 160 million videos watched since 2006 and 234 countries and territories where the Khan Academy is used. The Khan Academy has gained significant funding from the Gates Foundation, Google and Netflix. The Khan Academy is an example of the 'flipped classroom'. Pupils use online videos and similar resources at home after the school day – complete with assessment, feedback and guidance as to next steps. Pupils then use what they have learned at home to complete exercises at school the following day. This leaves the teacher free from whole-class instruction and able to deal with individuals with their particular learning problems according to what they had learned at home the previous evening. Pupils would be able to progress at their own pace through the mathematics curriculum and traditional whole-class, didactic teaching would become a thing of the past.

Some mathematics educators are unconvinced by the approach. Karim Kai Ani, a former middle school teacher and mathematics tutor, voices a typical criticism suggesting that there are basic errors in teaching simple concepts and these set the pupil on a path of misunderstanding which hampers their long term mathematical development, although it will give short-term success in high-stakes assessment. They do not decry Khan's achievement in creating such a vast and varied library. They acknowledge that he deserves to be recognised and to be praised. They see him as a good guy with a good mission – but a bad teacher whose teaching adopts a 'do this then do this approach' that presents mathematics as a meaningless series of steps.

Michael Pershan has contrasted the Khan Academy approach with that used to teach mathematics in Japan. A key point for him is the extent to which Japanese teachers allow their pupils to struggle with conceptual problems in contrast to the way American teachers spend little or almost no time on such activity. He argues for 'getting smarter by struggling' and notes that there is little if any struggle in the Khan Academy approach and that this is an inherent limitation in the approach.

If a school uses the Khan Academy approach to teaching mathematics where would that leave teaching mathematics in the light of STEM? One position might be that it forces mathematics into its own silo with a limited and perhaps even an inadequate pedagogy, which would make such teaching difficult if not impossible. The collective discussions so highly valued in the ICCAMS project could be difficult to facilitate with different pupils following their online, individual, isolated paths. The opposite position might be that with some orchestration pupils' conversations with the teacher in the flipped classroom could just as easily relate mathematical learning to science and design & technology.

Having considered both concerns with regard to mathematics education in schools and some of the ways in which the education community is responding to these concerns, we now consider how to address these through teaching mathematics in the light of pupil's learning in science and design & technology.

How might teaching mathematics in the light of STEM help?

In this section we will consider how pupils' learning in science and design & technology might be used to enhance their learning mathematics. Our approach will be to identify the mathematical requirements of some topics taught in science and design & technology. An obvious requirement for both subjects is the need to quantify observations for length, area, volume, mass, time and to develop compound measures such as speed, density and strength. In the case of science, it is important to be able to find patterns in data and use these to develop explanations so that these can be used in turn to inform design decisions in design & technology. Let us begin with chemistry and the move from a qualitative to a quantitative approach.

Deriving chemical formulae
A common experiment is to burn a weighed amount of magnesium ribbon in a lidded crucible and then weigh the amount of magnesium oxide formed. This is a tricky experiment to perform well. First, the crucible and lid should be weighed, then the magnesium ribbon added to the crucible in the form of an

open coil so that it can burn and the whole assembly reweighed. Then, the crucible must be heated to cause the magnesium to ignite and the lid must occasionally be raised ever so slightly to allow more air into the crucible to ensure complete combustion. But it is important not to allow any of the oxide being formed to escape.

Once the reaction appears to be complete then the whole assembly must be left to cool before it is reweighed. The weighing data can be used to find the mass of oxygen that has combined with the starting mass of magnesium. The challenge now is to turn this data about combining masses into a formula for magnesium oxide. There are several simple possibilities. If one atom of magnesium combined with one atom of oxygen the formula would be MgO. If one atom of magnesium combined with two atoms of oxygen the formula would be MgO_2. If two atoms of magnesium combined with one atom of oxygen the formula would be Mg_2O. The calculation also has to take into account the differing atomic masses of magnesium and oxygen. Magnesium has an atomic mass of 24 whereas oxygen has an atomic mass of 16. Hence for a formula of MgO the ratio of combination would be 24:16 equivalent to 3:2, whereas for a formula of MgO_2 would require the ratio of combination to be 24:32 equivalent to 3:4. Given that pupils will be handing masses of magnesium between 0.5 and 1.5 g the arithmetic can become complicated. One way forward here is to plot the data obtained on a chart which shows line graphs for different possible formulae of magnesium oxide. Such a graph is shown on Figure 5.2. Pupils in the class can share their results and then plot them on the graph. The result will be a scatter of points and the position of this scatter should enable the class to decide which of the three possible formulae is correct according to their experiments. Of course, the chemistry teacher will want her pupils to know and remember the correct formula of magnesium oxide (MgO) but the point of this experiment is to reinforce the idea that formulae are derived from experimental data. Later in the chemistry course the pupils will learn about atomic structure and valency and be able to use these ideas to explain why the formula of magnesium oxide is MgO and not Mg_2O or MgO_2. Clearly, the pupils will be using significant mathematics in this experiment.

It is possible to view the data manipulation and presentation as a series of mathematical operations. Each operation is not complicated but the overall sequence of operations is demanding. This requires a clear understanding of the purpose of the endeavour, experimental skill in obtaining the required data, competence in presenting the data graphically, an understanding of ratios and the ability to interpret the data once presented graphically. It is a worthwhile opportunity for pupils to use their mathematics in a chemistry lesson. Conversations between the chemistry teacher and the mathematics teacher are necessary to ensure that pupils are encouraged to use mathematical thinking and justify their procedures as

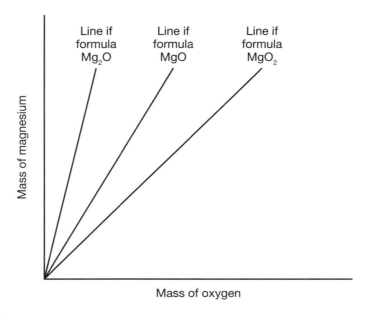

FIGURE 5.2 Graphical presentation of possible formulae for magnesium oxide.

opposed to simply following instructions. It might even be possible for the mathematics teacher to include the 'work up' of the results in a mathematics lessons. This would require a deliberate intervention to teach mathematics in the light of STEM. If the mathematics teacher felt that the pupils had sufficient mathematical knowledge and skill before such an intervention then the 'work up' lesson can be seen as an opportunity for revision and assessment of previous learning. If the pupils are going to be using unfamiliar mathematics then the work up session provides a novel way to introduce such topics.

Calculations from equations

In attempts to show the application of chemistry in everyday life, teachers often consider simple medicines such as indigestion remedies. The basis of such remedies is sometimes the neutralisation of excess stomach acid. Such products are often called 'antacid tablets' and the key ingredient will be a substance that reacts with the acid in the stomach. In some cases this is a carbonate. The reaction of the carbonate with the acid causes the production of carbon dioxide so that the reduction of acid content in the stomach is accompanied by the formation of a gas. In such cases those taking the tablets often 'burp'. In other cases the key ingredient is a hydroxide. Here the neutralisation of the acid is not accompanied by the production of carbon dioxide.

For those producing indigestion remedies it is important to know how much of the antacid ingredient to put in each tablet. Too little and the remedy will fail; too much and the reduction of acid in the stomach will be so great that food cannot be properly digested. The acid in the stomach is hydrochloric acid and the equation for the reaction of magnesium hydroxide with hydrochloric acid is as follows:

$$Mg(OH)_2(s) + 2HCl(aq) \rightarrow MgCl_2(aq) + 2H_2O(l)$$

The challenge is to use this equation to calculate how much magnesium hydroxide is needed to neutralise some of the acid in the stomach. Typically, an adult's stomach contains about 200ml of gastric juice with a concentration of 0.1 mol/l. To ensure that not too much of the acid is neutralized we can assume that only half the acid in the stomach should be neutralized. What are the steps in the calculation?

a) Decide on the amount of acid to be neutralised.
b) Use the equation to decide on the number of moles of magnesium hydroxide and hydrochloric acid that are reacting together.
c) Use the answer from a) to decide on the number of moles of hydrochloric acid that need to be neutralized.
d) Use the answers from b) and c) to decide on the number of moles of magnesium hydroxide needed to neutralize the hydrochloric acid.
e) Convert the answer to d) into grams of magnesium hydroxide needed for a single antacid tablet.

Underpinning this lengthy calculation are the important ideas of ratio and proportion. The question for the chemistry teacher is how the use of ratio and proportion in the calculation relates to the way this is taught in mathematics lessons. The question for the mathematics teacher is how might the way pupils are taught about ratio and proportion in mathematics support their thinking in such chemistry calculations. It is clear that a conversation is necessary to explore these questions and develop an approach in which the learning in both chemistry and mathematics is enhanced. Let us now move on to physics.

Understanding waves

Waves are a fundamental concept in physics and the behaviour of waves is used to explain a wide variety of phenomena. These include earthquakes, (seismic waves), sound waves, the electromagnetic spectrum and the properties of light (propagation, refraction and diffraction). Fundamental to understanding the behaviour of waves is the wave equation

Wave speed = Frequency x Wavelength
(metres per second, m/s) (hertz, Hz) (metres, m)

The unit hertz refers to cycles per second, a unit named in honour of the physicist Heinrich Hertz who discovered radio waves. This is sometimes abbreviated to

$$v = f \times \lambda$$

where

v = wave speed
f = frequency
λ = wavelength

This can be shown diagrammatically as a sine wave (see Figure 5.3). The amplitude of the wave can change without any change to the wavelength or frequency.

FIGURE 5.3 Sine wave.
Adapted from Millar et al. (2011)

It is possible to use this wave equation to calculate any one of the features in the equation if values are known for the other two features. The equation can be used to explain the colour of visible light. The speed of light can be treated as a constant, hence the frequency × wavelength is also constant. But if the frequency is decreased then the wavelength must increase. Similarly, if the frequency is increased then the wavelength must decrease. In the visible spectrum blue light has a higher frequency and lower wavelength than red light. The numbers get scary because of the units. Blue light has a frequency 606–668 THz and a wavelength 450–495 nm. Red light has a frequency 400–484 THz and a wavelength of 620–750 nm. T stands for tera which means x million million – 1 000 000 000 000 or 10^{12}, so the frequency of blue light is in the region of 460 million million cycles per second (or Hz); n stands for nano which means one thousand millionth – 0.000000001 or 10^{-9}, so the wavelength of red light is in the region of 700 thousand millionths of a metre.

Where might this lead in a conversation between the physics teacher and the mathematics teacher? There's certainly the possibility of discussing how students might learn to understand very large and very small numbers. There's also the possibility of discussing how students might develop an understanding of direct and indirect proportional relationships described by simple $y = mx$ type equations, or even simple trigonometry functions. Such conversations could lead to mathematics lessons in which such topics were introduced or revised in the context of waves and the simple wave equation.

Measuring particle size

An interesting part of teaching the particle theory of matter is to engage pupils in the measurement of the actual size of particles. The 'penny dropping' moment when pupils realise just how small particles are is worth striving for.

Practical Physics, developed by the Institute of Physics and the Nuffield Foundation, has a useful experiment to estimate the size of a molecule using an oil film.[1] The diameter of a tiny droplet of olive oil is measured and the droplet placed on a water surface covered with lycopodium powder. The drop is spread out to form a circle and it is assumed the circle is one molecule thick. The basis for this assumption is that the oil molecule has a hydrophilic end that is attracted into the water and a hydrophobic chain that is repelled by the water and stands up out of the water. The diameter of the circle is measured. (See Figure 5.4)

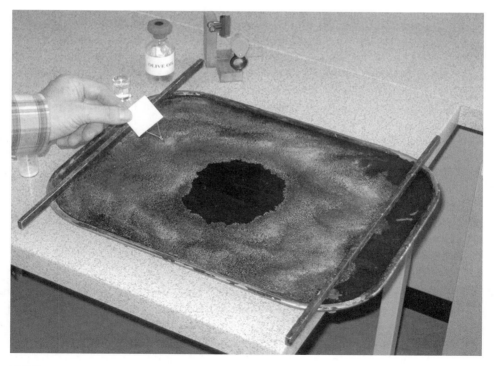

FIGURE 5.4 The Practical Physics oil drop experiment.

Mathematical thinking is required to turn the measurements into an estimate of molecular size.

- The volume of the oil drop is proportional to the diameter cubed.
- The oil drop spreads out to form a cylinder one molecule thick.
- The volume of the cylinder is given by area of the circle times its depth.
- The area of the circle is proportional to the diameter squared.
- If the diameter of the circle is D, and the diameter of the oil drop of d, and the length of the molecule is l, then $d^3 = D^2 \times l$.
- A typical diameter of the initial oil drop would be 0.5 mm.
- A typical diameter of the film would be 250 mm.

Hence

$$0.5 \times 0.5 \times 0.5 = 250 \times 250 \times \text{length of the molecule (in mm)}$$
$$\frac{0.5 \times 0.5 \times 0.5}{250 \times 250} = \text{length of molecule (in mm)}$$

Using a calculator:

$$0.000002 = \text{length of molecule (in mm)}$$
$$0.000000002 = \text{length of molecule (in m)}$$

Using standard notation this becomes:

$$2 \times 10^{-9}\text{m} = \text{approximate length of the oil molecule}$$

There are approximately 12 atoms in the olive oil chain the size of an atom is given by $2 \times 10^{-9} \div 12$.

Hence the approximate size of an atom is 1.7×10^{-10} m

This can be written as 0.000000000017 m
$$\approx 0.00000000002 \text{ m}$$
$$\text{or } 0.2 \text{ nanometres}$$

The above is of course an approximation, as the precise formulae for the volume of the initial drop and the cylinder have not been used in order to keep the calculation relatively simple. The result is however of the correct order of magnitude, the size of a carbon atom being 0.7×10^{-10} m

So what sort of conversation might the mathematics teacher have with the physics teacher about this experiment? A discussion on accuracy of measurement and the impact of inaccuracies on the estimate of molecule size is a possibility. The formulae for the volumes of spheres and cylinders might feature along with the possible effect of the approximations in the calculations shown above. The arithmetic involved in the calculations, the use of power of ten notation, and the prefix nano meaning one billionth. With so much varied mathematics embedded in the activity it is unlikely that the mathematics teacher can use the experiment to introduce these topics in the mathematics curriculum. However, discussing the experiment would provide an interesting revision exercise across a wide range of topics and could be used as an assessment for learning exercise. Discussion of the results of the experiment and how to derive an estimate for molecular size would reveal where pupils were comfortably confident and where they were experiencing difficulties. Let us now move on to biology.

Estimating population size

Deciding on the number of particular animals or plants in a particular location is a challenge for professional biologists. In most situations it is impossible to count the actual number of flora or fauna present so experimental procedures for estimating the population from a small sample have been devised. Pupils are introduced to these procedures in most biology courses and these estimation procedures are underpinned by mathematical understanding.

Using quadrats

This procedure is relatively simple and involves using a metal or wooden frame called a quadrat. It is usually used to count plants but can be used for slow moving insects. The most basic approach is as follows:

a) Placing the quadrat on the habitat under investigation.
b) Counting the number of a particular plant present inside the quadrat.
c) Estimating how many quadrats are needed to cover the habitat.
d) Multiplying the answer to c) by the answer to b) to estimate the number of the particular species in the habitat.

It is possible that the number of plants within the quadrat will vary from place to place in the habitat. A habitat could be variable in terms of abiotic factors, e.g., light and shade, exposure to wind, availability of water and minerals and biotic factors involving competition from other organisms. Hence the procedure often involves placing several quadrats at different positions in the habitat in order to improve the estimate and avoid bias. Part of a typical examination question might include the results of such an experiment as follows:

quadrat	number of dandelions
1st	5
2nd	1
3rd	0
4th	2

- Each quadrat has an area of 0.25m^2
- The total area of the habitat, a playing field, is 20,000 m^2

Q: Estimate the total number of dandelion plants in the playing field.

If the candidate realises that the sum of the area of the four quadrats is 1m^2 the task becomes simple. Simply add the number of dandelions in each quadrat to find the number of dandelions in 1m^2 and then multiply the result by 20,000. Surprisingly teachers report that many pupils find this sort of question confusing and use inappropriate arithmetical techniques – multiplying the areas and dandelion numbers instead of adding them giving 10 dandelions in .0039 m^2; averaging the number of dandelion in a quadrat and then miscalculating the number of 0.25 m^2 in the field. It is as if the requirement to 'be mathematical' presses a panic button. A conversation between the biology teacher and the mathematics teacher to explore why pupils tried such apparently illogical approaches would be a start to overcoming pupil's poor responses. A further step would be for a quadrat exercise to be undertaken as part of a mathematics lesson and the results then considered in a biology lesson.

Using mark, release, recapture

Mark, release, recapture is a common approach to estimating the size of an animal population in a habitat. A portion of the population is captured, marked, and released. Later, another portion is captured and the number of marked individuals within the sample is counted. This method assumes that the study population is 'closed'. In other words, the two visits to the study area are close enough in time so that no individuals die, are born, move into the study area (immigrate) or move out of the study area (emigrate) between visits. It is usual in biology texts book to simply provide the following formula which allows the population of the particular animal to be estimated.

$$N = \frac{MC}{R}$$

Where

N = Estimate of total population size
M = Total number of animals captured and marked on the first visit
C = Total number of animals captured on the second visit
R = Number of animals captured on the first visit that were then recaptured on the second visit

I must admit that I did not find the formula easy to understand intuitively. I wasn't sure why it worked. Some teachers try to provide insight by talking pupils through a situation in which 10 labelled ladybirds are released in a greenhouse and on recapture of 10 ladybirds some time later only one is marked indicating that the ladybird population in the greenhouse is 100. However, I do wonder whether this insight is sufficient to provide genuine understanding. Then I found out how the formula was derived.

The method assumes that in the second sample, the proportion of marked individuals that are caught (R ÷ M) should equal the proportion of the total population that is caught (C/N).

This can be written

$$\frac{R}{M} = \frac{C}{N}$$

This can be rearranged to give

$$N = \frac{MC}{R}$$

This is the formula often given to the pupils without explanation. I wonder whether it is worth pupils understanding where the formula comes from i.e., how it is derived, to better understand the logic behind the technique. Before attempting to do this with a class it would be wise for the biology teacher to have a conversation with the mathematics teacher. The result of this conversation might well be that the mathematics teacher would be happy to use the derivation of the formula as a means of teaching or reinforcing algebraic manipulation. Once the formula had been derived in mathematics, pupils could ideally use it in actual investigations of populations of small creatures in a local environment, e.g., wood lice or ground beetles. If this were not possible then second hand data from some original investigations could be used. Either way the pupils would be in a stronger position to understand the mathematical basis of the experimental procedure. Before moving on, let us look at another example in biology.

Probability and genetics

Some diseases are genetic. They are passed from the parents to their children. For example, causes and probability of a child having the genetic disorder cystic fibrosis is taught in most biology courses. The explanation requires pupils to understand several concepts: dominant and recessive alleles, faulty alleles, the production of two sets of alleles by each parent, and the combination of alleles during sexual reproduction, some of which give rise to the disease, some of which don't. These concepts are embedded in explanatory diagrams like the one shown in Figure 5.5.

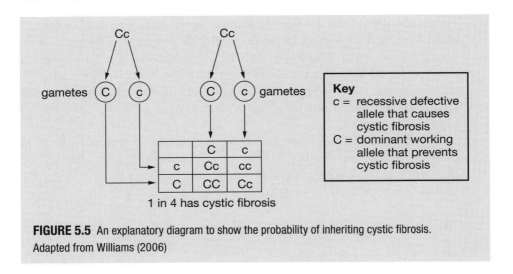

FIGURE 5.5 An explanatory diagram to show the probability of inheriting cystic fibrosis. Adapted from Williams (2006)

So if both parents carry the recessive defective allele (c) and the dominant working allele (C) there is a one in four chance that their child will inherit the disease because only one in four of the possible combinations gives two recessive defective alleles.

Parents whose genetic make up is Cc are known as carriers as they can pass on the defective allele but do not themselves have the condition. It is possible to test an embryo in the womb to discover if it has two defective alleles in which case the child would suffer from cystic fibrosis. It is now possible for parents to have their DNA tested to discover if they are carriers. But even if they find they *are* carriers, the chance that their child will be born with cystic fibrosis is only one in four. And probability has no memory. Hence if a couple who are carriers have three children, all of whom are healthy, the chance of their next child having cystic fibrosis would still be one in four. And a couple who were carriers might have just one child and that child could have cystic fibrosis even though the chance of that child having the disease is one in four. Without some understanding of probability it seems likely that pupils could become confused with regard to the factors effecting parent's decision making. Hence a conversation with the mathematics teacher might not go amiss. Indeed the mathematics teacher might consider using recessive/dominant allele combination as a way of teaching probability. A difficulty with this as an introductory approach might be that the science terminology gets in the way of understanding the probability. If this occurs, then it might be preferable for the mathematics teacher to use this as revision exercise in probability once pupils are familiar with the science. Now let us move on to design & technology.

Choosing materials

Choosing which material to use for the components of a design is always a challenge. In most of the products designed and made by pupils in schools the choice is inevitably limited. Often the choices made are based on a combination of precedent – what others have used when they have designed similar products – and availability – what the school has in stock or can afford to purchase. This experience, whilst defendable on grounds of practicality, does not engage pupils with serious thinking about material choice with regard to matching the required physical characteristics with those of available materials.

Questions concerning both strength (will the part break?) and stiffness (how much will the part deform?) are important, as poor choice of material will lead to poor product performance. Investigations into the properties of materials can give pupils insight into the behaviour of materials. The results of such investigations can be presented graphically and the interpretation of such graphs requires mathematical thinking. The simplified stress versus strain graph for a metal under tension shown in Figure 5.6 provides a good example. The behaviour of the metal in the linear part of the graph shows elastic behaviour. In this part of the curve the metal will stretch under load and when the load is removed return to its original size. In the non-linear part of the curve the metal deforms but when the load is removed the metal stays permanently deformed. The metal becomes thinner in the final downward part of the curve (known as 'necking') and eventually breaks when the loading exceeds the strength of the metal.

Conversations between the design & technology teacher and the mathematics teacher are essential here if pupil interpretation of such graphs is to be sound. Indeed it might be possible to go further than a conversation. The mathematics teacher could use stress-strain graphs for different materials as a means of teaching 'interpretation of graphs' and the understanding of compound measures – stress has units of force/area, strain has no units as it is a ratio of extension: original length. The stress/strain ratio (slope of the line in the linear region) gives Young's modulus for the material and is a measure of the materials elasticity. Because strain has no units, the units for Young's modulus are the same as the units for stress. Hence the units for elasticity have the same units as strength – a cause of confusion for many pupils. Of course the above consideration is an oversimplification of the thinking required to decide on which material to use for a component but it does open the way for the design & technology teacher to ask questions, such as how strong does it need to be? How stiff does it need to be? How will your design decisions about form and material ensure that the component is strong enough and stiff enough? When pupils become intrigued by such questions and how they may be answered they are beginning to appreciate STEM as an holistic approach to designing.

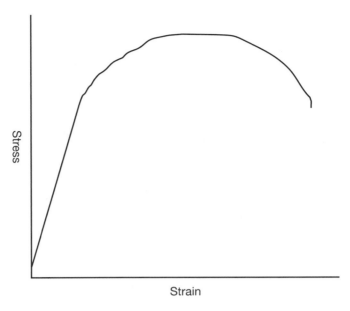

FIGURE 5.6 Simple stress strain graph for ductile metal.

Designing mechanisms

There is no shortage of mathematics embedded in the design of mechanical systems but some design & technology teachers have questioned the contexts into which such designing is embedded. Their position is summarised by the question 'Just how many pupils in the twenty-first century really want to make a mechanical toy or point of sale device?' They also argue that technically the results are generally unsophisticated and use technology from the nineteenth if not eighteenth centuries – which should not be the hallmark of modern technological learning. Whilst I have some sympathy with this argument, I am reminded of a conversation I had with a friend and colleague who trained as a mechanical engineer. 'You know David,' he said, 'four bar linkages are bloody amazing!'

This comment made me wonder about the intrinsic interest there might be in some mechanisms and that a more purist approach might pay dividends. What if one were to consider a mechanism as just an item of intrigue and did not worry too much about a context for use? I realise that this flies in the face of the conventional wisdom that the context for designing is of paramount importance and provides significant motivation for the pupil, but when I read a little more about four bar linkages I became convinced that this almost reactionary idea might have some worth. I found out about Grashof's rule. Franz Grashof was a distinguished nineteenth century German engineer whom in 1883, came to the conclusion that with regard to four bar linkages:

> If the total length of the shortest and longest bars is equal to or shorter than the lengths of the remaining two bars, then the shortest link can make complete revolutions.
>
> (Hartenburg and Denavit, *Kinematic Synthesis of Linkages*, 1964, p. 77)

This rule struck me as a having great mathematical potential and the possibility of simple practical work involving card strips and split pin paper fasteners. In a delightful book, *Mathematics Meets Technology* the author Brian Bolt describes three cases in which a four bar linkage obeys Grashof's rule: the crank and rocker, the double crank mechanism and the double rocker mechanism (see Figure 5.7). I can

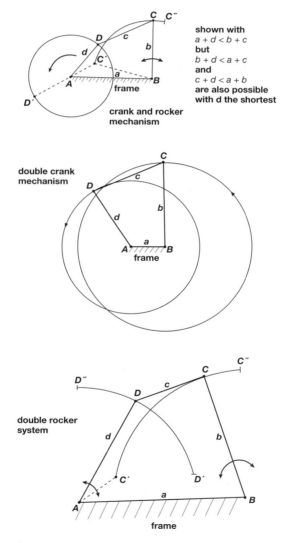

FIGURE 5.7 Three possible arrangements of the four bar linkage.
Adapted from Bolt (1991)

envisage mathematics lessons in which the teacher takes four bar linkages as a topic for practical and theoretical investigation with a view to pupils formulating Grashof's rule for themselves. If this investigation took place at a time when pupils were being asked to learn about mechanisms in design & technology and develop products which used mechanical systems this would provide them with a new mechanism to consider and a mathematical way of considering its design.

Considering robots

Simple robots feature in many design & technology curricula and an important aspect of working with robots is exploring the different ways they can be programmed to perform their various functions. This will involve both mathematical and computational thinking and will be considered in Chapter 9. The physical design of robots, as opposed to their programming, can involve significant mathematics.

Consider three basic types of robots: Cartesian robots, cylindrical robots and spherical robots – shown in Figure 5.8. The working envelopes of the robots are an important design feature. This describes the space in which the end effector of the robot can operate. In the case of the Cartesian robot, the position of the end effector at any one point will be described by three numbers – the x coordinate, the y coordinate and the z coordinate. The design of the robot governs the possible sizes of these coordinates and hence the size and shape of the working envelope, which is a cuboid. In the case of the cylindrical robot the radial arm can extend and retract horizontally, rotate about a vertical axis and the entire arm can be raised and lowered. The position of the end effector at any one point is described by its distance along the horizontal axis, (r), the angle it has rotated about the vertical axis (θ) and the distance it has moved along the vertical axis (z). The design of the robot governs the possible sizes of these cylindrical coordinates and hence the size and shape of the working envelope, which is cylindrical. In the case of the spherical robot the arm can extend along its length (r), rotate about a vertical axis (θ)) and can be rotated about a horizontal axis (φ) to elevate it above or below the horizontal. The design of the robot governs the possible sizes of these spherical coordinates and hence the size and shape of the working envelope, which is a spherical. The design & technology teacher can engage pupils with the design of these different types of robot quite easily with the use of construction kits such as Lego or Fisher Technic and the mathematics teacher can give such work a significant mathematical dimension by introducing pupils to three different ways of defining points in three-dimensional space.

There are many places in which robots are being used in society. Robots are finding their way into homes as domestic cleaning machines, into hospitals to perform surgery, in care homes for the elderly, in military operations such as bomb disposal, in search and rescue, in autonomous transport, in teaching, in manufacturing and in data collection. There will almost certainly be mathematical dimensions to their design in these different situations.

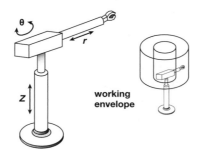

Cylindrical robot

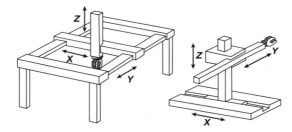

Cartesian robot

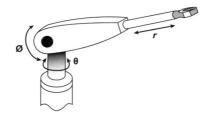

Spherical robot

FIGURE 5.8 Three types of robot arms: Cartesian, cylindrical and spherical.
Adapted from Bolt (1991)

Surface decoration
Surface decoration plays a large part in many textile courses. Repeat patterns of various sorts are one of the main ways of achieving surface decoration and, of course, the mathematics of symmetry underpins such pattern generation.

Starting with a simple geometric shape, a triangle or half circle perhaps it is a relatively simple exercise to use basic transformation operations such as translation, reflection and rotation to produce a variety of different patterns. More complex transformations such as glide translation and helical translation can be added to the mix of operations. Assigning colours as the result of particular sequence of transformations can add even more visual interest, e.g., every time a reflection is followed by a rotation the colour changes from red to blue. So it is possible for pupils to write algorithms of transformations to generate patterns. Traditionally, such algorithms can be applied to fabric by using block printing techniques with the block undergoing a particular set of transformations between the making of each print on the fabric. And it is possible to carry out this activity pattern generating activity on screen and then use sublimation printing to produce the patterned fabric. The basic unit of the pattern need not be confined to a simple geometric shape. Suitable shapes can be derived from natural form via observational drawing and simplification, abstract form by assembling a variety of curved and straight lines into an enclosed shape. However the shape is derived, the way it can be used to produce a repeat pattern can be developed using transformations. School mathematics courses often include an introduction to symmetry and transformation geometry. The generation of patterns for use as surface decoration in a textiles component of a design & technology programme provides an interesting context for the application this mathematics. Hence a conversation between the mathematics teacher and textiles teacher would seem to be in order. The motivation for learning the somewhat abstract ideas of symmetry transformations can be enhanced if the teaching by the mathematics teacher acknowledges explicitly with the class that they will be able to use the learning in their textiles lessons. Indeed the development of the algorithms to produce patterns in the mathematics lesson can be seen as an essential first step in the overall textiles task of designing and making a patterned fabric. It is of course important that the ultimate use for the patterned fabric is considered so that the pattern is appropriate for the garment or furnishing that is being designed. An interesting possibility is that the mathematics teacher, having introduced the pupils to pattern design using transformations, consults with the class as they develop patterned textile products. In this way the teacher can use the students' efforts in design & technology to assess their understanding of transformations and where appropriate intervene to help pupils overcome misunderstandings.

Developing 3D textile structures

School mathematics courses deal with 3D geometry and this often requires pupils to understand the structure of polyhedrons. The simplest is the regular tetrahedron, consisting of four triangular faces and this polyhedron is often used as the basis for constructing juggling balls. The regular dodecahedron consists of twelve regular pentagonal faces. This polyhedron is often used as the basis for children's soft toys giving an almost spherical shape which can be used in mobiles, pram toys and squashy footballs. With slightly stiffer fabric polyhedron or part-polyhedron can be used as the basis for lampshades. The mathematics of polyhedron is intriguing. Regular polyhedron obey Euler's theorem which can be written

$$V + F = E + 2$$

Where

V = the number of vertices
F = the number of faces
E = the number of edges

In the case of a cube

$$V = 8, F = 6, E = 12$$

In the case of an octahedron

$$V = 6, F = 8, E = 12$$

Each regular polyhedron has a dual polyhedron which is also regular. Duals are created by using the midpoints of the faces in the original polyhedron to form the vertices of the dual polyhedron. Hence the dual of a cube is a regular octahedron as shown here in Figure 5.9.

A polyhedron can of course be opened out flat to form nets. These nets can form the basis for templates for designing and making the items noted above. So, as with teaching transformations, the motivation for learning the somewhat abstract ideas of 3D geometry can be enhanced if the mathematics teaching acknowledges explicitly with the class that they will be able to use their learning in textiles lessons. Designing nets is an inherently mathematical process and asking students how many different nets they can find for a cube or cuboid encourages mathematical thinking and problem solving. Hence the basis for the conversation between the mathematics teacher and the textiles teacher might consider using the mathematics lessons on 3D geometry to provide the pupils with the design tools to develop appropriate forms for products. And again, the mathematics teacher could visit design & technology lessons to observe pupils using their knowledge of 3D geometry as a useful means of assessment. If this proves unrealistic then it should be possible for the design & technology teacher to report back to the mathematics teacher on the extent to which the pupils were able to use their understanding of 3D geometry to make design decisions. Alternatively, pupils might use an e-portfolio to share examples of 3D geometry work in textiles with their mathematics teacher.

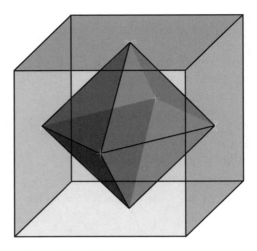

FIGURE 5.9 Duality of the cube and the octahedron.

Considering the energy content of food

Concerns about the levels of obesity in the population surface at regular intervals in the United Kingdom and the USA. One such example of this is the Foresight report, Tackling Obesities – Future Choices (2007), which is in little doubt as to the significance of the problem and the difficulty in developing a solution.

Sir David King, Chief Scientific Adviser to the UK government, captures this well in the foreword to the Foresight report.

> The project's findings challenge the simple portrayal of obesity as an issue of personal willpower – eating too much and doing too little. Although, at the heart of the problem there is an imbalance between energy intake and energy expenditure, the physical and psychological drivers inherent in human biology mean that the vast majority of us are predisposed to gaining weight. It's not surprising that the median body mass index in the UK is now above that considered to be in the 'healthy' range. We evolved in a world of relative food scarcity and hard physical work – obesity is one of the penalties of the modern world, where energy-dense food is abundant and labour-saving technologies abound.
>
> Creating an environment that better suits our biology and supports us in developing and sustaining healthy eating and activity habits is a challenge for society and for policymakers. It's not simply a health issue, nor a matter of individual choice. The current and likely future scale of the obesity problem is daunting, but the encouraging findings are that there is considerable scope to align policies to tackle climate change and sustainability, for example, with policies for public health.
>
> (Department for Business, Innovation & Skills, 2007, p. 1)

Foresight also commissioned the production of an educational resource, 'Take Shape', for use in secondary schools to help pupils aged 14–16 years appreciate the complex nature and extent of the problem. Many school food technology programmes deliberately educate pupils about the nature of consumer products developed by the food industry with a view to informing individual's food choices. Although this deals with only a minor contribution to the overall obesogenic environment it is significant in that it empowers pupils and their families to make decisions about their personal eating. Understanding the extent to which the ingredients in a product might contribute to an obesogenic environment relies on significant scientific and mathematical understanding. From the science perspective there is the nature of the ingredients and their ability to act as energy dense food. From the mathematics perspective there is the quantification of the scientific perspective. Overall the total number of calories in a portion will be important and products that are high in sugar and fat will be energy dense and contribute large numbers of calories. Fats in the diet, depending on their nature, may also lead to arteriosclerosis. For example, let us consider the energy intake from breakfast cereal. Calculating the calorie intake from a week's consumption of breakfast cereals is not a trivial task. It requires the pupils to take information from the packaging and consider it in the light of a typical portion size and the number of days per week it is eaten. It would be instructive to compare different cereals. This would be an intricate arithmetic exercise requiring the ability to perform a sequence of calculations and comment on the significance of the results. Enabling pupils to use arithmetic sensibly is a requirement of many school mathematics courses and using it to compare food energy content in the context of the looming obesity crisis provides the basis for collaboration between the mathematics teacher and the food technology teacher. Note that this task is made less demanding in terms of arithmetical manipulation if the pupils used a spreadsheet. This would also enable consideration of the questions 'What if I ate this instead of that?'

Ending hunger

Foresight has also produced a report: *Foresight – The Future of Food and Farming* (2011). Chapter 6 of the report deals with the problem of hunger which is significant. The report notes:

> Today, there are an estimated 925 million people hungry, and perhaps an additional one billion who are not hungry in the usual sense but suffer from the 'hidden hunger' of not having enough vitamins and minerals. Hunger is the antithesis of human development. It is important for policy makers to take a broad view of the nature and causes of hunger and its many impacts, including the severe and long-lasting nature of the effects that hunger and undernutrition can cause, particularly in children.
>
> (Department for Business, Innovation & Skills, 2011, p. 116)

Throughout this chapter there is a wide range of graphical information depicting various features relevant to world hunger. All school mathematics courses teach the accurate interpretation of graphs. For many pupils this can become an abstract exercise of little interest unless the information encapsulated by the graphs are of some interest to them. Few pupils will be unmoved or disinterested in the plight of hungry people, and the opportunity to use graphs dealing with this important issue provides the basis for collaboration between the mathematics teacher and the food technology teacher. It would require some effort on the part of both teachers to analyse the contents of Chapter 6 of the report and extract a range of graphical material that told a coherent story about world hunger which pupils would only be able to understand by interpreting the graphs. However, this would provide an interesting opportunity to show how this aspect of mathematics is a useful communication tool and to provide a contrast to the situation in the UK and USA where virtually all people have more than enough to eat. And by including this in food technology it will be possible to begin to engage pupils with the complex global system of food production/consumption and help them consider the moral dimension of a world where there is much hunger and the role that food technologies might play in tackling this problem.

Having presented a range of examples concerning the teaching of mathematics in the light of STEM we will revisit the 'life mathematical' in school.

Revisiting the 'life mathematical' in school

Enabling success in international tests as a key requirement of the life mathematical in school has been questioned. In an article in the *New Scientist* (2013) MacGregor Campbell challenges the conventional wisdom that PISA and TIMMS test scores are important in gauging how well pupils will be in working effectively in a knowledge-based global economy. He argues that several researchers have shown that there is little if any correlation between test scores and measures of economic success such as per capita GDP, Growth Competitiveness Index and entrepreneurship. As a specific example, he notes that Japanese students have always been near the top of the TIMMS and as such you might expect such students to go on to drive a high-flying economy. Yet the Japanese economy stagnated throughout the 1990s and 2000s. He concludes that fixating on international tests as a way to promote the importance of mathematics (and science) is likely to prove counterproductive and that more emphasis should be placed on developing creativity and initiative. Being able to use mathematics fluently in subjects other than mathematics, as proposed and advocated in the above examples, will support the creative use of mathematics and help pupils show initiative in bringing mathematics to bear in learning both science and design & technology. It is of course unlikely that government ministers will ignore PISA and TIMMS rankings, but engaging pupils with the utility of mathematics as indicated is likely to develop a more positive attitude overcoming the 'hate it' disposition and leading to better overall mathematical confidence and attainment.

The life mathematical in school in England is now likely to be extended to include all pupils to the age of 18 as advocated in reports from the Nuffield Foundation and Carol Vorderman and Roger Porkess. But it will be important that such programmes do not provide more of the same diet that many pupils found so unpalatable. In December 2012, ACME responded to these imperatives by recommending that a new mathematical qualification, based on problem solving in realistic contexts, should be developed and introduced as part of wider A level (years 16–18) reforms. According to ACME this qualification would:

- be distinct from A level mathematics, with an emphasis on solving realistic problems, using a variety of mathematical approaches.
- give students confidence in using and applying pre-16 mathematics.
- be designed to be studied over two years.
- be designed so that it is not in competition with either AS or A level mathematics.

Many of those pupils who have enjoyed being taught mathematics in the light of STEM will continue their study of mathematics at AS and A levels but some will not. This is most likely to be the case for some pupils who choose to study design & technology. Yet as we have seen, being able to use mathematics is useful in a variety of design & technology contexts. Hence if this recommendation led to the development of such a qualification it could capitalise on an approach pre-16 in which pupils were taught mathematics in the light of STEM. Indeed, it is extremely likely that some of the problems which pupils tackled in this new course would be design & technology problems. Of course, assessment will be an issue here but the work being carried out by Ian Jones, described earlier, gives hope that it will be possible to develop assessment schemes that deal with and reward the mathematical problem-solving abilities that could be developed through this new qualification.

As we finish writing this chapter the Nuffield Foundation has published a report entitled 'Towards universal participation in post-16 mathematics: lessons from high performing countries'. Amongst the report's recommendations are that appropriate qualifications would focus on mathematical fluency, statistics and application of mathematics. Again, the accent on fluency and application indicates that previous experience of teaching mathematics in the light of STEM would pre-dispose young people to see the value of such a qualification

The NCETM report 'Developing Mathematics in Secondary Schools' noted that schools in which mathematics teaching is successful value highly the links between mathematics and other subjects in the curriculum. Clearly, the authors of this book value highly the links between mathematics and science and design & technology and perhaps it would not be going too far to argue that if a school deliberately forges such links then the mathematics teaching overall is likely to become more successful. Underpinning many of the activities that embody such links is the idea of the conversational classroom in which pupils actively discuss their approaches to using mathematics, the difficulties they are experiencing and how they overcome them. This was a key feature of the 'Increasing Competence and Confidence in Algebra and Multiplicative Structures' (ICCAMS) Project. This can be seen to mirror the conversations between mathematics teachers and teachers of other subjects. The importance of conversations cannot be underestimated in a school's life mathematical. One can see the failure to develop conceptual knowledge and the ability to solve problems, noted by the most recent Ofsted report into mathematics teaching, as being compounded by the classroom of certainty in which tentative attempts to understand and use difficult ideas through discussion find no place.

And what of the life mathematical in schools that embrace the Khan Academy's approach to teaching and learning mathematics? Will it be possible to extend the highly-focused approach to teaching particular aspects of mathematics to include a broader approach in which mathematics is used in the teaching and learning of other subjects? Proponents might argue that this is what teachers will do in the classroom with pupils who have learned particular mathematics online at home. It will be interesting to see if this actually happens. Another intriguing possibility is that the online activities in the Khan Academy are extended to engage with teaching mathematics in the light of STEM. This would be a departure from the current approach but given the enhanced funding now available it would not be impossible. And this development would to some extent meet the criticisms of those who consider that the Khan Academy approach denies pupils the opportunity to learn through conceptual struggle.

Conclusion

So what are we to make of this chapter? There is no doubt that in both the USA and the UK there are serious concerns about the response of many young people to the teaching and learning of mathematics. Perversely it might seem, those schools that acknowledge the conceptual struggle involved in learning mathematics and enable pupils to articulate this struggle have more success than schools which, with the best intentions, over-simplify and fragment the learning, denying pupils the opportunity to construct their own personal robust understanding and in the process gain significant mathematical skills. We advocate an approach that supports the importance of conceptual struggle, and suggest that one way to achieve this is to take the mathematics necessary for learning science and design & technology into the mathematics classroom.

We have developed the examples of teaching parts of the mathematics curriculum in this way to illustrate that it is both possible and worthwhile. If you are able to use these examples we will of course be delighted, but if you find them inappropriate then we believe that this should not deter you from developing ideas that will work for you in your situation. Our conversations with science and design & technology teachers have led us to the view that there is no shortage of possible examples that require the use of mathematics in those subjects. Our foray into presenting such examples is, of necessity, limited but we are convinced that conversations between mathematics teachers and those teaching science and design & technology will be able to identify many more examples, importantly, examples that will be successful in the individual circumstances of their particular schools. We have noted the importance of conversations in this endeavour: the initial and probably short conversations between teachers exploring possibilities; the subsequent more detailed and time-consuming conversations required to outline what might be done to respond to the possibilities and a consideration of the conversations to take place in the classroom between pupils as they learn mathematics through using it for other STEM subjects. It is this final set of conversations that will both enable and reveal the effectiveness of our suggested approach. Hence we suggest that you discuss with colleagues what sort of conversations you want to happen, how you might support such conversations and how you might monitor the conversations that do take place with the view to improving their effectiveness. In this way, we believe that you will be able to make a significant contribution to the life mathematical in your school, one which pupils will value and enjoy. Hence in teaching mathematics in the light of STEM our advice is don't neglect the importance of regular conversations with colleagues from science and design & technology.

Note

1   Details of the oil drop experiment can be found at http://www.nuffieldfoundation.org/ practical-physics/estimating-size-molecule-using-oilfilm

Background reading and references

ACME (2011) 'Mathematical Needs: The Mathematical Needs of Learners' report. Available at: www.acme-uk.org/media/7627/acme_theme_b_final.pdf (accessed 10 February 2014).

ACME (2012) 'Past 16 Mathematics: A Strategy for Improving Provision and Participation' report. Available at: www.nationalnumeracy.org.uk/resources/49/index.html (accessed 10 February 2014).

Bolt, B. (1991) *Mathematics Meets Technology*. Cambridge: Cambridge University Press.

Campbell, M. (2013) 'West vs. Asia Education Rankings are Misleading'. *New Scientist*, 217, (2898) 22–23.

Department for Business, Innovation & Skills (2007) 'Foresight – Tackling Obesities: Future Choices' report. Available at: www.bis.gov.uk/foresight/our-work/projects/published-projects/tackling-obesities/reports-and-publications (accessed 10 February 2014).

Department for Business, Innovation & Skills (2011) 'Foresight – The Future of Food and Farming'. Available at: www.bis.gov.uk/foresight/our-work/projects/published-projects/global-food-and-farming-futures/reports-and-publications (accessed 10 February 2014).

Duncan, A. (2009) Secretary Arne Duncan's Remarks at OECD's Release of the Program for International Student Assessment (PISA) 2009 Results. Available at: www.ed.gov/news/speeches/secretary-arne-duncans-remarks-oecds-release-program-international-student-assessment- (accessed 10 February 2014).

Gove, M. (2012) 'Education for Economic Success'. Speech to the Education World Forum. Available at: www.education.gov.uk/inthenews/speeches/a0072274/michael-gove-to-the-education-world-forum (accessed 10 February 2014).

Hodgen, J., Pepper, D., Sturman, L. and Ruddock, G. (2010) 'Is the UK an Outlier? An International Comparison of Upper Secondary Mathematics Education'. Nuffield Foundation Report. London: Nuffield Foundation. Available at: www.nuffieldfoundation.org/uk-outlier-upper-secondary-maths-education (accessed 10 February 2014).

Hodgen, J., Marks., R. and Pepper, D. (2013) 'Towards Universal Participation in Post-16 Mathematics: Lessons from High Performing Countries'. Nuffield Foundation Report. London: Nuffield Foundation. Available at: www.nuffieldfoundation.org/sites/default/files/files/Towards_universal_participation_in_post_16_maths_v_FINAL.pdf (accessed 10 February 2014).

ICCAMS Project. Available at: http://iccams-maths.org/ (accessed 10 February 2014).

John-Steiner, V. and Hersh, R. (2011) *Loving and Hating Mathematics: Challenging Myths of Mathematical Life*. Princeton, New Jersey: Princeton University Press.

Jones. I, Swann, M. and Pollitt, A. (in press) Assessing Mathematical Problem Solving Using Comparative Judgement. *International Journal of Science and Mathematics Education*.

Millar, R., Sang, D., Swinbank, E. and Tear, C. (2011) *21st Century Science: GCSE Physics*. Oxford: Oxford University Press.

NCETM (2009) 'Developing Mathematics in Secondary Schools' report. Available at: www.ncetm.org.uk/Default.aspx?page=41&module=file&fileid=651176 (accessed 10 February 2014).

Ofsted (2012) 'Mathematics: Made to Measure'. Ofsted report ref 110159. Available at: www.ofsted.gov.uk/resources/mathematics-made-measure (accessed 10 February 2014).

Pershan, M. (2012) 'What if Khan Academy was Made in Japan?' YouTube video. Available at: www.youtube.com/watch?feature=player_embedded&v=CHoXRvGTtAQ (accessed 10 February 2014).

PISA. Available at: www.oecd.org/pisa/ and www.oecd.org/pisa/pisaproducts/ 48852548.pdf (accessed 10 February 2014).

Porkess, R., Budd, C., Dunne, R. and Rahman-Hart, P. (2011) 'A World Class Mathematics Education for All Our Young People'. Developed by a task force chaired by Carol Vorderman and lead author Roger Porkess. Available at: www.tsm-resources.com/pdf/VordermanMathsReport.pdf (accessed 10 February 2014).

Russell, B. (1957) *The Study of Mathematics in Mysticism and Logic*. New York: Doubleday.

Strauss, V. (2012) 'Khan Academy: The Hype and the Reality'. Washington Post blog: The Answer Sheet. Available at: www.washingtonpost.com/blogs/answer-sheet/post/khan-academy-the-hype-and-the-reality/2012/07/22/gJQAuw4J3W_blog.html (accessed 10 February 2014).

TIMMS. Available at: http://nces.ed.gov/timss/index.asp and http://timssandpirls.bc.edu/ (accessed 10 February 2014).

Webley, K. (2012) 'Reboot the School', *Time*. Available at: http://content.time.com/time/magazine/article/0,9171,2118298,00.html (accessed 25 November 2013).

Williams, G. (2006) *Biology for You*. Cheltenham: Nelson Thornes.

6

Project work and problem-based learning through STEM

Introduction

In Chapters 1 and 2 we considered the processes involved in the STEM subjects and along with systems thinking, we identified that 'problem solving' was a key feature that the subjects have in common. This chapter takes problem solving further and looks at the issues that need to be considered in the planning and organisation of project work and problem-based learning.

One of the first school courses in technology of the late 1960s was called 'project technology', and Nuffield science courses often had a project that students could carry out independently. On-going practical work and its related tasks tend to have a range of names depending to some extent on the emphasis fashionable when the name was coined; in technology and engineering examples include 'capability tasks' and 'design-and-make tasks'. In science 'project work' the terms 'project-based learning' or 'problem-based learning' are used to describe activity where the focus is on discovering an aspect of the natural world for oneself, and in Chapter 2 we listed the nature of mathematical tasks that can be truly characterised as problem solving. Whatever the title in vogue, work linked to authentic real-world tasks is the principal driver in STEM activities and for many pupils, doing a project – in class or extracurricular – is what it is all about.

Interest in the importance of problem solving practical work is not new. Early in the twentieth century (and before), practical work was seen as an aid to learning and separate from vocational preparation. John Dewey, for example, working in Chicago set up an innovative school in 1896 where cookery and carpentry were seen as important in providing insights into natural materials and processes.

Practical work, then, has a long history and project work has received a more recent impetus through what have been termed 'twenty-first century skills'. For example, in *The Global Achievement Gap* (2008) Wagner advocates seven survival skills for the twenty-first century:

1. Critical thinking and problem solving;
2. Collaboration across networks and learning by influence;

3. Agility and adaptability;
4. Initiative and entrepreneurialism;
5. Effective oral and written communication;
6. Accessing and analysing information;
7. Curiosity and imagination.

You notice that 'critical thinking and problem solving' lead the list. This list also includes 'agility and adaptability', which are also characteristics of project-based work. An additional consideration is the extent to which 'authenticity' can be brought into project work – where the project is based on a real-world problem, and engages students in authentic practice, involving situations that are real to the student, their lives, and also presenting students with situations they may encounter in the future workplace.

Although continuous assessment at home has been a cause for concern (who is actually doing the work? The pupil or their parents?), the ability for a pupil to take a personal interest in an aspect of their STEM work and to apply what they have learnt to a novel situation is clearly of benefit. However, the word 'project' is used in many subjects to describe an aspect of teaching, learning and assessment; the label begins to be used differently in different contexts. To help clarify this, and investigate how project work can be done successfully and coherently, this chapter will consider the following questions:

- What is 'project work', i.e., project-based learning and problem-based learning, and why are they important?
- How are successful projects and related tasks organised?
- What is the relationship between project work and assessment?

What are project-based learning and problem-based learning – and why are they important?

Features of project-based learning

If teachers were asked to describe the characteristics of project work, their ideas would probably include the following:

- It is a substantial task and can take a considerable amount of time.
- The exact outcome is open-ended and unpredictable.
- The pupil takes responsibility to conduct the project as much as possible. The choice of a project is based upon a need which the pupil can see and identify with, and is based on an authentic 'real-life' situation – a project may be chosen by the pupil.
- A range of skills, knowledge and concepts are required to complete a project successfully, as technological problems do not respect subject boundaries.

Project-based learning, therefore, emphasises learning activities that are long-term, interdisciplinary and student-centred. Of course, teachers are a resource to the students, but should act more as facilitators, requiring students to organize their own work and manage their own time and compelling them to communicate and collaborate with one another. Project-based learning engages students in complex tasks based on challenging or 'driving questions'.

The examples below illustrate a board-prescribed science investigation project; tasks such as these carry 25 per cent of the final examination marks.

Fresh milk is heat treated to 132°C for one minute before it is sold to customers. This is known as ultra-heat treatment.

A milk manufacturer is trying to find ways to cut their production costs and has suggested that temperatures lower than 132°C might achieve the same results.

You are a microbiologist investigating the effect of temperature on the levels of bacteria in milk samples. You will report your findings to the milk manufacturer.

Or

Research has shown that the foods and drinks that are given to young children can affect their development and how well they progress at school later on in childhood and adolescence.

Fruit juices can seem like a healthy option for young children but there are concerns by the NHS because different juices contain differing amounts of vitamin C, sugar, acidity and fibre.

You are a food analyst working for the Food Standards Agency (FSA). You have been asked to investigate 5 different fruit juices. Your investigation could include:

- pH tests
- food tests
- vitamin C content
- acid concentration
- mass of suspended matter

You should write a report on your findings which could be used by the NHS to help parents, nurseries and child minders choose the best fruit juice for toddlers and young children.

(AQA, 2013)

These science examples of 'controlled assessments' match some of the general characteristics of project-based learning as described above. For instance, they would clearly take an extensive period of time to complete and some concepts borrowed across STEM subjects would have to be appropriately applied to produce the outcome.

Another example of project-based learning in the area of technology and engineering is offered by the Design and Technology Association (DATA, 2013). The significant driving question here is: What can nature offer architectural design? In this case, the issue of significance is sustainability and the project-based learning unit of work is focused on education for sustainable development. A project-based learning approach will allow the pupils to turn their critical faculties on the way buildings do or do not achieve sustainability and if they do not, what might be done about it. They will not be able to do this without the requisite knowledge, understanding and skill and it is important that the pedagogy used in this unit of work provides this. There are some suggested 'big tasks' (or projects) and some contributory 'small tasks' from across the STEM subjects that might be useful in undertaking the big task. The following is taken from the teachers' guide:

The students can formulate their project through a big task for example:

- Re-designing an existing building in order to make it more sustainable
- Designing a new building on a given plot of land to ensure that it is sustainable.
- Taking a department from within the school and redesigning it to make it more sustainable
- Identifying an existing building with sustainable credibility.
- Developing a presentation to explain how it achieves this sustainability.

The projects at the centre of this unit of work pose considerable challenges for students. To support the students in meeting these challenges there are a range of small tasks that provide structured opportunities for learning that will be useful in tackling the big tasks. There are three sets of tasks, one set for each of the contributing STEM subjects

For design and technology the small tasks are concerned with:

- architecture informed by nature
- sustainable architecture
- product life cycle analysis

For science the small tasks are concerned with:

- reducing heat loss
- wind power
- materials
- forces and structures.

For mathematics the small tasks are concerned with:

- exploring the Fibonacci Series and the Golden Ratio
- scale drawings, plans and elevations
- power from the wind and calculating wind power.

(DATA, 2013)

Features of problem-based learning

Problem-based learning (PBL) can be traced back to McMaster University in Canada in the 1960s where the instructors at McMaster's medical school wanted to find a way to link the vast amount of content knowledge of the medical students to a way of applying it to the vital activity of real-life medical practice. They developed a teaching approach that would force the students to use their textbook knowledge in case study situations and, in turn, staff could assess students' ability to work as practicing doctors. Today, PBL is a curriculum model constructed around real-life problems that, by their very nature, are ill-structured, open-ended and ambiguous.

A type of the PBL approach more common in schools are model-eliciting activities (MEAs) which are designed to help pupils apply the mathematical procedures they have learned to create mathematical models. To initiate MEAs, typically, the teacher sets up a context for the pupils and this is often a simulated newspaper article about the real-life topic to be considered and pupils respond to some questions based on the article. The problem is then posed to the pupils who work in groups to model possible solutions. Often, such problems have multiple solutions or the students are working towards a 'best fit'. Chan Chun Ming (2008) gives this example below:

The hiring problem

Mission: Your group is in charge of hiring some workers to help clean, paint, and move furniture in the school. These workers must complete the job within four days.

  Conditions:

1. You can hire only from one company once, and you have to accept the number of workers for that company.

2. You have a worksite supervisor who can only supervise at most 12 workers per day, so you try to hire as many as 12 per day. Assume that each worker to be hired works the same amount of time, and produces the same amount of work per hour.

3. You need at least: 14 workers for moving furniture, 14 workers for painting, and 14 workers for cleaning within the four days.

Presentation: You have to present your case to your class. Show in full detail (with different solution options) how you arrive at hiring the workers. Show your *productivity index* and use it to make your decision.

The hiring problem data

Cleaning services:

Company	A	B	C	D	E
No. of Workers	4	2	6	3	5
Cost $	160	76	270	120	175

Painting services:

Company	F	G	H	R	J
No. of Workers	3	6	7	4	5
Cost $	114	240	315	160	210

Moving services:

Company	K	L	Q	N	T
No. of Workers	7	4	3	6	4
Cost $	245	160	135	225	140

Productivity index is calculated as follows:

(Total no. of workers / Total Cost) × 100 {Give index to three decimal places}

Are you getting value for money? The larger the index the better.

From a teacher's point of view, some of the managerial problems that such work presents may be evident too: the teacher has suggested the task, not the pupil – who may or may not see it as relevant to them – and if the pupil lacks appropriate knowledge, that knowledge to complete the work must be gained somehow. These issues will be considered later.

Tamara Moore and Gillian Roehrig at the University of Minnesota believe that MEAs allow for a more 'thoughtful and inclusive approach' to gauging student understanding of STEM subjects which is impossible with a textbook-based approach, and set out five characteristics of MEAs:

1. Model-eliciting, meaning that students are required to develop a model to not only solve the problem at hand, but also others like it. This usually looks like a step-by-step method for *how* to solve the problem, rather than just an answer to one question. This is important because it helps students understand the mathematical structure of the problem.
2. Self-assessable, meaning the individual or student team can critique their own work for accuracy and effectiveness.

3. Open-ended to allow for creative and thoughtful interpretation of the lesson. Rarely in the real world is there one way to solve a complex problem –and you can't find the answer in the back of a textbook! MEAs let students develop their own ways of thinking about the problem, in that they design the model for the problem based on their own prior knowledge and experiences, thus improving their problem-solving capabilities.

4. Realistic to connect students with familiar topics, like solar energy or paper airplanes. MEAs illustrate how STEM subjects can help solve the problems – big and little – of the world.

5. Generalisable in that MEAs are useful tools for *all* STEM disciplines: Science, Technology, Engineering and Math.

(Moore and Roehrig, 2013)

The difference between project-based learning and problem-based learning is essentially one of *ownership* of the learning activities. PBL has tended to be a way of configuring the curriculum and relating what the students know to actual, real-world problems which in turn leads them to find out new knowledge and skills to bring to bear on the problem. Rather, project-based learning has been more about a pupil choosing an extended activity that they are interested in and using it as a vehicle for demonstrating their current capabilities, but also including demonstrating their abilities in researching and investigating new knowledge and acquiring skills as required. But these tend to be two-sides of the same coin as the degree of latitude actually allowed to the pupils to follow their own interests in project-based learning has to be tempered by restraints of available resources and time, classroom management issues (particularly in large lower-school classes) and the ever-pressing need to 'cover the syllabus'.

Why is this type of work important?

Project-based and problem-based learning are particularly valuable in that they enable pupils to:

- integrate skills (in applying knowledge; speculative thinking; communication skills; ability to manipulate ideas and materials; etc.) and knowledge from a variety of sources in the process of developing useful outcomes.
- become more autonomous through taking increasing responsibility for the direction of their own work.

The aim of encouraging pupils to become autonomous – i.e., able to plan, investigate and research aspects of their own learning – has long been part of the rationale for many of the STEM subjects.

A balanced, practical-based curriculum will include many activities such as teacher demonstration, discussion work and also 'focused activities' or 'resource tasks' which are specific inputs that are pertinent to the work in hand and matched to the programme of study. In one sense, 'projects' could be considered to be just one teaching technique among many, but the qualities pupils require to solve problems and engage in successful project work cannot be inculcated by teacher-directed activities alone. It has been argued that project work is able to encourage people to 'create and do' rather than just 'know and understand'.

Such capability is important in many aspects of life and particularly, it is argued, in industry and commerce. Barlex reports that one school so highly valued the attributes promoted by project work that it included the following on its references for pupils:

Employers please note:
The qualities engendered in students who successfully complete a project are of value to Britain's industrial needs and your firm:

The capacity to acquire new skills when they are needed;
Industriousness over a long period of time;
Perseverance in the face of disappointment and problems;

Research skills necessary to become familiar with established ideas in the fields related to the project, be they technical, scientific or aesthetic;

The ability to use such ideas in the new and unique context of the project;

The ability to communicate clearly and effectively the development and final outcome of the project in both written and graphic form.
(Barlex, 1987, p. 7)

It is clear that project-based learning enables pupils to express their capability in a way that written papers alone cannot do. Teachers' enthusiasm for project work has influenced its inclusion in Key Stage 3 as well as for GCSE, but the characteristics of open-ended project work – so laudable for small groups of older pupils – must be examined more critically in the light of managing the capabilities and numbers of pupils in the lower school.

The ability of a teacher (or a team of teachers) to ensure that the national curriculum programme of study is followed progressively using open-ended projects is severely stretched by the characteristics of very long time schedules, an unpredictable outcome with unpredictable knowledge needs, and facilitating the concept and skill requirements of a class of twenty pupils on a 'when needed' basis. One strategy is to reduce the unpredictability by designating specific problems and assignments for pupils to tackle.

Technology, engineering and design-and-make assignments

A design-and-make assignment is a type of project work in engineering or design & technology that conforms to the following general characteristics:

- The *exact* outcome is unpredictable (although the framing of the task reduces the possible number of outcomes).
- The pupil takes responsibility for the conduct of the project as much as possible.

It is based upon a need that the pupil can identify with and perceive as a 'real-life' situation.

There are some important differences, however. Assignments are chosen by the teacher to highlight aspects of the programme of study. The direction and outcome is more controlled than in the open-ended major projects typical of many GCSE schemes, so that skills and knowledge can be introduced progressively. One drawback is that greater control over the content and timing of what is taught reduces the autonomy of the learner, but the resultant controlled development of learning, and successful management of the project development, may be more beneficial. Clearly, it depends on the degree of prescription versus the degree of openness. The previous experience of the pupils will largely dictate the teacher's approach.

Consider the following example. This is an identified task chosen by the teacher and presented to the class, but the outcome is only loosely specified and further work is needed to identify the likely learning outcomes.

Key Stage 3: Design-and-make assignment

Context: Safety in the home.

Task: To design and make a device that will give warning of potential hazards in the home.

Outcomes: Warning devices for intruders, overflowing vessels, high temperature and needless energy loss.

Materials and wood, metals, composites, range of switches and/or components: sensors, resistors, LEDs, ICs, batteries, connectors.

This task could be presented to the pupils in different ways to recognise the differences of individuals and also the depth of knowledge and skills pupils possess at the start of Key Stage 3 compared with the end of it. A range of project briefs might include:

- Task 1: Design and make an intruder alarm that will trip when someone treads on a mat.
- Task 2: Design and make an intruder alarm that is tripped (and stays on) when someone enters a room.
- Task 3: Design and make a device that will give warning of an intruder in the home.

Depending on the age and experience of the pupil, these tasks for lower secondary students could be very different to the science investigations set out above, in particular in the ways the teacher structures the activities to help and direct the work, basing the structuring on the previous experiences of the pupils. The organisation of activities will be considered next.

How are successful project-based learning and related tasks organised?

The starting point in organising successful project work depends, to some extent, on the *level* of that organisation. Before considering the organisation at a teacher-in-classroom level, the higher level of planning a 'scheme of work' (the collection of projects and associated activities) for a whole Key Stage should be thought through by all teachers involved. If learning is to be meaningful, the work done must:

- be differentiated, i.e., able to be tackled at a number of levels so that individual pupils understand what is expected of them and the work makes appropriate demands;
- build progressively on previous activities – a new project must offer new challenges which, at least at a general level, are supported by previous tasks;
- not become a treadmill where pupils 'go through the motions' but learn few new skills or ideas;
- be relevant to pupils, i.e., pupils must see the point of the project, particularly if it is more open-ended and steered by the enthusiasm of the individual.

Considerable planning is required to ensure that this happens in practice.

When planning project work it is important that you are clear on the following:

- The capabilities, resources and awareness that pupils are likely to bring with them to the project;
- The resources the pupils will reinforce and develop by means of the project;
- The capabilities the pupils will be required to demonstrate by means of the project;
- The awareness that will be highlighted by the project.

Here the term 'resources' includes knowledge and skills, and 'awareness' means the way the project affects and impinges on our everyday lives, with the consequent consideration of values.

The rest of this section looks at the important issues to consider when planning projects: teaching knowledge when needed, or as structured development and the relative importance of skills and problem ownership and motivation

Teaching knowledge when needed, or as structured development and the relative importance of skills

Pupils may know what they want to do but not be able to realise their goals because they do not have the required knowledge or skills. For instance, the example design-and-make assignment illustrated above indicates a need for knowledge of switches and transducers before the tasks can be successfully accomplished. More critically, when planning their work pupils may not consider certain approaches to a problem because they are ignorant of the existence of equipment or a technique which might help them. For these pupils 'problem solving' is doing little more than applying their common sense.

So what is the best approach? Should pupils learn skills in isolation, which might prove useful later but for which they perceive little immediate value? Should pupils learn skills 'as needed' within projects when they appreciate the usefulness of what they are learning but without a coherent structure and without realising that there *was* something new that they should know, to transfer to future work? The best approach is probably to steer a middle line as is illustrated by the 'big tasks' and 'small tasks' in the aforementioned DATA example. A carefully planned selection of shorter projects or small tasks emphasises particular aspects of the programme of study, skills and techniques, together with the longer, more open task (big task) which allows pupils to develop their capability by drawing on their accumulated experiences. In these longer big tasks, new skills and knowledge will have to be covered, just as the shorter small tasks will need to be meaningful and situated in an appropriate context to make sense. Learning skills for skills' sake – as sometimes happens in design & technology when pupils have to move from teacher to teacher in a 'skills circus' – can be unsatisfactory as the point of the activity is lost on some.

Problem ownership and motivation

As discussed above in relation to differences in emphasis between project-based learning and problem-based learning, if pupils choose a project themselves they may be more motivated to work independently and with interest, but they may have insufficient the knowledge and/or skills to complete it successfully. A teacher-decided project may be better suited to build progressively on pupils' previous work, be more controlled in the materials and equipment needed to resource it, and easier to manage as part of whole class work; however, students may not be so interested in what they have been asked to do. This issue assumes great importance as pupils progress through the school and are engaged in more open project work, but the issue is still relevant in earlier stages. The careful introduction of the project is vital and ways in which the pupils can themselves identify a need to investigate and work on is important. Brainstorming work in small groups will help an individual identify a possible line of work, but a teacher's knowledge of a pupil's background and interests certainly enables smooth negotiation of a project which is worthwhile from everyone's point of view.

Organising project work in the classroom

The word 'classroom' is used generically to denote any space where STEM education takes place. It has already been suggested that much of the strategic planning of project work should be done at a department team level to satisfy the statutory requirements of each stage and the examination boards, tempered with important education issues concerning the individual pupil. What is left for the individual teacher to organise?

The 'process' in projects

The teacher is responsible for the conduct of the project planned by the whole team and the teaching and implementation of what many books refer to as 'process'. There are as many different interpretations and critics of process as there different subjects in STEM! In design & technology and engineering, the criticism centres on the simplistic use of process as a linear movement from 'identification of need' to 'ideas' to 'specification' to 'product' to 'evaluation of product'. People do not actually design like that. Similar criticisms can be made about problem-based learning in mathematics. The thinking process is not linear but a complex activity where new possible solutions and evaluations of current ideas continually circle back and permeate every part of the activity at every stage. The over-emphasis on particular aspects of the process, perhaps because of a need to award marks, can be unhelpful and leads to such distortions as pupils inventing 'initial ideas' after their design is finished.

While accepting the shortcomings of the descriptors, many projects will contain the following activities:

- Researching: finding out information from books, magazines etc.
- Investigating: experimenting with equipment, materials, processes etc.
- Specifying: stating clearly the criteria that the chosen solution has to meet.
- Developing ideas that might make a contribution to the chosen solution.
- Optimising ideas to formulate the details of a chosen solution.
- Planning the making or organisation of the chosen solution.
- Making.
- Evaluating.

The skill of the teacher is to integrate these activities within the constraints of the resources, materials and equipment available and the timetable restrictions. The best lessons feature some or all of the following:

- Pupils are taught safely by specialist teachers who are confident and familiar with the media, tools and equipment being used, and who know the standards they should expect;
- The work is well planned, with systematic teaching of skills, knowledge and techniques;
- Teachers provide a good range of resources and materials, and encourage pupils to use these to investigate, design, make, test and evaluate their work;
- Specialist teachers use a variety of teaching techniques, and provide pupils with a good balance of activities both as part of an individual lesson and as part of their long-term planning;
- Teachers know the pupils for whom they are responsible, know the most appropriate moment to intervene, and are able to respond flexibly to the requirements of individual pupils;
- Teachers set a brisk pace and provide work which is realistic and interesting to pupils.

However, a well-planned scheme of work, a lively introduction, carefully prepared resources for skill enhancement and teacher inputs, and 'a good balance of activities' will still produce disappointing results if there is insufficient attention given to the allocation of short-term targets within the big task. There should be a clear purpose to each lesson.

By helping pupils to know what they need to have accomplished by strategic points throughout the project, they can be guided to a successful outcome. This does not mean that all pupils should do exactly the same thing in a rigid undifferentiated way, but there should be an awareness of the way pupils can get sidetracked by a particular facet of the work and lose sight of the whole task or problem presented.

What is the relationship between project-based learning and assessment?

It has been observed that the influence of assessment can alter the nature of STEM project work (see Banks, 2009). The assessment criteria of GCSE and the attainment targets of the national curriculum are important, but sometimes teachers can insensitively force pupils through a research or evaluation process for the sake of gaining marks on a particular scheme, rather than helping them develop their own ideas in a natural way. In contrast, and when assessing design & technology project-based learning, Barlex advocates a 'minimally invasion' approach:

What is required is the means to allow pupils to reflect on and reveal their progress in making design decisions as the task progresses. Essentially the assessment exercise has to probe and record chronologically the pupil's thinking. Such probing must take place as a pupil moves through the design task. I suggest that probes are required at three junctures in any design and make activity.

The first probe will be used when a pupil has developed his or her first ideas for a product. A pupil will be asked to consider whether his or her proposals meet the requirements of the brief and to clarify and justify the design decisions made so far. The pupil will also be required to review these decisions and consider whether what he or she is proposing is likely to be achievable in relation to resources of time, materials, equipment and personal skills.

The second probe will be used when most of a pupil's design decisions have been made through sketching, 3D modelling, and experimenting. This will be at the point where making is imminent or has just started. Again, the pupil will be asked to clarify and justify the design decisions made so far. Again, the pupil will also be required to review these decisions and consider whether his or her design fully meets the requirements of the brief and whether his or her plans for making are achievable.

The third probe will be used when the product is complete and will include an evaluation against the brief and the specification.

These probes will be used by pupils working in pairs or small groups under structured guidance with their work on the design task available for reference. The probes will provide a script through which pupils can reflect on and justify their design decisions.

(Barlex, 2007, p. 53)

So assessment needs to be integrated naturally into lessons and assessments need to be made during a project as well as at the end. The burden of assessment needs to be spread out; indeed, some important attributes can only be assessed as the work is being done. Such assessment opportunities need planning. Pupils can help in recording assessments by noting points in their books, project folder or design portfolio; for example, the outcome of a discussion which led to a decision, a new idea or modifications to a design. Internal moderation between teachers is necessary to come to a shared meaning of what is required for specific levels. A collection of evidence in the school will help to establish common agreement.

Several projects are needed to build up a view of the capability of a pupil as different projects bring different types and levels of responses from pupils. This is a case where 'looking sideways' not only helps with the construction of the curriculum but also an understanding of the capability of the pupils. The aims and purposes of project work should not be unduly affected by the assessment process. As described above, certain procedures will be suggested by teachers because 'it earns marks in the exam', but the relationship between the pupil and the teacher and the desire of the pupil to take ownership of the task should not be compromised.

A complementary and in some ways contradictory approach, however, has been advocated by Richard Kimbell through the e-scape project (2007). This project rejects criteria-based assessment as a fallacy – the criteria gets more and more detailed, teachers still don't agree that the end 'result' is valid and so fiddle the contributory criterion marks to make it 'right'. Instead, the project worked up the concept of a six-hour structured activity (two consecutive three-hour mornings) in which pupils take a design task from its starting point up to the point of a working prototype but rather than constructing a separate portfolio of assessment 'evidence', the pupils use a hand-held PDA (personal digital assistant) to create an e-portfolio online. Kimbell says:

> The clever bit of this project (at the classroom end) lies in the fact that the e-portfolio is unlike anything that currently exists by that name. Typically such things are second hand re-constructions of real designing – in PowerPoint (PP) or some other sequential software. The construction of the e-portfolio is typically a different task to the designing that it seeks to illustrate. First do your designing – then tell the story in your PP e-portfolio. By contrast the e-scape system uses hand-held digital tools directly in the nitty-gritty of the designing activity in workshops and studios. As learners do their thing, the hand-held digital tools up-link the work dynamically into a secure web-space, where their e-portfolios emerge before their eyes as they work through the activity. These are real-time design e-portfolios.
>
> (Kimbell, 2007, p. 68)

So the tasks are given to the pupils and are timed, scripted activities devised explicitly for assessment. This will inevitably undermine the authenticity of the activities and may lead to a one-size-fits-all approach, however, within that constraint, the accumulation of evidence is very 'minimally invasive' and the illustration of their thinking is very much – and literally – in the hands of the pupil.

Conclusion

Many of the issues to consider when supervising project-based learning are context-dependent. The school environment, the subject traditions of the teachers in the STEM subjects, the whole-school timetable, and the financial resources delegated to the different departments – all are highly influential and important for successful project work. Consumables on projects, for example, may have to be paid for by pupils or their families, but sponsorship from industry or assistance from a parent support group may help. The type of projects tackled may reflect the expertise of the staff and be hampered by the class size, which is determined by the school management team.

However, the most important factor is general to all teachers in every school. Project and investigation work will be most successful when pupils are matched to a task they find challenging but manageable and that is relevant to a need they can perceive. This means that teachers need to know the pupils' background – both personal and in their subject. Some of this will be on record cards in the different departments, but another way to find out is to hold STEM staff meetings regularly. The crucial information to help a teacher in project work may well be in a colleague's head.

In more ways than one, the key to successful projects is teamwork. As we have said before, it is important to engage in regular conversations with colleagues.

Background reading and references

AQA (2013) 'Additional Applied Science Exemplars'. See www.aqa.org.uk/ (accessed 10 February 2014) for link to examples.

Banks, F. (2009) 'Research on Teaching and Learning in Technology Education'. In A. Jones and M. de Vries (eds) *International Handbook of Research and Development in Technology Education*. Rotterdam, The Netherlands: Sense Publishers.

Barlex, D. (1987) 'Technology project work, ET887/897, Units 5–6, Module 4', *Teaching and Learning Technology in Schools*. Milton Keynes: The Open University Press.

Barlex, D. (2007) 'Assessing Capability in Design & Technology: The Case for a Minimally Invasive Approach'. *Design and Technology Education: An International Journal*, 12.2, 9–56. Wellesbourne, Design and Technology Association.

DATA (2013) 'What Can Nature Offer Architectural Design? A STEM Project Based Learning Unit Suitable for Key Stage 3 Teacher Guide. Wellesbourne, Design and Technology Association.

Kimbell, R (2007) 'E-assessment in Project E-scape'. *Design and Technology Education: An International Journal*, 12.2. 66–76, Wellesbourne, Design and Technology Association. Available at: https://ojs.lboro.ac.uk/ojs/index.php/DATE/article/view/Journal_12.2_0707_RES6 (accessed 10 February 2014).

Ming, C. C. (2008) Using Model-eliciting Activities for Primary Mathematics Classroom. *The Mathematics Educator*, 11(1), 47–66.

Moore, T. and Roehrig, G. (2013) 'Beyond the Textbook: MEAs in Action'. University of Minnesota Vision 2020 blog. Available at: http://cehdvision2020.umn.edu/cehd-blog/stem-meas-in-action/ (accessed 31 March 2013).

Wagner, A. (2008) *The Global Achievement Gap*. New York: Basic Books.

7

Enabling the 'E' in STEM

Introduction

This chapter has been divided into four parts. The first part was written by Matthew Harrison who is Director, Engineering and Education at the Royal Academy of Engineering. Matthew is extremely knowledgeable and both passionate and partisan with regard to engineering education. Matthew has been at the heart of the development that led to the introduction of the engineering diploma into schools in England. This is followed by a brief commentary by the authors on Matthew's piece in which we question the extent to which his vision of engineering as a school subject might come about. This is followed by a short discussion on the position of engineering in high schools in the USA. Finally there is a set of questions for you to consider concerning ways of moving forward engineering as a school subject.

Enabling engineering amongst 14–16 year olds in schools in England

Matthew Harrison

The nature of engineering in the context of a school

The word 'engineering' turns out to be surprisingly slippery, with multiple definitions offered. These range from defining the scope of engineering activity (Malpas, 2000) to providing a vision of the social and economic purpose of engineering (National Academy of Engineering, 2008). As discussed in Chapter 1, the tendency to use the single term 'science' (or at best 'science and technology') as shorthand for any publically funded science, technology or engineering activity is unhelpful. The terminology used in economic analysis adds to the confusion as the contributions made by engineering activity are obscured by inappropriately broad classifications such as 'manufacturing', 'construction' and 'industry' and also excluded consideration of the 'service' sectors where many engineers practice as engineers in technical roles (Harrison, 2012).

Some of the slipperiness in the school context comes from the intertwining of the terms 'engineering' and 'technology' (Harrison, 2011) and more generally from a widespread presumption that engineering qualifications are occupation-specific and therefore their adoption for the 14–16 year olds phase is controversial. This will be discussed later in the chapter.

Let us focus on the way students, parents and teachers identify with the subject of 'engineering'. The dominant identity for engineering in schools is instrumental in nature: something practical and technical that is explicitly connected with making things and economic prosperity. The UK finance minister George Osborne concluded his budget announcement speech on the 23rd March 2011 thus:

> We want the words 'Made in Britain', 'Created in Britain', 'Designed in Britain', 'Invented in Britain' to drive our nation forward. A Britain carried aloft by the march of the makers. That is how we will create jobs and support families.
>
> (Osborne, 2011)

The willingness of HM Treasury to link economic prosperity to making things (engineering), even in schools, is not new nor is it actually exclusive to engineering. The origins of the use of 'STEM' in UK education policy circles appear to come from HM Treasury.

> Science, Technology, Engineering and Maths have a core role in the future health of sustainable higher value added activity in the UK. As such, the Department for Education and Skills will play a more strategic role in the coming years towards monitoring the quality and quantity of outputs from the education system, at all levels, in STEM subjects, and acting decisively to redress emerging mismatches between supply and demand for skills.
>
> (HM Treasury, 2004)

These pronouncements on the value of engineering and other STEM skills are clearly provoked by recognition of the contribution that STEM makes to national economic prosperity. Engineering activity accounts for 28% of the Gross Value Added (GVA) to the UK economy and engineering and engineers pervade the whole economy (Harrison, 2012).

The pronouncements may also be provoked by concerns over the creeping changes in the overall shape of the UK economy and the vulnerabilities that might result. The Heseltine review (Heseltine, 2012) voices unease over 'the worst economic crisis of modern times' and shows that the long-term decline in the UK share of global exports in goods since 1980 coincides with the emergence of household consumption as the dominant contributor to GDP growth. The loss of growth since the global economic crisis of 2008 illustrates the vulnerability of an economy lacking in export-led trade in products based on engineering activity (i.e., making things).

To this identity, linked to economic prosperity, we must add the identities of:

- a professional occupation with threshold standards of competence, an ethical code of behaviour, an expectation of continuing professional development and a network of professional institutions to support professional membership and registration (Engineering Council, 2010).
- a subject of strategic importance in higher education (Saraga, 2011) deemed worthy of close monitoring, assessment of the balance of supply and demand and government intervention and support.
- a source of valuable wage returns in the labour market (Greenwood et al., 2011) where engineering occupations exhibit good returns when compared with wages generally.
- a significant contributor to the provision of STEM skills to adults (Harrison, 2012b) with associated gains in productivity (Harrison, 2012).
- a real-world and practical context for teaching and learning of STEM more widely (National Science Learning Centre, 2008).
- a subject in its own right in schools and colleges and frequently a subject cast as vocational or even occupation specific.

We will now consider the last two bullets in more detail.

Engineering as an enabler of a STEM curriculum in schools

Extra-curricular engineering activities have been promoted in schools for more than 30 years. Long before any government endorsed the 'STEM Programme' (National Science Learning Centre, 2008) engineering firms, charities and professional bodies funded a wide range of engineering outreach in schools. A comprehensive view of this STEM 'pre-history' is provided in the 2008 guide, *Shape the Future* (Royal Academy of Engineering, 2008). More recent guides are provided by the STEM Directories project and by the Tomorrow's Engineers initiative showing contributions from outside the schools system continue at a fairly large scale.

The motivations behind some long-term and very deep investments are personal to those that fund them, but are likely to include (in no particular order):

- Attainment in STEM subjects (curriculum enrichment);
- Charitable mission (many funders and deliverers of engineering activities are registered charities);
- Corporate social responsibility ('good neighbour' educational outreach);
- Corporate sponsorship opportunities ('good employer' profile);
- Equality and inclusion (gender imbalance in engineering, widening participation in the professions);
- General public engagement with STEM (raising STEM literacy, STEM awareness);

- Helping young people to form career intentions;
- Progression with STEM subjects;
- Provision of professional role models for young people;
- Raising staff morale through motivating work with young people;
- Securing a talent pipeline for engineering in the UK.

The last motivation listed seems to be a particularly enduring one:

> Students are motivated to enter engineering and perform better in industrial training through achievement in planning and making something that works, works well, and is something of which they are proud; not by merely being told all about it.
>
> (Matthews, 1977)

More recently, many programmes have emphasised the value they bring to the continuing professional development of teachers across the STEM disciplines. In this way, engineering takes on the identity of a real-world and practical context for teaching and learning of STEM more widely. An example of this if offered in Figures 7.1 to 7.3.

The context of the Royal Academy of Engineering's resource 'Winning Medals' was chosen because it was considered to be motivating to young people in the UK who had just witnessed the very positive coverage of wheelchair sports at the London 2012 Olympics. In its design and through trials undertaken in and with schools, the following characteristics were developed:

- A 'big question' or 'driving question' (See Chapter 6) to promote critical reasoning amongst pupils. In this case the driving question is 'Does engineering design make a difference to wheelchair competitors' quest for competition medals?' There is an underlying dilemma here, deliberately brought to the fore, in which the identity of the wheelchair athlete, frequently cast as heroic in the media, is called into question when they rely on engineered technology for their success.
- A practical and technical ethos where pupils are encouraged to build realistic physical models to explore the behaviour of engineered systems. In the example in Figure 7.2 pupils build and launch model sprint wheelchairs to investigate directional stability and therefore explore why wheelchairs take on the exaggerated shape they do for high level competition. The links to design & technology as a subject in school are obvious.
- Active learning. In Figure 7.3 pupils use simple calculations (not shown here) to arrive at an average speed of travel for a competition wheelchair. They are then supported through a physical investigation to determine the limits of the athlete in terms of the cyclic movement of their hand and arms. The comparison of average speed of hand and wheelchair make pupils think about how the system

TEACHER'S
VERSION

WINNING MEDALS:
does engineering
design make a
difference?

This resource aims to give students the
opportunity to investigate the impact
of science, technology, engineering and
mathematics (STEM) on wheelchair sport.

FIGURE 7.1 Teaching resource: Winning medals.
Source: Nolan (2012)

Making instructions

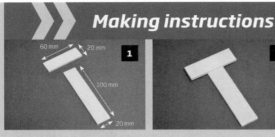

1
Cut two lengths of corrugated plastic for the wheelchair's chassis.

2
Join the corrugated plastic with hot glue or double-sided sticky pads.

3
Fix a 60 mm length of drinking straw to the chassis with hot glue.

4
Make a rear axle by cutting an 85 mm length of the 3 mm steel rod.

5
Insert the steel rod axle into the drinking straw on the underside of the chassis.

6
Cut one 130 mm length of the 3.2 mm aluminium rod. Make a 90° bend 30 mm from one end of the rod.

7
Cut one 160 mm length of the 3.2 mm aluminium rod. Make a 90° bend at its midpoint.

8
Insert the 130 mm bent aluminium rod into the corrugated plastic chassis. This will become the front wheel's axle.

9
Slide the 75 mm diameter wheels onto the steel axle.

10
Slide a 10 mm length of drinking straw onto the front wheel's axle.

11
Add the 39 mm diameter wheel to the front axle. If the wheel does not easily slide on and spin freely you will need to use a 4 mm drill to increase the size of wheel's hole.

12
Insert the 160 mm bent aluminium rod into the rear of the model wheelchair's chassis. This part will help you to launch the model.

FIGURE 7.2 Teaching resource: Modelling a wheelchair.

Source: Nolan (2012)

So the fastest world class wheelchair athletes can currently travel at an average of approximately **8 m/s**, which is equivalent to **17.9 miles per hour**.

The athletes achieve these speeds by providing a burst of muscle force to the hand-rims of the wheelchair – an *impulse* – and over long distances *coasting* between impulses. The velocity of the athlete's hands must be equal or greater than the *tangential velocity* [3] of the hand-rim if they are to apply a *positive torque* and increase the rotational speed of the wheel, that is, accelerate the wheelchair – increasing its travelling velocity. If the athlete's hands are travelling slower than the hand-rims they will have the effect of *slowing the hand-rims down*, absorbing torque and therefore *decelerating* (slowing down) the wheelchair.

 Visit **www.youtube.com/paralympicsporttv** and observe how T54 wheelchair athletes accelerate their wheelchairs in track events, such as the 100 m and 200 m races.

When accelerating in a straight line, the maximum speed of the wheelchair occurs when the tangential velocity of the hand-rims reaches the maximum velocity of the hand movement that the athlete can produce.

 Time to COMPETE

What is the maximum hand velocity possible when powering a wheelchair? Do a controlled test!

- Take two tables and position them with a 50 cm gap between them.
- Lay a 30 cm ruler on the edge of each table as shown in Figure 7.
- Stand between the tables with your hands comfortably by your sides and your palms stretched out.
- See how fast you can move your hands backwards and forwards over the 30cm distance as if you were powering a wheelchair. A friend should count the number of times your hands can make a 30 cm 'trip' down the length of the ruler and back again in 20 seconds.
- Work out an average velocity, in terms of metres travelled per second, for your hands using the equation below.

$$\text{velocity (m/s)} = \frac{\text{distance (m)}}{\text{time (s)}}$$

- At what point do you think your hands have maximum velocity?

[Answers provided to the STEM activity leader]

- The maximum repetition rate of the entire hand motion cycle will rarely be more than 3 Hz (3 cycles per second) as this is the commonly known maximum 'control frequency' of the human. One cycle is represented by a 'trip' down the length of the ruler and then back again. See if the repetition rate is higher when the subject moves their arms 'in phase' with each other (both moving forward at the same time) or in 'anti-phase' (when one moves backwards as the other moves forwards).

- The distance the hand travels in one cycle is 60 cm, so at 3 Hz this is 180 cm which is an average velocity of **1.8 m/s**.

$$\text{velocity (m/s)} = \frac{3 \times 0.60\text{m}}{1\text{ (s)}}$$

[3] The velocity of the hand rim at the point at which the athlete's hand makes contact.

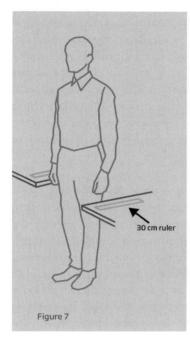

Figure 7

30 cm ruler

FIGURE 7.3 Teaching resource: Exploring human performance.

Source: Nolan (2012)

really works. Subsequent mathematics (not shown for brevity) allows the students to investigate the difference between the maximum speed of the hand and a cycle average. This, combined with thinking on the relationship between speed (a scalar quantity) and velocity (a vector) and the relationship between the diameter of the wheel and the tangential velocity of the rim, develops deeper understanding of the complex behaviour of the wheelchair as an engineered system and the adaptive, tacit control imposed by the athlete. The links to both science and mathematics as curriculum subjects is deliberate in order to foster a more coherent understanding of how knowledge gained through the study of each subject is applied to solve problems across all three.

Throughout this example, and others like it, scaffolding for a dialogic approach to learning is provided through prompts to teachers that encourage discussion between pupils, between pupil and teacher, and wherever possible to provide an external actor such as an engineer to model the behaviours of engineers in complex situations. This discussion, not just about what is being learned but also *how* it is being learned, challenges the presumption that engineering in schools will always be vocational or even occupation-specific. Borrowing from Papert's ideas on computing in schools, engineering activities can produce 'objects to think with' thereby 'concretising formal knowledge' (Papert, 1980) and applying it to new problems. Such feats of critical thinking start to look like advanced intellectual accomplishments and not narrow skills training for the workplace.

Engineering as a curriculum subject in schools

It must be recognised, however, that as well as occupying an extra and intra-curricular role, engineering is frequently cast with the identity of a vocational subject in schools. For example, it is cited in the Wolf Review (Wolf, 2011) and in the tables of vocational qualifications that count in school performance measures and school league tables (DfE, 2011). With that positioning comes the probability that in the minds of some, engineering is for the 'less able' (Claxton and Lucas, 2012) and that qualifications will be occupation-specific.

The Royal Academy has tried to counter this view, positioning engineering as a valued component of STEM and entirely relevant to pupils on academic pathways with accompanying qualifications that are respected in the labour market and for progression in the subject (Harrison, 2011). Here the case is made *against* occupation specific-qualifications at 14–16:

> Qualifications adopted for 14–16 year olds must be a 'portable qualifications' and therefore must include a significant transferable knowledge core: evidenced by significant STEM in key content and learning outcomes. Therefore [they] must not be solely based on National Occupational Standards.
>
> (Harrison, 2011)

However, despite its apparent purposefulness, its STEM-value and the commonly-held view that it links to economic prosperity, engineering is only taken by a small minority of 14–16 year olds in schools in England. Let us look at some possible reasons for this.

Data on the qualifications completed in England obtained from the Further Education STEM data project (Harrison, 2012b), from the Joint Council for Qualifications and from Parliamentary questions show that 16,000 school pupils in England achieved Level 1 or Level 2 engineering qualifications at Key Stage 4 in 2010/11. Between them, these pupils achieved more than 18,000 engineering qualifications, suggesting that a few pupils took more than one engineering qualification. Whilst this figure involved around 40 different qualifications, most had relatively few pupils enrolled and only a few had more than 500 enrolments. More than two thirds of the achievements were in just three qualifications: BTEC qualifications, the GCSE in engineering and the Principal Learning from the 14–19 Diploma in Engineering.

Given a total examination cohort size of around 650,000 and just 16,000 pupils choosing engineering, why is engineering as a subject in its own right such a relative rarity in schools? One cause must be the well-documented ambivalence to engineering careers amongst young people leading to the conclusion that engineering will be relatively unpopular as a subject. Only 38% of 12–16 year olds in the UK see engineering as a desirable career (Engineering UK, 2012). This varies with gender as another survey found (Becker, 2010) that in the UK 18% of young women and 50% of young men are willing to become engineers. Therefore, vocational or occupational engineering qualifications will only have limited, gendered appeal: only 7% of completions of the Higher Diploma in Engineering were by girls and for the Double Award GCSE it was 8%.

However, looking beyond pupil choice, there might be further issues of prioritisation in schools. Engineering is far more common amongst young people in the Further Education (FE) sector than in schools: nearly 40,000 Level 2 engineering qualifications were completed by 14–19 year olds in the FE and skills sector in 2010/11 (data from Harrison 2012b). Therefore in the complex balancing of 16–19 STEM provision between FE colleges and local schools it appears that, perhaps due to its practical and vocational requirements and identity, engineering is often left to the FE sector and twice as many young people seek it out there than take it at school.

Further indications of prioritisation in schools seem evident in an analysis of year-on-year trends in subjects that might compete for the attention of, predominantly male, 14–16 year-old pupils in schools such as physics and aspects of design & technology.

Table 7.1 shows completions in these subjects in England, again taken from the Joint Council for Qualification (JCQ). It is not possible to disaggregate JCQ data by age of learner or by whether the qualifications were taken in schools or in FE Colleges. However, inspection of FE STEM Data (Harrison, 2012b) suggests that the majority will have been completed in schools.

TABLE 7.1 Completions.

	GCSE physics	GCSE design and technology (all product areas)	GCSE double award engineering	Higher 14–19 Diploma in engineering
2009	84,197	287,965	5,002	15
2010	113,216	270,401	4,132	871
2011	132,402	238,483	1,430	1,521
2012	149,179	226,656	1,640	1,463

Source: Joint Council for Qualifications (2012)

Table 7.1 clearly shows that GCSE physics completions have been rising steeply whilst completions in engineering and design & technology have fallen. It is well known that physics has increased in popularity in recent years as a direct influence of the focus on 'triple science' in schools in England. It is also commonly known that, since being removed from the core of the National Curriculum, design & technology has struggled to maintain a position in schools hard pressed to deliver on other competing priorities and this is seen in falling completions (noting that those shown in Table 7.1 are for all product areas in design & technology including female-dominated food and textiles and male-dominated resistant materials and systems and control).

It is worth focusing, however, on the characteristic of the Higher Diploma that most influenced teaching and learning of engineering: applied learning. The Higher Diploma is a wrapper around 'Principal Learning' (the core subject specific content for a line of learning), generic learning (work experience, personal learning and thinking skills, functional skills in English, mathematics and ICT, a project) and additional specialist learning (further subject specific content). The Higher Diploma specification requires half of the guided learning hours taken up by the Principal Learning to be spent on 'applied learning' defined as:

> Acquiring and applying knowledge, skills and understanding through tasks set in sector contexts that have many of the characteristics of real work, or are set within the workplace. Most importantly, the purpose of the task in which learners apply their knowledge, skills and understanding must be relevant to real work in the sector.
>
> (QCA, 2007)

The development of applied learning in 14–16 engineering in the years since 2006 has produced curriculum materials that have been carefully collated at the National STEM Centre in York and on the Learning and Skills Improvement Service (LSIS) *Excellence* gateway. Much is the product of collaborative work between teachers within the consortia of schools and colleges set up for delivery of the diplomas (DFES, 2005) and for the Diploma in Engineering it is frequently related to the design and manufacture of engineered products. In such cases, learning for work and learning through work can take the form of realising a realistic engineered product, perhaps using an industrial specification or technique or perhaps solving a real-world problem in the context of an engineering firm. For example the Technology Enhancement Programme curriculum resources on smart materials have proven very useful to teachers of the Higher Diploma in Engineering, which requires knowledge of the characteristics and behaviours of materials and an understanding of how materials are selected for use in a product.

In 2008, the Royal Academy of Engineering set out to complement such curriculum support materials with learning resources that looked at the more human-centred aspects of the Diploma in Engineering and provided learning for work and learning through work by encouraging pupils to adopt the behaviours of an engineer and to think like an engineer. In other words to *become* an engineer and not just to study engineering.

For example, the final learning outcome from Unit 8 of the Higher Diploma in Engineering is to 'know about the environmental and social impact of engineering and sustainability of resources'. Figure 7.4 shows an activity developed to get pupils active in considering the application of their new engineering knowledge to real-world problems acknowledging the dilemmas that are commonly characteristic of complex real-world situations. Such examples encourage the use of critical reasoning and dialogic approaches to making decisions. They support pupils in exploring circumstances where there are multiple influences and constraints on a problem, many of which will be contradictory.

A rebirth of engineering as a curriculum subject in schools?

In 2012, UK Minister for Skills and Enterprise Matthew Hancock announced the re-development of the Principal Learning from the 14–19 Diploma in Engineering as follows:

> If Britain is to compete and thrive in the global economy then we must lead the way in science and technology. These new engineering qualifications will give young people the skills that they want, and that businesses need, to be at the forefront of this race.
>
> (Osborne, 2012)

The need for a redevelopment can be seen in the fall in completions in the Higher Diploma in Engineering in 2012, which only hint at a wider picture. The diploma was effectively stopped as a qualification by the closure of the mechanism through which the attainment of students was aggregated across the many separate qualifications taken within the diploma 'wrapper' (Ofqual, 2011). The Principal Learning component of the diploma remained as a qualification in its own right but was cast as 'vocational' by the DfE simply because any qualification taken by

SUSTAINABLE engineering

WINNERS & LOSERS

Description of activity

Divide the class into pairs and give each pair a copy of the Winners and Losers worksheet (overleaf).

Ask students to write the product or issue they are going to explore, e.g. should each student in the school be given a laptop instead of using exercise books? in the centre circle of the Winners and Losers diagram.

Now ask them to write in the people who will be most affected by the issue, e.g. paper manufacturers, students, waste disposal company, school bursar, laptop parts manufacturers in the middle segments.

Finally, ask your students to write in the outer segments how that group will be affected by the issue, both positively and negatively. It is helpful to write positive and negative results in different colours to help students work out whether the net result will be good or bad for a more sustainable future.

As a plenary, pairs then report back on their discussion to the rest of the group with their overall conclusion as to whether the issue has a more positive or negative impact on people.

★ **NB: You could also use the Winners and Losers activity to assess positive and negative impacts on the environment.**

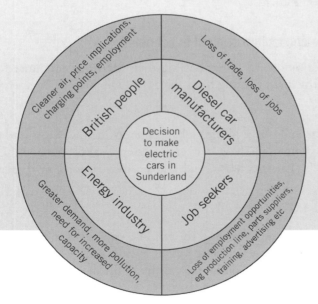

The Royal Academy of Engineering

PRACTICAL ACTION
Technology challenging poverty

FIGURE 7.4 Teaching resource in support of unit 8 of the Higher Diploma in Engineering
Source: Practical Action and the Royal Academy of Engineering (2012)

14–16 year olds other than a GCSE, IGCSE or AS is deemed vocational (DfE, 2011). With a change in the way that school performance measures were calculated to remove the notion of 'equivalences' for vocational qualifications (where larger qualifications counted as more than 'one' in school league tables) schools could see powerful disincentives to offering non-GCSE qualifications that are much larger than a single or double GCSE in size. The result is that the Principal Learning qualification was all but abandoned, and only a few schools with a particular technical ethos continued to offer it after 2011.

The task of leading a redevelopment of the Principal Learning qualification in engineering, and in doing so shaping it into a suite of smaller qualifications that fit the requirements of school performance measures (league tables), has been accepted by the Royal Academy of Engineering, an organisation that has led on most of the developments in 14–19 engineering education in recent years.

The challenge in this will be in preserving the valued characteristics of the Principal Learning in engineering qualification seen to be:

- The applied nature of the learning, including sufficient practical experiences for pupils to build self-efficacy with the physical domain and, for those who want it, to extend their personal identity as practical people.
- The deep engagement of employers in developing and delivering the curriculum.
- The authenticity of the engineering content, essential if engineering employers are going to be successful in developing and delivering the curriculum.
- The strong links to other STEM subjects.
- A focus on preparing Level 2 learners for progression towards higher wage return qualifications and eventually higher wage occupations.

whilst linking several qualifications together in such a way to preserve constructive alignment of learning outcomes. When taught well, the cohort of pupils, their teacher and other significant adults should become a community of practice (Lave and Wenger, 1991) with pupils able to construct a self-image of themselves 'becoming engineers'.

The issue of whether the re-developed Principal Learning qualification in engineering will be occupation-specific is being tackled head on. The Department for Education, in experimenting with 'outcomes' measures for school leavers at age 16 and 18 shows that only 6% of 16 year olds in 2010 were not captured in a definition of continuing education that includes enrolment in a school sixth form, sixth form college or FE college or on an apprenticeship (DfE, 2012). Only a subset of the 6% will be in work, and even fewer will be in engineering employment. Therefore, with a vision of making a significant contribution to the engineering skills of the nation, the re-developed qualifications must be aimed at securing progression in STEM education or training, being relevant to all pupils with the required aptitude and attitudes and not just the very few who will transfer post-16 to engineering employment. In short, the qualifications should not and will not be occupation-specific. They will be applied qualifications that foster reflective and self-conscious thinking in the acquisition of STEM knowledge. They will always be taken alongside academic subjects prescribed by the National Curriculum: English, mathematics, science, computer science, languages and humanities.

Taken as a set, the content of the re-developed qualifications will be almost identical to that of the Principal Learning in engineering qualification and is listed in the box below.

Purpose statement for 14–16 Engineering, 28th November 2011, Royal Academy of Engineering

Engineering today

The UK is in the business of high added-value, high-technology, sustainable engineering and manufacturing. In addition, it needs to maintain capability in civil engineering, engineering construction, electricity production and distribution, gas, water and sanitation, transportation, process manufacture, nuclear, electronics, food manufacture, fuels, high-value materials, consumer products, IT, software and healthcare services. All depend on engineering knowledge and skills and all are signalling increasing demand and experiencing a scarcity of supply of suitably qualified young people.

What is engineering for 14–16 year olds?

Engineering is one of the STEM (Science, Technology, Engineering, Mathematics) subjects prioritised by Government and employers in the UK and in every successful nation. It is readily associated with progression through sixth forms and apprenticeships, further and higher education and towards rewarding employment in sectors of the global economy that are vital to sustainable growth.

What is the relevance of engineering to 14–16 year olds?

Engineering provides a creative and practical curriculum vehicle, enabling the application of mathematics and science to realistic problems that involve purposeful design, innovation, technology, computing, the realisation of functional artefacts and commercial enterprise. It directs pupils to see how they can use what they have learned to solve problems and improve lives.

14-16 engineering curricula promote successful progression to a wide range of next steps in education and training. Building on a strong foundation in science, technology and mathematics in Key Stages 1–3, engineering curricula provide an inspirational context for STEM and an opportunity for pupils to explore their identity as an engineer or technician through the solution of realistic technical problems.

Respected engineering qualifications for 14–16 year olds, such as the Principal Learning in the 14–19 Diploma in Engineering provide the STEM learning outcomes required for progression to STEM apprenticeship, Further Education or University along with significant opportunities to design, create, and test engineered products (Harrison, 2011b). These engineering qualifications at Key Stage 4 are entirely relevant to pupils on academic pathways.

What is the purpose of engineering for 14–16 year olds?

- To link theory and practice in STEM, engaging with employers and industries to provide a creative engineering environment in schools through authentic, directly relevant applied learning
- To provide a worthwhile addition to the education of a broad range of pupils
- To foster an interest in and understanding of engineering approaches to problem solving
- To appreciate engineering as an economic and social benefit
- To maintain UK engineering leadership in the world by inspiring the next generation of engineers and technicians
- To help pupils understand the personal value of careers in engineering
- To increase the numbers of young people, female and male, who want to go on to be engineers and technicians

What is the content of Engineering for 14–16 year olds?

14–16 year olds should learn about: engineering enterprise and the diverse career opportunities available; engineering design and development; sustainability; computerised manufacturing and process control; planning and producing engineered solutions; electronics and electrical principles; modern production processes; engineering maintenance.

Source: The National Committee for 14–19 Engineering Education (2011)

The subject content is being classified as:

- Engineering knowledge and understanding: that content seen as the most fundamental technical knowledge relevant to the engineering domain.
- Technical knowledge with practical skills: the wider technical content relevant to the engineering domain applied using appropriate practical skills.
- Professional knowledge: knowledge of the nature of engineering enterprise; professionalism; social and environmental responsibility.
- Interpersonal skills: the employability skills – communication, managing projects, managing people, teamwork – required for success in engineering occupations and re-distributed as evenly as practicable across the set of linked qualifications so that each qualification has integrity and usefulness in its own right.

The challenge of re-developing the Principal Learning qualification is being cheerfully accepted by the teachers, curriculum developers, awarding bodies, educators and others assembling around the task. The prize is a set of qualifications that can form the core of a 14–16 technical curriculum, providing the authenticity required for progression in engineering but with a relevance to the concerns of young people to mean that more are attracted to study engineering than before.

The aim is to have the qualifications accredited for first teaching in September 2014 and for them to be included in the 2016 school performance measures (league tables). Success will be to meet the wider vision for engineering amongst 14–16 year olds set out in the Royal Academy of Engineering's Purpose statement for 14–16 Engineering above, with an annual uptake of the qualifications of at least 50,000. Nearly 60,000 Level 1 and 2 engineering qualifications are achieved by 14–19 year olds in schools and colleges each year and it is hoped that those who might have achieved at Level 2 aged 17 or 18 will, in future, be encouraged and supported to do so by age 16. This is important as progression to Level 3 is key to accessing high wage engineering employment and those who are still at Level 2 post-16 are at a significant disadvantage.

This scale of uptake will depend on two factors. The first is the incentive for schools to offer engineering at Key Stage 4 and this relies on qualifications counting in school performance measures. The second is the quality of the provision which will determine the progression options for those that take the qualification. Quality of provision does rely on availability of equipment and space to undertake the practical elements of engineering qualifications but it also depends on having expert teachers. In 2012, equipment and space were still available in around 500 schools in England as a legacy from their involvement in the Diploma in Engineering. In addition, data obtained from the Department for Education by the Royal Academy of Engineering shows that more than 5,000 teachers in secondary schools hold degrees in engineering. There are therefore capital and human resources out in schools through which this ambition could be met.

As a final thought it is worth reflecting on the progress made amongst educationalists and engineers in understanding and refining the position of engineering within a school. Over the last decade ever more care is taken in the development of engineering learning materials, taking account of published literature and undertaking evaluation within a pilot before attempting wide dissemination. This new dual-professionalism, combining deep engineering expertise with an understanding of pedagogy, will stand the emerging engineering education community well and provides a more effective platform for collaboration with subject practitioners in other disciplines.

Summary

I have provided a brief overview of the history and role of engineering as a subject for 14–16 year olds in schools in England as a context for interdisciplinary STEM, as outreach by the engineering profession and as a curriculum subject in its own right. We considered the nature of engineering in the economy and hence in public policy and showed how this has affected the identity of engineering as a curriculum subject. We explore too how extra and intra curricular engineering learning resources can link to other STEM subjects and provide an educational experience for young people in which they exhibit practical and technical learning, applied learning, dialogic approaches to collaborative learning and tackle dilemmas to strengthen their powers of critical reasoning. These higher cognitive characteristics are in sharp contrast to the common positioning of engineering as only a vocational or even a narrow occupation specific subject in schools with implied assumptions that it is therefore most suited to the less able pupil. The tension between this and the casting of wider identities for engineering as a curriculum subject in schools was investigated through the lens of the development, delivery and now re-development of the Higher Diploma in Engineering.

Engineering as a school subject?

So what are we to make of Matthew's arguments for introducing engineering as a school subject? He has made a strong case that in studying engineering there is significant cognitive content as well as psychomotor skill development and that labelling the subject as 'vocational', and by implication suitable only for the less able, is unwarranted. Many of those schools which support the engineering diploma do so in response to local employer engagement and these employers see the qualification as an important stepping-stone in the recruitment of engineering technicians. The schools do not see the course as only suitable for the less able, but they *do* see it as a subject that is occupationally orientated. Hence we are not completely persuaded by Matthew's argument of the weak link to vocationalism. The rhetoric surrounding the STEM agenda at national level is often couched in terms of economic instrumentalism so it still remains to be seen whether it is possible for engineering to find its place as a legitimate component of a general education for all.

The 14–19 engineering diploma grew slowly after its introduction and at the same time the GCSE double award engineering lost ground as shown in Table 7.1. This was accompanied by a much greater loss of ground with regard to design & technology – a fall of some 60,000 entries overall compared with a loss of 3,400 entries in GCSE double award engineering, but with a growth of 1,500 entries in the 14–19 engineering diploma. So we must acknowledge that the increase in uptake whilst encouraging was not so significant numerically. Certainly the reduction in numbers of students taking design & technology was not offset by the increase in those students studying the engineering diploma. The classification of the engineering diploma as 'vocational,' and hence a change in the way the qualification could be counted towards school performance measures, was a cruel blow that prevented any further immediate growth and led to a dramatic fall in uptake. But all is not lost. At the time of writing, the engineering diploma qualification is being re-developed so that it to avoids the pitfall of being seen as narrowly occupational-specific and is being slimmed down to ensure that time spent on the course is not disproportionate to the extent it counts towards school performance measures. Much to Matthew's delight, this appears to be giving school engineering a second chance.

There is no doubt that Matthew is ambitious in his estimates for the uptake of engineering as a school subject in response to this new opportunity. In broad terms he hopes for an annual uptake of 50,000 students. The question is, just how realistic is this? One imponderable is the extent to which the qualification can indeed contribute to school performance measures, however, we know that those developing the new qualification will do all they can to ensure that this criterion is met. The second is the extent to which schools have the resources, both human and capital, to teach the course. We think Matthew is perhaps overly optimistic with regard to human resources. Although there may be 5,000 teachers in secondary schools with degrees in engineering many of these are employed to teach physics, mathematics and design & technology. And it is likely that some teachers whose engineering degrees provides a knowledge and understanding of computer programming will soon find themselves teaching on the new computer studies courses that the government is keen to introduce into schools (See Chapter 9).

You would not expect an organisation as astute as the Royal Academy of Engineering to put all its 'eggs in one basket' and it is significant that the E4E (Engineering for Education) group within the Academy has spent some considerable effort in developing a re-conceptualisation of the school subject design & technology. The key proposals were launched in March 2013 and the accompanying documentation is available online. Interestingly, there is an explicit acknowledgement that the subject is *not* a vocational subject and the way the subject has been redefined enables design & technology courses to offer learning experiences that mirror engineering activities to a considerable extent. Given the large uptake of design & technology compared with the engineering diploma, it may be that in its redefined form design & technology enables many aspects of engineering to find their place as a legitimate component of a general education for a majority if not all students.

The situation in the USA could not be more different. Here engineering is being subsumed into the science curriculum. The US *Framework for K-12 Science Education* (NRC, 2012) indicates that engineering should be taught as part of the science curriculum. Of the over 160 pages that form the second part of the document (i.e., the majority) Scientific and Engineering Practices counts for 42 pages, and Disciplinary Core Ideas – engineering, technology, and applications of science counts for 15 pages. Hence this is not a tokenistic approach. Christine Cunningham and William Carlsen (2013) have reviewed this approach and acknowledge that the broad rationale for the approach is to teach engineering before teaching science. Such a teaching and curriculum strategy avoids teaching science first, which students often find abstract, unappealing and difficult to understand. Instead, science can be embedded in an engineering experience in a way that will predispose students to learn science later, when they have been motivated by the engineering experience. Cunningham and Carlsen comment at length on the way the document considers scientific and engineering practices as having parallel features although a different intent. This epistemic similarity is shown diagrammatically in Figure 7.5. We think it is worth considering some of the features of practice and question to what extent they will achieve their espoused aims of enhancing science education.

First, let us consider the practice of *developing* and *using models*. Cunningham and Carlsen argue that that science deals with conceptual models, whereas engineering deals with concrete models which are more accessible. However, in many science courses these are physical models that students use to explore concepts – for example, the bubble raft for explaining the properties of metals, ball and spoke models for exploring mechanisms in organic chemistry, different coloured beads representing dominant and recessive genes and, more recently, computer-based models have been developed for exploring the rules governing the behaviour of objects under various forces. Such models can then inform the scientific imagining that takes place in the 'mind's eye' when pupils are constructing and reconstructing their science understanding. Students can be asked to construct physical models to develop science understanding. Engineering models often start with sketches as opposed to 3D models, and these can present students with a considerable conceptual challenge: lines on a 2D surface representing a 3D item. Such modelling skills require teaching, as indeed do 3D modelling skills. We have to ask the question, will the science educator know about different sketching/drawing/modelling techniques and be able to teach them?

Second, let us consider the practice of *analyzing* and *interpreting data*. Here the thrust seems to be that giving students design/construction problems that they can solve as opposed to engaging them with ideas they find difficult to understand will develop students' self efficacy and that this will somehow spill over into disciplinary agency in other disciplines. What seems to be missing here is any sense of just how wonderful a really good explanation based on ideas derived from interpreting data can be. The argument is almost anti-intellectual with regard to scientific thinking.

Third, let us look at the practice of *engaging in argument from evidence*. This feature is clearly important for both science and engineering. With pressure to cover a large amount of content, science teachers often teach the prevailing paradigm as something to be memorised as opposed to something to be developed through reflection and arguing from evidence. This is understandable, if regrettable, but if engaging in argument from evidence is important for developing science understanding, will skills in arguing about aspects of engineering transfer to science understanding when it is required, especially as the item under scrutiny in science will not be a physical object but an explanation? We must also take note of Matthew Harrison's position that engineering is a coherent discipline in its own right and should be taught as such, not subsumed within the science curriculum. Some find it difficult to make the case for engineering education for all at pre-college level, after all we don't teach nursing or doctoring at pre-college level. In England, the Royal Academy of

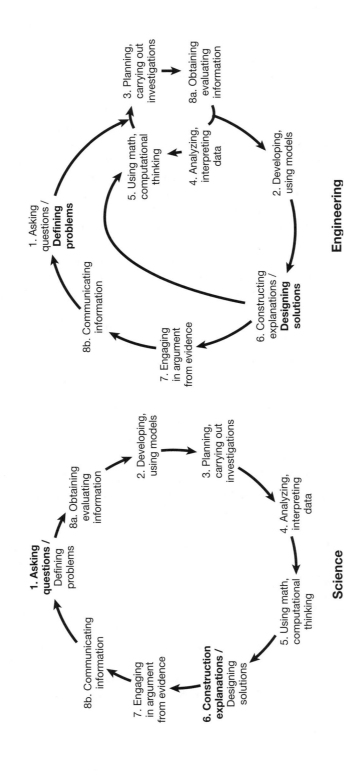

FIGURE 7.5 Cycles of epistemic practices in science and engineering.

Source: Cunningham and Carlsen, 2013.

Engineering is currently arguing that design & technology is the only subject in the high school curriculum that introduces young people to the knowledge and skills needed for creative design, innovation and engineering. Design & technology is seen as a general academic subject with its own fundamental body of knowledge, principles and concepts which are not provided elsewhere in the curriculum.

Finally, we must consider the practical question of *who* will teach the engineering activities that are expected to enhance science learning? Engineering, as Cunningham and Carlsen rightly state, leads to the investigation and creation of products in which to some extent science understanding is embedded. If such products are to be other than construction-kit based then the quality of manufacture becomes a serious issue. The generally applicable scientific principles underpinning the site-specific design of a bridge amount to naught if the bridge is so poorly constructed that it fails. In the USA those teachers who have themselves a wide range of appropriate construction skills and are able to teach these to students are likely to be technology teachers but will not necessarily have the science understanding required to engage with teaching science by design through engineering type projects. By the same token the science teacher who has the science understanding to help pupils use their developing science knowledge in designing products is unlikely to be able to teach construction skills and may well lead pupils to develop designs that are well beyond their construction capabilities.

Hence the issue here seems to us to be one of achieving suitable collaboration as opposed to poorly prepared science teachers invading and acquiring the 'construction' territory of technology teachers. So we think that in the USA situation it would be worth exploring how science and technology teachers might collaborate, with science teachers teaching science in the light of the learning that students are achieving in technology lessons and technology teachers teaching technology in the light of the learning that students are achieving in science lessons – a mantra which we have already chanted in this book!

Now we come to the questions for you to consider concerning ways forward for engineering as a school subject. The basic question is where do you stand with regard to teaching engineering to secondary (high school) students? Do you think it is appropriate?

Matthew Harrison has argued that it need not be considered a vocational course as the study of engineering meets the criteria for an academic course of study. The reality is that when engineering is available as a school subject, schools that opt to teach it do often see it as vocational. A key practical point from the experience of the engineering diploma in England is that it is costly, complex and demanding. But if you were committed to the idea this should not deter you. Or would you prefer to see it as part of the science curriculum as is being promoted in the USA? As a science teacher, you might feel that this was asking too much of you and that you wouldn't be able to meet the practical requirements of such a programme. However, you might feel that by collaborating with technology teacher colleagues it would indeed be possible to meet the requirements. This might take diplomacy as some technology teachers might see engineering within science as 'stealing' their curriculum territory. Or would you reject the option of teaching engineering and instead opt to teach design & technology in such a way that it provided young people with the knowledge and skills needed for creative design, innovation and engineering without being overtly vocational as is being suggested in England? This approach is not without its curriculum development burden. An approach to design & technology that did not have strong links to mathematics and science would not meet these intentions. And what if you are a mathematics teacher? How might you be involved in teaching engineering if your school decided it was to be on the curriculum? There would certainly be many opportunities to support both science and design & technology colleagues as they integrated the use of mathematics for engineering purposes into their teaching.

Where you stand will depend on your school situation, your professional knowledge and skill and your views on the purpose of secondary school (high school) education. Whatever your position, we would suggest that it will not be tenable if you do not engage with colleagues across the STEM subjects.

Background reading and references

Applied Learning Materials for Engineering. Available at: www.nationalstemcentre.org.uk and www.excellencegateway.org.uk (accessed 10 February 2014).

Becker, F. S. (2010) Why Don't Young People Want to Become Engineers? Rational Reasons for Disappointing Decisions, *European Journal of Engineering Education*, Vol. 35, No. 4, 349–66.

Claxton, G. and Lucas, W. (2012) Is Vocational Education for the Less Able? In P. Adey and J. Dillon (eds) *Bad Education: Debunking Myths in Education*. Buckinghamshire: The Open University Press.

Commission on Social Justice (1994) Social Justice Strategies for National Renewal, London: IPPR.

Cunningham, C. and Carlsen, W. (2013) Pre-College Engineering Education. In N. G. Lederman (ed.) *Handbook of Research in Science Education*, 2nd edition, Abingdon: Routledge.

DATA 'Believe in D and T Campaign'. Available at: www.believeindandt.org.uk (accessed 10 February 2014).

Department for Education (2011) Qualifications for 14–16 Year Olds and Performance Tables: Technical Guidance for Awarding Bodies. London: Department for Education (DfE).

Department for Education (2012) Statistical First Release: Destinations of Key Stage 4 and Key Stage 5 Pupils, 2009/10. London: Department for Education (DfE).

Department for Education and Skills (2005) 14–19 Education and Skills. London: Department for Education and Skills (DFES).

Department for Education and Skills (2008) Promoting Achievement, Valuing Success: A Strategy for 14–19 Qualifications. London: Department for Education and Skills.

Engineering Council (2010) UK Standard for Professional Engineering Competence (UKSPEC). London: The Engineering Council.

Engineering UK (2012) '2012 Engineers and Engineering Brand Monitor'. Fresh Minds Research for Engineering UK. Available at: www.engineeringuk.com/_resources/documents/EEBM2012.pdf (accessed 10 February 2014).

Greenwood, C., Harrison, M. and Vignoles, A. (2011) Labour Market Value of STEM Qualifications and Occupations. London: Institute of Education and Royal Academy of Engineering.

Harrison, G. (2000) The Continuum of Design Education for Engineering. Engineering Council. Available at: www.nationalstemcentre.org.uk/elibrary/resource/8391/the-continuum-of-design-education-for-engineering (accessed 10 February 2014).

Harrison, M. (2011a) Supporting the 'T' and the 'E' in STEM: 2004–2010. *Design and Technology Education: An International Journal*, Vol 16(1), 17–25.

Harrison, M. (2011b) 'Respected', Technical Qualifications for Use in University Technical Colleges. London: Baker-Dearing Education Trust, Edge Foundation and Royal Academy of Engineering.

Harrison, M. (2012a) Jobs and Growth: The Importance of Engineering Skills in the UK Economy. London: The Royal Academy of Engineering.

Harrison, M. (2012b) 'FE STEM Data Project' November Report. London: The Royal Academy of Engineering.

Harrison, M. and Ota, C. (2008) Nuts and Bolts Guide to Delivering the Engineering Diploma. London: Department for Children, Schools and Families. Available at: www.eriding.net/diplomahandbook/docs/lines_learning/100223_14-19_dip_lines_of_learning_nutsandbolts_engnandb2.pdf (accessed 10 February 2014).

Heseltine, Lord M. (2012) 'No Stone Left Unturned in Search of Growth'. London: Department for Business, Innovation & Skills.

HM Treasury (2004) UK Government Science and Innovation Investment Framework 2004–2014, HM Treasury.

Joint Council for Qualifications (2012) 'GCSE Results for 2012'. Available at: www.jcq.org.uk/examination-results/gcses (accessed 10 February 2014).

Lave, J. and Wenger, E. (1991) *Situated Learning: Legitimate Peripheral Participation*. Cambridge: Cambridge University Press.

Malpas, Sir R. (2000) The Universe of Engineering: A UK Definition. London: The Royal Academy of Engineering.

Matthews, D. (1977) Relevance of School Learning Experience to Performance in Industry. Watford: Engineering Industry Training Board.

National Academy of Engineering (2008) *Changing the Conversation: Messages for Improving Public Understanding of Engineering*. Washington, DC: The National Academies Press.

The National Committee for 14–19 Engineering Education (2011) 'Purpose Statement for 14–16 Engineering'. London: The Royal Academy of Engineering. Available at: www.raeng.org.uk/education/scet/pdf/Statement_of_purpose.pdf (accessed 10 February 2014).

National Research Council (2012) *A Framework for K-12 Science Education: Practices, Crosscutting Concepts, and Core Ideas*. Washington, DC: The National Research Council.

National Science Learning Centre (2008) The STEM Framework, National Science Learning Centre.

Nolan, D. (2012) *Winning Medals: Does Engineering Design Make A Difference?* London: The Royal Academy of Engineering. Available at: www.raeng.org.uk/education/eenp/engineering_resources/pdf/Winning_medals_teacher_version.pdf (accessed 10 February 2014).

Ofqual (2011) 'Consultation on Changes to Diploma Regulation'. Available at: http://core.kmi.open.ac.uk/download/pdf/9063643.pdf (accessed 10 February 2014).

Ofsted (2010) 'Diplomas: The Second Year'. Ofsted report ref 090240. Available at: www.ofsted.gov.uk/resources/diplomas-second-year (accessed 10 February 2014).

Osborne, G. (2011) 'Budget Statement by the Chancellor of the Exchequer, the Rt Hon George Osborne MP'. Available at: http://webarchive.nationalarchives.gov.uk/20130129110402/http:/www.hm-treasury.gov.uk/psr_reporting_centralgovernment.htm (accessed 10 February 2014).

Osborne, G. (2012) 'Chancellor Announces Boost for Engineering Skills'. London: HM Treasury. Available at: www.gov.uk/government/news/chancellor-announces-boost-for-engineering-skills (accessed 10 February 2014).

Papert, S. (1980) *Mindstorms: Children, Computers and Powerful Ideas* (2nd edition). New York: Basic Books.

Practical Action and the Royal Academy of Engineering (2012) *Winners and Losers*. Rugby: Practical Action and London: The Royal Academy of Engineering. Available at: http://practicalaction.org/winners-and-losers (accessed 10 February 2014).

QCA (2007) 'The Diploma: An Overview of the Qualification'. London: Qualifications and Curriculum Authority. Qualifications data available at www.jcq.org.uk and D. Johnson (2013). Question from Diana Johnson MP, 9th January 2013. Available at: www.publications.parliament.uk/pa/cm201213/cmhansrd/cm130109/text/130109w0003.htm#13010973001322 (accessed 10 February 2014).

Royal Academy of Engineering (2008) 'The Shape the Future Directory of Engineering and Technology Enrichment Activities for Schools and Colleges' report. London: The Royal Academy of Engineering.

Saraga, P. (2011) 'Strategically Important and Vulnerable Subjects: The HEFCE Advisory Group's 2010–11' report. Higher Education Funding Council for England. Available at: www.hefce.ac.uk/pubs/year/2011/201124/ (accessed 10 February 2014).

STEM directory. Available at: www.stemdirectories.org.uk (accessed 10 February 2014).

Tomorrow's Engineers. Available at: www.tomorrowsengineers.org.uk (accessed 10 February 2014).

Triple Science. Available at: www.triplescience.org.uk (accessed 10 February 2014).

Wolf, Alison (2011) Review of Vocational Education. London: Department for Education.

8

The role of STEM enhancement and enrichment activities

Introduction

Recently, I reviewed some of the comments I've heard whilst eavesdropping on pupil's informal 'corridor' conversations.

> Student A: Miss said we've got a STEM careers day coming up – all sorts of science and technology stands to visit; all of Year 9 have got to go. And in the evening there's an info session for our parents.
> Student B: Are your Mum and Dad coming?
> Student A: I think so; my Dad said I needed to think about what I wanted to do.

> Did you hear about the STEM club the science teachers are setting up? Sounds as if you get to do cool stuff – like what we don't get to do in lessons.

> Sir said he's organising a STEM Challenge Day for us at the local college. Something about robots and there'd be the chance to build one and talk to some engineers. You have to be picked to go though. Should we ask if we can go together?

These indicate some of the activities that make up enhancement and enrichment activities. Generally, they are outside the mainstream curriculum that we considered in Chapter 2. In many countries the main rationale for these activities is an economic one. Their aim is seen as supporting and encouraging a larger number of pupils in considering, and ultimately entering, a STEM-based career; the economic argument that has underpinned a variety of STEM initiatives. This is in contrast to the other main rationale for STEM which is epistemological in nature and contends that the contributing subjects, although different in nature and intention, have sufficient in common and such reciprocal utility that it makes good educational sense to see them in some sort of curriculum relationship.

A question immediately arises. Why are such activities necessary? Is the mainstream curriculum experience not engaging enough to attract young people into STEM-related careers? We have seen in Chapter 3, the intrinsic nature of science may render it unattractive to many young people and, as indicated in Chapter 5, a significant proportion of young people in both Europe and the USA become alienated towards mathematics as they move through secondary education. This apparent disenchantment with STEM is corroborated by the findings of the ROSE (Relevance of Science Education) project (2010). This is a well-regarded international study investigating young peoples' attitudes towards science and technology. Participating countries range across northern Europe, Africa, India, the Far East and South America. A info graphic produced in 2012 describes the STEM talent gap in the USA and identifies a particular issue for the USA. There is an under representation of minorities and women in STEM fields and this, coupled with population shifts indicating that more women and minorities will be entering the workplace, will exacerbate the STEM talent gap. Given disenchantment with the in-school STEM curriculum, and governments' concerns over growing STEM skills gaps, it is easy to see enhancement and enrichment activities as a solution to persuading young people to overcome their resistance to so-called 'hard' subjects such as science and mathematics and gain STEM qualifications and move onto a STEM career track.

In this chapter we explore a variety of STEM enhancement and enrichment activities at different scales of implementation. We begin by considering some initiatives that are global in scale and discuss their nature and intentions. Then we consider two individual countries, America and England, and describe and discuss developments that are taking place. Then we consider ways in which enhancement and enrichment activities might be evaluated and the results of such evaluations.

Global STEM enhancement and enrichment activities

I will consider here four enhancement and enrichment activities that are global in scale. The first two are competition based and concerned with developing relatively traditional STEM products and systems: FIRST Lego League, which focuses on robotics and F1 in Schools, which focuses on utilising CAD/CAM in the context of Formula One (F1) racing. The third is Hackedemia, which is not a competition and participants are able to follow their individual interests in developing hi-tech artefacts. The fourth is the iGEM Competition, which operates in the sphere of synthetic biology and from this perspective is completely different from the first three.

FIRST Lego League

FIRST Lego League (FLL) is a well-established STEM enhancement and enrichment activity. FIRST is an acronym – For Inspiration and Recognition of Science and Technology. It operates in over 61 countries and representatives from these countries can attend the annual FLL World Festival. It is a robotics program for 9–16 year olds (9 to 14 in the USA, Canada and Mexico), which the organisers say is designed to get children excited about science and technology and teach them valuable employment and life skills. The challenge facing the participants is in two parts: the Robot Game and the Project, both of which are underpinned by the FLL Core Values. Teams of up to 10 young people, with one adult coach, participate in the challenge by programming an autonomous robot to score points on a themed playing field (the Robot Game) and developing a solution to a problem they have identified (the Project). The FLL Core Values are significant. They are listed in Panel 8.1.

The terms 'Gracious Professionalism' and 'Coopertition' are significant. The term 'Gracious Professionalism' was coined by Dr Woodies Flowers, National Adviser to FLL. He defined this as 'learning and competing like crazy, but treating one another with respect and kindness in the process'.[1] Gracious professionals avoid treating anyone like losers. This is strongly linked to 'Coopertition', which requires displaying unqualified kindness and respect in the face of fierce competition. According to the organisers, Coopertition is founded on the concept and a philosophy that teams can and should help and cooperate with each other even as they compete.

The FIRST Lego League presents pupils with a socially relevant task. In 2012, the Project concerned identifying a problem faced by senior citizens as they age and to develop an innovative solution to help them deal with the particular problem. Participants are required to develop a presentation that describes the problem and the solution. The Robot Game is strongly related to this and teams and their robots have to manage a mix of challenges and activities related to being independent, engaged or connected. These are features that are particularly important for senior citizens as their problems become more challenging with advancing years. There is a wide range of information to support the participants available on the FFL website. For the team members there is extensive information on building with Lego and programming the NXT 'brick' which is the processor controlling the robot. For the adults who act as coaches and mentors there is also advice and guidance.

PANEL 8.1 FIRST Lego League Core Values.

- We are a team.
- We do the work to find solutions with guidance from our coaches and mentors.
- We know our coaches and mentors don't have all the answers; we learn together.
- We honour the spirit of friendly competition.
- What we discover is more important than what we win.
- We share our experiences with others.
- We display Gracious Professionalism® and Coopertition® in everything we do.
- We have FUN!

Source: www.firstlegoleague.org/mission/corevalues

Similar Lego resources are available to schools, for example, Mindstorm kits, so it would be possible to build FLL into a school curriculum. But the vast majority of FLL activity occurs as part of afterschool clubs very often with parental support. Teams who take part in FLL can attend official tournaments organised by so-called Operational Partners such as National Instruments, Rockwell Automation and 3M. There are in fact a wide range of FIRST Lego programmes of which FLL is just one.

F1 (Formula One) in Schools

F1 in Schools is a multi-disciplinary challenge in which teams of students aged 9 to 19 deploy CAD/CAM software to collaborate, design, analyse, manufacture, test, and then race miniature gas powered balsa wood F1 cars. It is the brainchild of Andrew Denford the Managing Director of Denford Limited a UK manufacturer of CAD/CAM machines and technology. F1 in Schools is a well-established enhancement and enrichment activity. Over the past 10 years it has grown from operating in just England to involve students from 34 countries. The organisers claim that it provides a global platform for the promotion of Formula One and partners to a youth market. In order to compete, teams must raise sponsorship and manage budgets to fund research, travel and accommodation. A criticism that these events will not appeal to girls has been rejected by the Fédération Internationale de l'Automobile (FIA) who have appointed Monisha Kaltenborn one of FIA's Women in Motorsport Ambassadors, to become a patron of F1 in Schools India.

The challenge faced by competing teams is as follows:

1. Working in teams of between three and six students, each member is assigned a role. The team prepares a business plan, develops a budget and raises sponsorship. Teams are encouraged to collaborate with industry and forge business links.
2. Using 3D CAD (Computer Aided Design) software, the team designs a model Formula One car of the future.
3. Aerodynamics are analysed for drag coefficiency in a virtual reality wind tunnel using Computational Fluid Dynamics Software (CFD).
4. Using 3D CAM (Computer Aided Manufacture) software, the team evaluates the most efficient machining strategy to make the car.
5. Aerodynamics are tested in wind and smoke tunnels.
6. In the race the cars travel at more than 60kph and compete side-by-side along 20-metre straights.
7. Teams are judged on car speed, as well as supporting evidence of their design, verbal presentation and marketing display stand in 'the pits'. Teams compete regionally, nationally and internationally for the Bernie Ecclestone F1 in Schools World Championship trophy.

Teams who enter the competition are bound by extensive competition regulations – the manual runs to 31 pages. Teams also have to abide by strict technical regulations defined in a 24-page manual. These include a requirement to use CAD/CAM in the production of the car and the organisers recommend the use of Solidworks for the CAD and the use of DENFORD QuickCAM PRO software for CAM. It is a requirement that the body is manufactured from balsawood by material removal using a CNC router/milling machine. The organisers recommend the use of a DENFORD CNC Router.

An interesting aspect of the competition is that in the schools World Championship each competing team is made up from two teams each from a different country. The organisers believe that this will develop participants' communication and collaboration skills and raise levels of tolerance and understanding. It is possible for schools to build F1 in Schools activities into their curriculum. There are clear possibilities for design & technology with the CAD/CAM development of the cars themselves but this can be linked to strongly to science and mathematics in considering and taking into account the drag on particular designs. However, to compete at regional level and above requires considerably more commitment. The organisers believe that participating in the competition will help change young peoples' perceptions of engineering, science and technology and enable them to develop an informed view about careers in engineering, Formula One, science, marketing and technology.

Comparing FLL and F1 in Schools

Whilst there are similarities between FLL and F1 in Schools: their economic justification, global scale and the fact they are both competition based, there are two significant differences. The main curriculum difference is that FLL introduces a new challenge each year that deals with quite different STEM domains. In recent years the problems faced by the participants have involved nanotechnology, climate change, transportation and disaster management. The F1 in Schools challenge has remained essentially unchanged since its inception and does not differ significantly year from year. There is a more explicit identification and emphasis throughout FLL on their Core Values of 'gracious professionalism' and 'coopertition' than is apparent in F1 in Schools. At the World Championship level in F1 in Schools such values do become apparent to some extent by the requirement that each competing team is made up from teams from different countries.

Hackidemia

Hackidemia is a newcomer to providing enhancement and enrichment in different countries in the world. It is the brainchild of Stefania Druga, Bobi Rakova and Brent Dixon and this team are supported by mentors in different parts of the world with a wide range of technical and educational expertise. The approach consists of a mobile 'invention laboratory' that can be set up in different locations to engage young people in developing and prototyping a wide range of artefacts. Quite deliberately, it extends the area of activity to include the arts and has a wide portfolio of activities. Recently, Hackidemia has run workshops in France, Cambodia, Bulgaria, Romania, Brazil, Germany, Australia, Malaysia and Nigeria. In some cases the workshops are part of a 'maker fair' and all the workshops reflect the maker philosophy of enjoyment and education from making an eclectic selection of things that work. The Hackidemia team believe that a very important aspect of their work is that it teaches young people to develop and use a wide range of tools that are applicable to many different sorts of problem solving.

The Hackidemia approach makes heavy use of 3D printing and encourages young people to design and test new learning activities and games, many of which are linked to story telling. This is in considerable contrast to the much more formal approach taken by FLL and F1 in schools which are based on competitions with rules. The organisers believe that these activities spill over into the home exposing families and communities to the possibilities of new technologies. They argue that this highly interdisciplinary approach provides an alternative to that adopted in most schools and is successful in engaging young people in highly technical activities. This in turn is likely to lead to young people opting for STEM-related career plans. They also suggest that the approach provides a successful pilot which schools can see is successful and begin to adopt as part of their pedagogy. There can be little doubt as to the enthusiasm of the core team or the enjoyment and learning that could be taking place in their workshops although it does remain to be seen whether this approach is sustainable or has significant impact.

The International Genetically Engineered Machine (GEMI) Competition

Biology is not usually seen as a science subject that has a significant contribution to STEM where the accent is often on physics and to a lesser extent chemistry. It is noteworthy that in the USA the technology curriculum includes agricultural technology and related biotechnologies and in New Zealand biotechnology is an identified area of optional study. Hence it is possible that topics within biology that inform biotechnology might be seen as part of STEM. Any study of biology will of course deal with genetics but it is unlikely that that there will be any in-depth consideration of synthetic biology. This is a new area of research in which engineering principles are combined with knowledge of genetics to enable the design and construction of new biological functions and systems not found in nature.

The iGEM Challenge

iGEM is a worldwide synthetic biology competition initially aimed at undergraduate university students but now extended to high school students. Given that the treatment of synthetic biology is at best very limited in school science courses iGEM can be seen as a global example of STEM enhancement and enrichment. Student teams are given a kit of biological parts at the beginning of the summer from the Registry of Standard Biological Parts. The iGEM competition facilitates this by providing a library of standardised parts (called BioBrick standard biological parts) to students, and asking them to design and build genetic machines with them. Student teams can also submit their own BioBricks. Working at their own schools the teams use these parts and new parts of their own design to build biological systems and operate them in living cells. Successful projects produce cells that exhibit new and unusual properties by engineering sets of multiple genes together with mechanisms to regulate their expression. Information about BioBrick standard biological parts, and a toolkit to make and manipulate them, is provided by the Registry of Standard Biological Parts. This is a core resource for the iGEM program, and one that has been evolving rapidly to meet the needs of the program.

The organisers of the iGEM competition believe that the competition has goals beyond that of just building biological systems. They identify these as:

- Enabling aspects of biology to be considered as engineering.
- Promoting the open and transparent development of tools for engineering biology.
- Helping to construct a society that can productively apply biological technology.

The organisers argue that requiring the teams to be self-organised and engage with the imaginative manipulation of genetic material provides a new way to arouse student interest in modern biology and to develop their independent learning skills.

In 2012, 41 high school teams registered for iGEM; 31 were from the USA, seven were from Asia and four were from Europe. All the projects submitted indicated significant sophisticated synthetic biology. The winner was a team from Germany supported by the Heidelberger Life Science Laboratory. The team describe their project as follows:

We have developed a synthetic measurement toolkit consisting of standardised parts for the precise quantification of both UV and radioactive radiation. Our toolkit is applicable in a variety of everyday life settings – from checking the exposure of your body to UV-light during sunbathing to detecting sources of radioactivity in high-risk-areas.

We have developed a body adornment collection which can hold UV sensitive E-coli bacteria that change colour according to UV dosage thus providing a biological warning of over exposure to sunlight. Through this product we want to raise the public awareness of the invisible danger and exemplify the great perspectives offered by synthetic biology.

(Heidelberger Life Science Lab, 2012)

Comparing global STEM enhancement and enrichment activities

The organisers of all of these global enhancement and enrichment activities use an economic rationale to justify themselves. Their aim is to engage school pupils with STEM-related activities in the expectation that this will lead them to consider a STEM-based career and so ensure an increase in the numbers of young people who can be employed in STEM-based occupations. Three are competition based – FIRST Lego League (FLL), F1 in Schools and iGEM. FLL gives the highest profile to collaboration but all cases require collaboration through teamwork to some extent. The websites of these activities show that the teams of young people taking part are highly involved and derive considerable enjoyment from participating. There can be little doubt that their engagement will be a highly formative experience. Hackidemia does not use a competition-based approach, relying instead on the intrinsic appeal of designing and making hi-tech artefacts and giving participants a large degree of choice in the nature of the artefact they produce. There is little information on the Hackidemia website as to participants' response. Whereas FLL, F1 in Schools and Hackedemia focus on 'traditional' STEM content, for example, hi-tech making, computing and the physical sciences, the iGEM competition is different in that it focuses on synthetic biology which is a newly emerging area of technological activity taught to only a limited extent in school science courses. Indeed, for young people who cease to take science courses at 16 years of age it is likely that they will have learned little about synthetic biology. Given that this technology is likely to have a significant if not disruptive impact in the near future the iGEM competition is particularly important in raising public awareness.

STEM enhancement and enrichment activities in the USA

This section will consider two significant STEM enhancement and enrichment activities currently taking place across the USA: the Making the Future initiative being developed by Cognizant and the DARPAR MENTOR programme. Both these initiatives relate strongly to the Maker Movement which bases its philosophy on a constructionist view of education. Those in the Maker Movement not only promote making things as a fun and enjoyable activity but insist that making activities develops a wide range of cognitive skills.

Cognizant: Making the future initiative

Barack Obama made a plea for STEM education to the National Academy of Sciences as follows:

> Think about new and creative ways to engage young people in science and engineering, like science festivals, robotics competitions and fairs that encourage

young people to create, build and invent—to be makers of things, not just consumers of things.

(Obama, National Academy of Sciences Annual Meeting, 2009)

Cognizant is a major business consultancy, listed in Fortunes 500, that specialises in the use of technology to develop new business models in ever-competitive global markets. Cognizant identified three troubling trends in the USA that underpinned Obama's plea:

1. A relative decline in math and science proficiency
2. A decline in interest in the STEM fields
3. A decline in measured creativity

Cognizant also noted that these trends threatened the competitiveness of the US economy and quality of life for future generations. Cognizant responded by initiating the Making the Future programme which has an after-school and summer programme as its flagship.

Developed in partnership with the Maker Education Initiative and the New York Hall of Science, the programme provides grants to community organisations to run hands-on, Maker-movement inspired programmes in an after-school or summer camp setting, or within the school day when conditions allow. Making the Future grants may cover costs for tools, materials, instructor fees, and other expenses essential to meeting the needs of the children participating in the programme.

Cognizant issued over 20 programme grants in 2013, based on an established pool of funding. Each grant was in the region of $15,000–$30,000'. For 2014 Cognizant expect to award funding for a further 24 programmes.

A flexible approach with guiding principles

Cognizant is very flexible on the format, structure, age group, demographics and types of activities that are conducted in the programmes it funds. However, it asks that grant recipients consider the following five guiding principles that shape quality Making programmes:

1. The programme must include fun, hands-on, project-based, and engaging activities.
2. Children should make something, versus doing experiments or activities that don't have a final product.
3. Programmes can follow a set of planned activities, but should allow for individual creativity, deviation, experimentation, and encourage trial and error.
4. Children should be able to keep the projects they make so that they can share their pride in their accomplishments, re-tell the Making process, and bring Making into their community.

5. Programmes should be long enough in duration that children can immerse themselves in a meaningful experience. This refers to both total programme duration (20–40 hours or more) and session duration (typically 90 minutes or more, although shorter for young children).

The types of project activities can be very wide-ranging so as to attract a broad range of children, and may include making electronic gadgets, robots, craft-oriented projects, digital fabrication, software oriented projects, music, hydroponics and clothing/wearable projects.

A variety of delivery schedules are possible, depending on the needs of the sponsoring organisation and the children they serve. Possibilities include:

- after-school, meeting once a week for 2 hours for 14 weeks
- week-long winter school vacation camp, meeting 4 hours per day
- two-hour programme embedded in a summer day camp, meeting for 8 weeks
- a summer-long series of workshops
- a Saturday programme, meeting 2 hours each Saturday from October through May
- an in-school programme, offered in 40-minute blocks once a week, to an entire grade level
- a school-day internship model, meeting for 5 hours twice a week, for 14 weeks

Cognizant acknowledge that a critical element to the programme is having one or more experienced Maker Coaches to lead and facilitate the programme. Grant funds are intended to be used by the sponsoring organisation to hire qualified instructors. Volunteer instructors from the community or the hosting organisation can be used, if available.

Making the Future has a clear and explicit economic rationale. Interestingly, it has more in common with Hackidemia than FIRST Lego League or F1 in Schools given the emphasis on personal choice and adherence to Maker Movement philosophy and practice. Hence it appears that the initial programme was successful and will increase on a year-by-year basis. It is interesting to note the emergence of the Maker Movement as an inspiration for STEM enhancement and enrichment activities.

The DARPA MENTOR programme

This brings us to the second example; the involvement of DARPA in supporting Maker Activity with young people through its Manufacturing Experimentation and Outreach (MENTOR) programme. This focuses on engaging high school-age students in a series of collaborative design and distributed manufacturing experiments. DARPA envisions deploying up to 1,000 Computer-Numerically-Controlled (CNC) manufacturing machines – such as 3D printers – to high schools across the USA. The goal is to encourage students across clusters of schools to collaborate via social networking media to jointly design and build systems of moderate complexity, such as mobile robots, go-carts, etc., in response to prize challenges. DARPA expects the MENTOR programme will expand to ultimately reach 1,000 high schools by the 2014–15 academic year. The Manufacturing Experimentation and Outreach (MENTOR) effort is part of the Adaptive Vehicle Make programme portfolio which seeks to revolutionise the design and build process for complex defence systems by compressing the development timelines at least five fold while increasing the nation's pool of innovation by several factors of 10.

Controversy over involvement with DARPA

The involvement of DARPA has been problematic for some members of the Maker Community who expressed concerns with regard to the involvement with the military and intellectual property rights. Mitch Altman, a San Francisco-based hacker and prominent member of the maker community withdrew from participating in Maker Fairs in 2012. Dale Dougherty, the editor and publisher of *Make*, felt required to publish a justification for involvement with DARPA and dispel misapprehensions. In particular he drew attention to the following.

> All software we develop under the DARPA program will be available as open source … This also applies to content and other materials that we develop for the program.

> Student work is not owned by DARPA … DARPA does not have any claim on student work … It is up to the students and educators what to build.

> The project will build … infrastructure for project sharing, which we believe engages more students in the process of making.
>
> (Dougherty, 2012)

Overall he justified the partnership 'as an opportunity to extend the Maker movement into schools'.

It is clear that there are considerable similarities between Cognizant's Making the Future and DARPA's MENTOR programmes. They both have an explicit economic justification, yet they are both underpinned by a Maker philosophy which values 'making' as an educationally justifiable activity for its own sake not necessarily associated with an economic justification. One interpretation of the economic justification, to provide the next generation of weapon's engineers, has given some in the Maker community cause for concern whilst others see this as a golden opportunity to develop tools and infrastructure that supports 'Makerism' as a powerful means of general education for all.

STEM enhancement and enrichment activities in England

This section considers six STEM enhancement and enrichment activities currently taking place in England. They are as follows: (1) the National Science and Engineering Week and the associated (2) National Science & Engineering Competition, (3) a Rocket Challenge day for pupils aged 14, (4) the CREST Award scheme, (5) Nuffield Research Placements and (6) the work of a single teacher who has developed a wide range of such activities.

National Science and Engineering Week

In England there is a National Science and Engineering Week (NSEW) each March. It is managed by the British Science Association, which coordinates the activities and provides an electronic newsletter to inform schools and colleges about possible activities. This is funded by the UK government's Department for Business Innovation and Skills. The organisers claim that the week 'shines the spotlight each March on how the sciences, technology, engineering and maths relate to our everyday lives, and helps to inspire the next generation of scientists and engineers with fun and participative events and activities'. According to the NSEW website in 2012 there were an estimated 4,500 events and activities from thousands of different organisers involving more than two million people at schools, museums, universities, shopping centres, cafes and more – generating £1.08m worth of press coverage nationwide. The climax of the week is the Big Bang Fair. In 2012, this received 56,000 visitors to a range of events and activities delivered by 170 organisations from the public, private and voluntary sectors.

National Science and Engineering Competition

The Big Bang Fair also hosts the finals of the National Science & Engineering Competition (NSEC). Open to all 11–18 year olds living in the UK and in full-time education, the competition rewards students who have achieved excellence in a science, technology, engineering or maths project. There are regional events in which students showcase their projects and the best of these are invited to present their work at the National Finals at the Big Bang Fair. Projects can take a wide variety of forms:

- A piece of original research;
- An original invention;
- A design for a new or improved item;
- Experimentation using new techniques or existing techniques in an original way;
- Use of media to demonstrate a scientific principle or concept;

- The application of a diagnostic and/or creative approach to a well-defined problem or research question;
- A piece of work which explores issues surrounding science or aims to improve the engagement of others with science, technology, engineering or mathematics.

The subjects or topics can also vary widely. For science and mathematics these include: agricultural science, anthropology, biochemistry, biology, chemistry, ecology, environmental science, electronics (theory), geography, geology, mathematics, physics, psychology and sociology. For engineering and technology these include: design & technology, electronics (design and use), engineering (all disciplines), food technology, graphic products, information technology and computing, resistant materials and textile technology.

The criteria for judging the projects are as follows:

1. Project concept: What was the motivation behind your project and what were your aims?
2. Project process: How well did you plan and organise your work? What sort of experiments and research did you do? Were you innovative or creative in your approach?
3. Project outcome: How well did your project achieve its aims? Is your final product or report of a high quality? Does your project have a 'real-world' application?
4. Personal skills: How well did you deal with any problems or challenges? How well do you communicate your project? Does your enthusiasm shine through?

In contrast to the competitions taking place in global enhancement and enrichment discussed above the judging criteria are concerned with a set of broader features that can be used to compare and assess work in significantly different domains. One of the difficulties of assessing such a wide range of projects is that judges can find themselves in the position of saying the equivalent of 'Well I think this orange is better than this apple'. The criteria developed by those responsible for the NSEC avoid this difficulty and enable a competition with a wide range of appeal where participants can choose their project so that this competition has some of the advantages of the non-competition approach espoused by Hackidemia.

STEMNET – A Coordinating Organisation

The NSEW and associated NSEC can be seen as a direct response to Action Plan 8 of the national STEM programme 'Improving the quality of advice and guidance for students (and their teachers and parents) about STEM careers, to inform subject choice'. But the NSEW and NSEC do not happen in isolation from a wide range of regional events. These are coordinated by a national organisation called STEMNET which manages 45 sub-regional contract holders each of which has two main responsibilities. The first responsibility is managing the STEM Ambassadors scheme by which young scientists and engineers visit schools to promote STEM careers. Currently over 3,000 employers release staff to act as STEM ambassadors. The second responsibility is to broker STEM enhancement and enrichment activities to schools and colleges in their area.

Rocket Challenge Day: A university-based challenge day

A typical example of the activities brokered by a contract holder is the Rocket Challenge Day at Roehampton University. Ruth Seabrook, head of the secondary PGCE programme for design & technology, always invites STEM ambassadors to meet her trainees but, in November 2011, she explained to the author that she wanted to do more. She went through how she achieved this: she suggested the idea of a collaborative STEM event with her colleagues in mathematics and science. They all agreed that it was important for trainees from each of the disciplines to have opportunities to work together and the result was a joint enterprise involving six local secondary schools. The schools each sent mixed age teams (11–14 years) to take part in a day-long challenge involving designing, making and testing simple rockets. Each team was supported by PGCE trainee teachers from science, mathematics and design & technology. Each team was able to use a STEM ambassador for technical advice. The event has been running since 2010. Roehampton University is also the STEMNET contract holder and now employs Beverly Ballie to carry out the necessary duties. Once Seabrook had explained the idea Ballie could see the value of what Seabrook wanted to do immediately. It brought together the science of 'Action and Reaction', and the notion of optimisation – what was the best balance between weight of propellant and height reached? Ballie's role was to identify and liaise with local schools and to provide the STEM ambassadors. She was able to do this relatively easily because she had access to the STEM ambassador database and part of her role was to develop and maintain a STEMNET database of local schools and their STEM curricula.

This made the whole exercise much more manageable from the teacher trainer point of view. Feedback from both teachers and pupils was extremely positive about both the nature of the event and the learning achieved. However this activity did more than support STEM education in local schools. It provided trainee teachers from across the STEM subjects with the opportunity to work together and learn something about each other's subjects. Thus it provided a significant introduction to collaboration across the STEM curriculum.

CREST Awards and Nuffield Research Placements

Two other national schemes are worthy of mention. These are the CREST Awards and Nuffield Research Placements. The CREST Awards scheme requires young people at school to undertake projects of their own choice in the STEM subjects and, depending on the demand of the project, pupils can achieve bronze, silver or gold awards. Bronze Awards are typically completed by 11–14 year olds; around 10 hours of project work is expected. Students experience the project process: improving their enquiry, problem solving and communication skills. Silver Awards are typically completed by 14–16 year olds; around 30 hours of project work is expected. CREST Silver Awards can be achieved through coursework (e.g., GCSE design & technology) and projects in work related learning. Gold Awards are typically completed by 16–19 year olds and allow these students to conduct some authentic research; these longer-term projects require around 70 hours work. Importantly UCAS (the organisation responsible for managing applications to higher education courses in the UK) have endorsed CREST Awards for inclusion in young people's personal statements in their application for admission into University. The CREST Award scheme places a high priority on student choice of project topic but also on progression so that young people's enthusiasm can be captured whilst they are young and then maintained by increasing the challenge but without a decrease in ownership of the projects.

Nuffield Research Placements provide over 1,000 students each year with the opportunity to work alongside professional scientists, technologists, engineers and mathematicians. Students in the first year of a post-16 Science, Technology, Engineering and Maths (STEM) course are eligible to apply. Placements are available across the UK, in universities, commercial companies, voluntary organisations and research institutions. The organisers are particularly keen to encourage students who don't have a family history of going to university or who attend schools in less well-off areas. To ensure that no one is excluded on a financial basis students' travel costs are covered. Some students may also be eligible for a weekly bursary in addition to travel expenses.

An exceptional teacher

The majority of teachers who engage in enhancement and enrichment activities in England do so via a wide range of existing schemes that broker their services through STEMNET. However, it is possible for an individual teacher to develop their own brand of enhancement and enrichment activities. David Baker has taken the position that although the initial 'D' is missing from STEM it is through design activities that young people can be engaged in STEM. Baker teaches at Latymer School in Hammersmith, London and organises a whole range of extra-curricular design-based activities including design days at weekends and design camps during the summer holidays. Pupils from neighbouring schools are invited to attend. Recently, he has organised some STEM activities under the banner of the STEM Academy, which were supported by funding from the charity Shine. The programme Scrape, Rattle and Blow was concerned with the science, design and mathematics of music and musical instruments and ran for five consecutive Saturday mornings. During this time pupils aged 14 years learned about sound and how it is produced and how it can be altered according to the size, shape and materials used in the instrument. They explored how a sound can be measured in terms of waveforms and frequencies, and how this links to the pitch of a note. They used mathematics to work out different formulae to create tuning systems. They used a variety of acoustic and electronic devices to amplify sound. They built their own design of musical instruments and produced a CD recording of their performance.

The work of David Baker shows that an individual teacher with energy can make a significant contribution to enhancement and enrichment activities. It is noteworthy that his approach was not predicated on the economic argument but rather on using a 'designerly' approach to show how science, mathematics and technology could come together under a single context, in this case musical instruments, and each contribute considerably to pupil's knowledge understanding and skill.

Although most of the enhancement and enrichment activities described here are justified on an economic argument it is noteworthy that to a large extent the young people involved can choose what they do and in many if not most cases they are involved in making. Although the organisations that promote these activities have little if any contact with the Maker Movement there are strong similarities in the adoption of an overall constructionist philosophy.

Evaluation of STEM enhancement and enrichment activities

The evaluation of STEM enhancement and enrichment activities is part of the wider evaluation of STEM educational initiatives. In some cases these initiatives involve large-scale mainstream curriculum change, as in the case of Nuffield Twenty First Century Science in England. In other cases they are quite small scale as in the case of collaborations between a few schools in a state district in the USA. In yet other cases they involve enhancement and enrichment activities outside the mainstream curriculum and these can vary considerably in scale as we have seen earlier in this chapter.

Workshops developing evaluation practice

Recently, the Royal Academy of Engineering held a series of workshops to develop evaluation practice amongst the STEM community. Delegates were invited to consider the shape of the future of STEM evaluations and the workshops were set up to focus on quantitative, qualitative and econometric methods, with consideration of the role of STEM evaluations in a challenging financial climate. They were to provide an opportunity to contribute, share, learn and apply ideas about effective (and cost-effective) methods of evaluation and to explore current thinking of leading STEM funders and evaluators. As such, the overall purpose of the programme of workshops was to promote quality debate and discussion on current and future evaluation practice amongst the STEM community.

An interesting outcome of the seminars was the realisation that there was an opportunity for the STEM community to achieve greater *impact* and potentially *value for money* by making better use of existing evidence of *what works* in education (looking wider than just STEM) and also *why it works*. This latter feature, the *why*, looked to be increasingly important. Exploiting knowledge of *why* things work the way they do would allow the STEM community to:

- appraise intervention options more effectively before committing resources.
- develop more effective interventions.
- construct interventions that align better with the environment in which they are deployed.
- use less expensive evaluation.
- focus evaluation effort on novel/untested components of an intervention.
- as a result deliver better interventions (more impact, better value for money).

Now we will consider two evaluations of STEM enhancement and enrichment in the light of the Royal Academy of Engineering seminars.

Evaluating the After-school Science and Engineering Club programme

The After-school Science and Engineering Club (ASSEC) programme was set up in England as part of the National STEM programme and operated from 2007 to 2010. It was managed on behalf of the Department of Education (known then as the Department for Children, Schools and Families) by STEMNET. Sheffield Hallam University's Centre for Science Education and Centre for Education and Inclusion Research was commissioned to evaluate the programme's early progress. The findings reported in the final evaluation are not entirely positive. More positive effects were seen for science than for mathematics and engineering. The report also notes that club activities were not always chosen such that they reflected the interests of the target group and hence retained their membership e.g., a prevalence of 'cars and rockets' activities may be counterproductive with girls. Significantly, the report notes that the impact of the clubs on the wider school beyond club sessions was limited if senior management weren't supportive and that there is need for more mathematics activities for clubs. In terms of the Royal Academy of Engineering seminars' findings that evaluations should consider the 'why', it is noteworthy that support from senior management is essential if clubs were to have impact beyond the clubs themselves. Clearly, it is likely that discovering ways to develop the support of senior management for enhancement and enrichment activities are an important area of further research. The evaluation of the Wellcome Trust Camden STEM Initiative in England revealed that developing club activities that were likely to support improvement in schools performance metrics was an important first step in gathering senior management support.

Unfortunately, funding was discontinued in 2012 and the majority of schools have not been able to find internal funding to continue such activities, which is not surprising given the limited impact revealed by the evaluation.

Evaluation of mathematical enhancement and enrichment activities

Royal Society Ogden Education Research Fellow Wai Yi Feng has conducted research into mathematics enhancement and enrichment activities (Feng 2012). Feng began with a literature survey and through this, was able to identify four types of mathematics enrichment activity:

Type 1: Development of mathematical talent;
Type 2: Popular contextualisation of mathematics;
Type 3: Enhancement of mathematical proficiency and learning processes;
Type 4: Outreach to the mathematically underprivileged.

The features of these activities are summarised in Table 8.1
Then Feng conducted four case studies on mathematics enrichment programmes:

1. A set of residential Mathematics Summer Schools, offered by the National Academy for Gifted and Talented Youth;
2. A series of Mathematics Master-classes, run by a Royal Institution Master-class group;
3. An after-school outreach and enrichment programme, targeted at students from a disadvantaged, inner-city area, run in collaboration with NRICH (http://nrich.maths.org/public);
4. The United Kingdom Mathematics Trust's (Junior and Intermediate) Mathematics Challenge competitions, undertaken in one school.

TABLE 8.1 Features of mathematics enrichment activity.

Type	Focus	Target audience	Provisions
Development of mathematical talent	■ Identify and develop mathematical talent ■ Meet distinctive academic needs ■ Cultivate elite group for leadership positions ■ Help students find fulfilment in mathematics ■ Recruit, train and retain mathematically-gifted students in mathematics and related fields	Mathematically gifted and high-attaining students	■ Introduce additional/more difficult topics not taught in school ■ Involve more advanced treatment of curriculum topics ■ Material matched to students interests and talents *(continued)* ■ Students given freedom to pursue their own enquiry

TABLE 8.1 (continued)

Type	Focus	Target audience	Provisions
Popular contextualisation of mathematics	■ Present powerful mathematical concepts in accessible terms ■ Translate powerful concepts into common consciousness ■ Expand students' mathematical horizons and experience ■ Raise public understanding of mathematics and its applications ■ Demonstrate importance and interest of mathematics ■ Overturn negative stereotypes	All students	■ Involve novel presentations/extended explorations of school topics ■ Draw on topics which may not appear to be linked to mathematics ■ Introduce accessible topics not covered by the curriculum ■ Highlight mathematical applications and relevance of mathematics in 'daily life'
Enhancement of mathematical proficiency & learning processes	■ Provide stimulating experience of mathematics ■ Promote and foster mathematical thinking in problem-solving situations	All students	■ Feature mathematical problems/activities requiring creative applications of taught ideas/techniques ■ Emphasise appropriate content differentiation and teacher mediation Integral and ongoing part of education not to be distinguished from 'everyday' teaching and learning
Outreach to the mathematically underprivileged	■ Increase access to mathematics learning opportunities ■ Raise engagement in mathematics among wider audiences ■ Enable underprivileged students to overcome barriers of engagement and gain access to valuable opportunities in life ■ Raise aspirations and higher education participation among disadvantaged groups	Underprivileged students and under-represented social groups	■ Aligned with concerns for social justice and equity ■ Include broadly-conceived 'mathematics' components

Complexity revealed

Feng was able to identify the contributions of each type of enrichment activity within each case study. Her analysis reveals a complex situation. The varying types of enrichment did not play out equally in the different studies and their intentions were in some cases in conflict with one another within a particular enrichment programme. Feng's research indicates that the nature of enrichment cannot be assumed, as it is context dependent and within enrichment programmes identifying and achieving common goals is not a simple matter requiring all the stakeholders to clarify their positions and develop practice that is consistent with agreed goals.

Feng's findings give pause for thought concerning both the setting up and evaluation of enhancement and enrichment activities. A clear identification of stakeholders and their reasons for supporting or being involved in the activities would seem an essential pre-requisite to avoid the confusion over the purposes of the intervention and to ensure as far as possible that the way the activities are carried out is in line with these purposes. A strategy for any evaluation which, in line with the Royal Academy of Engineering seminar findings, that looked at why or why not the enhancement and enrichment activities were successful would explore the extent to which stakeholders remained true to the initial purposes.

Conclusion

Several questions remain concerning the provision of enhancement and enrichment activities for all STEM subjects. Why is the school experience of such subjects perceived as being so impoverished that stakeholders feel that there is a need to initiate enrichment activities outside the mainstream school provision? We must acknowledge that some enhancement and enrichment activities e.g., F1 in Schools and FIRST Lego League do have a place in the mainstream curriculum but this is not seen as a key feature, although the involvement of school teachers in these activities through extra curricular activities is crucial to their success. We asked the same question in Chapter 2: should it not be possible to develop a 'business as usual' curriculum that does not require such enhancement or enrichment? Might some of the activities initially envisaged as sitting within enhancement and enrichment migrate into the mainstream provision?

One way of looking at the activities in enhancement and enrichment activities could be to see them as a means of curriculum development in which activities could be devised and piloted with pupils before transfer into the mainstream curriculum. A particular feature of some enhancement and enrichment activities which makes them attractive is the extent to which they allow those taking part to choose what they do. This can create problems when a syllabus requires certain features to be taught and pupils choose to do things that do not meet these requirements. However, it should be possible to run a mixed economy and provide significant choice at times and limited choice at others. Migration into the mainstream would in no way detract from the work of those currently engaged in supporting enhancement and enrichment. On the contrary, it could be argued that it would see their contribution to the curriculum having a more pervasive effect, concentrating on developing a curriculum with both appeal and intellectual coherence for all pupils, as opposed to a minority. Indeed, a useful intention for some enhancement and enrichment programmes would be to develop activities that could migrate into the mainstream and the evaluation criteria for such activities would be the extent to which this occurred. Taking the Royal Academy of Engineering Workshops finding that investigating *why* is important, identifying and explaining factors that enabled transfer into the mainstream would be very useful. An appreciation of such factors would provide useful insight for those who wanted mechanisms to modernise current curriculum offerings.

Note

1. 'Gracious Professionalism' and 'Coopertition' are explained at http://www.usfirst.org/aboutus/gracious-professionalism

Background reading and references

Altman, M. (2012) Google+ Post Regarding His Objections to MENTOR. Available at: https://plus.google.com/102168405388745526392/posts/8Kg6dMUrX6x (accessed 10 February 2014).

Barack, O. (2009) Remarks made at The National Academy of Sciences Annual Meeting. Available at: www.whitehouse.gov/the_press_office/Remarks-by-the-President-at-the-National-Academy-of-Sciences-Annual-Meeting (accessed 10 February 2014).

Big Bang Fair. Available at: www.thebigbangfair.co.uk/home.cfm (accessed 10 February 2014).

Carlson, R. H. (2012) *Biology is Technology: The Promise, Peril, and New Business of Engineering Life*. Cambridge, MA: Harvard University Press.

Cognizant Making the Future Programme: Available at: www.cognizant.com/aboutus/makingthefuture (accessed 10 February 2014).

CREST Award Scheme. Available at: www.britishscienceassociation.org/crest (accessed 10 February 2014).

DARPA Adaptive Vehicle Make (AVM) Programme. Available at: www.darpa.mil/our_work/tto/programs/adaptive_vehicle_make__(avm).aspx (accessed 10 February 2014).

DARPA Manufacturing Experimentation and Outreach (MENTOR) Programme (2012) DARPA Computer Science STEM program supports president's Educate to Innovate campaign. Details are at this url: www.darpa.mil/NewsEvents/Releases/2012/02/23.aspx (accessed 2 March 2014).

David Baker's Design Clubs. Available at: www.designcamp.org.uk (accessed 10 February 2014).

Dougherty, D. (2012) 'Makerspaces in Education and DARPA'. Makerspace.com. Available at: http://blog.makezine.com/2012/04/04/makerspaces-in-education-and-darpa/ (accessed 10 February 2014).

Feng W. Y. (2012) 'The Development of a Framework for Understanding Mathematics Enrichment: A Case Study of Initiatives in the UK'. Paper presented at BERA 2012. Available at: www.bera.ac.uk/bera2012/pdf/BERA2012_0695.pdf (accessed 10 February 2014).

FIRST Lego League. 'Core Values'. Available at: www.firstlegoleague.org/mission/corevalues (accessed 10 February 2014).

F1 in Schools. Available at: www.f1inschools.com/ (accessed 10 February 2014).

Hackidemia. Available at: http://hackidemia.com/ (accessed 10 February 2014).

Heidelberger Life Science Lab (2012) iGEMS Unveil the Invisible. Available at: http://2012hs.igem.org/Team:Heidelberg_LSL (accessed 10 February 2014).

iGEM. Available at: http://igem.org/Main_Page (accessed 2 March 2014) and http://2012HS.igem.org/Team:Heidelberg_LSL (accessed 2 March 2014).

Kelly OCG (2012) STEM Talent Gap in the USA. Available at: www.kellyocg.com/Knowledge/Infographics/The_STEM_Talent_Gap/ (accessed 10 February 2014).

Mannion, K. and Coldwell, M. (2008) After-school Science and Engineering Club Evaluation (ASSEC). Department for Children, Schools and Families. Research Report No DCSF-RW071. Available at: www.shu.ac.uk/_assets/pdf/ceir-ASSEC-DCSF-FinalReport.pdf (accessed 10 February 2014).

National Science and Engineering Competition. Available at: www.thebigbangfair.co.uk (accessed 10 February 2014).

National Science and Engineering Week. Available at: www.britishscienceassociation.org/national-science-engineering-week (accessed 10 February 2014).

Nuffield Research Placements. Available at: www.nuffieldfoundation.org/nuffield-research-placements (accessed 10 February 2014).

Nuffield Twenty First Century Science. Available at: www.nuffieldfoundation.org/twenty-first-century-science (accessed 10 February 2014).

Relevance of Science Education (ROSE). Available at: http://roseproject.no (accessed 10 February 2014).

Royal Academy of Engineering (2012) Report on Three Workshops Held November 2011, December 2011 and January 2012. Unpublished Report. London: The Royal Academy of Engineering.

Shine. Available at: www.shinetrust.org.uk/site/ (accessed 10 February 2014).

Sjøberg, S. and Schreiner, C. (2010) The ROSE Project: An Overview and Key Findings. Available at: http://roseproject.no/network/countries/norway/eng/nor-Sjoberg-Schreiner-overview-2010.pdf (accessed 10 February 2014).

STEMNET. Available at: www.stemnet.org.uk/ (accessed 10 February 2014).

Straw, S., MacLeod, S. and Hart, R. (2012) Evaluation of the Wellcome Trust Camden STEM Initiative. Berkshire: National Foundation for Educational Research. Available at: www.wellcome.ac.uk/stellent/groups/corporatesite/@msh_peda/documents/web_document/wtvm055664.pdf (accessed 10 February 2014).

UCAS. Available at: www.ucas.ac.uk/ (accessed 10 February 2014).

9

Computing, digital literacy, IT, computer science, TEL and STEM

Introduction

I am writing this on a small laptop computer on a train. I have Wi-Fi and have just gone through my emails. A three-year-old child is sitting opposite me playing on her mother's smartphone, and what is obviously a rugby team are noisily crowding together to have their photo taken on a tablet. It looks like the photographer is sending the picture to his social network site for the others to pick up later. On my laptop I am reading an article about Google Glass and the advantages of 'augmented reality'. However, I also read that despite the fact that we are immersed in technology in our daily lives apparently young children in England will be stopped from using calculators in their mathematics tests.[1] In fact, the reason that I am on the train is that I am returning home after watching some lessons in a school where the use of mobile phones has been banned. There seems a mismatch between how new technologies are increasingly a part of every-day life, and how we learn about and use them in school.

At the turn of the last century, Lord David Puttnam, chair of the then General Teaching Council for England appeared in an Open University video in which he considered what it would be like if a teacher and a surgeon from the year 1900 time-travelled to their equivalent jobs in the year 2000. What differences would they notice? Puttnam said:

> The doctor would be able to make the tea, take a pulse, and mop the patient's brow but not much else. That's because the technologies of the operating theatre would be an alien environment to him. Whereas the schoolteacher could walk in, pick up a piece of chalk and carry out a recognisable lesson in most subjects. That is to do with the fact that the technologies to do with teaching have not changed so much. I believe that in the next 20–30 years, we are going to go through a cycle of change similar to the medical profession. I see that as very exciting.
>
> (Open University, 2000, p. 20)

Leaving aside any objections we might have to this comparison – perhaps comparing a teacher to a GP rather than a surgeon would be fairer – in this chapter we will review how Puttnam's prediction for a radical change in the use of IT is progressing.

As I looked around me on my train journey, I thought about the first time I used a computer. It was in 1969, the year of the first Moon landing, and a teleprinter terminal had been installed in my school where I was a pupil, connected to the 'main frame' computer at County Hall. In fact, I never even saw that computer as it was guarded by the 'high priests' (the computer technicians). As I typed at the terminal, it produced a roll of punched tape which listed the computer commands – as I had to programme the computer to do what I wanted, which was mainly for simple calculations, I learned the computer language FORTRAN to do so.

In 1977, my brother-in-law bought himself a Tandy TSR-80 personal computer and I remember laughing out loud about it. Why would anyone want their *own* computer? But as it turns out, my brother-in-law was a personal-computing pioneer, and just a decade after I sat at that teleprinter I was using personal computers as part of my day-to-day teaching practice: Commodore PETs with far less memory capacity at 8Kb than a cheap mobile phone in 2013. Programmes for the machine could be saved onto cassette tapes – and that is the significant point. All these early personal computers and the cheap home hobby computers such as the Sinclair ZX 80 through to the BBC Micro of the 1980s had to be programmed, although now in the more user-friendly BASIC computer language. Everyone was learning programming in order to be 'computer literate'. In contrast, in 2012, exactly 30 years after the launch of the BBC Micro, the Royal Society wrote:

> The ICT National Curriculum has accommodated a wide range of teaching and content, and in the course of this study we have found examples of imaginative and inspiring teaching under the ICT heading. Sadly, however, these positive examples are in a minority, and we have found far too many examples of demotivating and routine ICT activity, and a widespread perspective among pupils that 'ICT is boring'. Fears now abound in the Computing community that we have somehow lost our way in recent years.
>
> (Royal Society, 2012, p. 4)

It seems there really was a golden age of personal computing where users could not only 'drive' the computer, they also knew in some detail 'what goes on under the bonnet'. Until the early 1990s it used to be the case that students entering computer science courses already knew about computer architecture and programming, and all who had used a computer had some understanding of the basics of computer science whereas now 'many pupils are not inspired by what they are taught and gain nothing beyond basic digital literacy skills such as how to use a word-processor or a database' (Royal Society, 2012, p. 5)

In this chapter we will consider the following issues:

- The use of computing in the STEM subjects and the contribution to digital literacy;
- The renaissance in computer science in schools;
- Technology Enhanced Learning (TEL), what we might be using computers, electronic displays and mobile phones for in our teaching, and where we might be going both in home and school learning through the almost ubiquitous use of these new devices.

Definitions

The terms used are rather confusing so I have adopted here the definitions set out by the Royal Society.

Computing The broad subject area; roughly equivalent to what is called ICT in schools and IT in industry, as the term is generally used.

ICT Information and Communications Technology; the school subject defined in the current National Curriculum in England.

Computer science The rigorous academic discipline, encompassing programming languages, data structures, algorithms, computer architecture etc.

Information Technology (IT) The use of computers, in industry, commerce, the arts and elsewhere, including aspects of IT systems architecture, human factors, project management, etc. (Note that this is narrower than the use in industry, which generally encompasses computer science as well.)

Digital literacy The general ability to use computers; a set of skills rather than a subject in its own right.

TEL (Technology Enhanced Learning) TEL is the support of any learning through the use of technology, so breaking down barriers of when and where one can learn and setting one's own level of the pace of learning. This is often done through the provision of a Virtual Learning Environment (VLE).

(Adapted from the Royal Society, 2012, p. 5)

Computing and STEM

Before we consider what we might use computers for in our teaching, we need to pause and think through our beliefs about the relationship between the pupil and the teacher. Who is in control of the learning process? What are our attitudes to 'hands-on' skills and processes rather than computer simulation and computer-aided activities? One of the most useful ways of thinking about these matters, although suggested a long time ago, was by Kemmis, Atkin and Wright in 1977. Their ideas, when applied to Information Technology (IT), are set out in Table 9.1.

Today, in most schools IT is used in several teaching modes:

- Mode 1: As a tool for demonstrating and illustrating e.g., using an electronic white board or data projector and screen.
- Mode 2: A computer is used as part of a circus of activities or as a when-needed support to class activities.
- Mode 3: Half a class uses up to six computers.
- Mode 4: A whole class uses computers e.g., in the computer room or a set of tablet computers or smart phones in the classroom.
- Mode 5: Independent use (e.g., at home, in the library, or the learning resource centre).

Although mobile devices are ubiquitous and access to information so easy that even pub quizzes are prone to teams illicitly searching for answers, we need to remember to consider the intended learning objectives of any lesson and the way that IT can support or detract from that learning. There are times when we would wish pupils to work unaided such as when searching for patterns, doing mental arithmetic or practicing some manual skills. But with blanket bans on the use of calculators or mobile phones, some schools seem to be in danger of separating school learning from everyday life. A camera on a mobile phone can keep a record of project work, record new ideas or capture group-work not only through filming but also by using the audio record function. Mobile phones can also connect to the Internet to look up information and receive stimuli for new ideas. It is now possible for everyone to have a virtual library in their pocket.

TABLE 9.1 Models of learning with information technology.

Instructional	Revelatory	Conjectural	Emancipatory
Drill and practice type programs	Playing a simulation game or adjusting the conditions on a simulation experiment	Looking at a set of data and drawing conclusions.	Using the computer as a tool to do calculations or other labour saving activities
Using YouTube or other 'how-to' video websites to follow a technique or process	Amending a given design	Modelling and testing a hypothesis Trying out a possible new design CAD	Data capture, word processing, constructing graphs CAM
Computer leads the learning	⟵――――――――――――――――――⟶		Pupil leads the computer

It is not only the way the computer is used as a learning tool that needs to be reconsidered but also how the use of computer programmes are taught. For example, taking pupils through all the different possible commands of a design package in a lockstep manner is very different from allowing the pupils, working in pairs, to explore different possibilities using supporting tutorial videos as and when needed.

Let us consider a selection of specific uses of IT in the STEM subjects.

IT and science

As we have already discussed in earlier chapters, process skills are very important in science and many science teachers cling to a 'seeing is believing' principle of practical work. I am a firm believer in 'doing' science too, but I recognise that new equipment can vastly improve learning.

Cameo 1

When I was at school, I was taught Newton's Laws of Motion using Fletcher's Trolley. A vibrating, inked paintbrush behind the trolley drew out a wavy line on a roll of paper. Interpreting it was a nightmare. Later, as a teacher, I used to use ticker-tape timers and runways. This was much simpler, but even then the majority of the pupils got bogged down in the process of counting, measuring and calculating the results. A series of measurements might take several lessons and the pupils often lost sight of the purpose of carrying out the procedure in the first place. Now they use light-gates connected to a computer and everyone can obtain a full set of results within a one-hour lesson. Teaching the topic this way is very much clearer than before.

Putting the pupil at the centre of their learning, Table 9.2 is a list of science activities and possible IT tools to support that learning.

A word of caution is necessary when using sensors and data-loggers. Sound experimental technique is, obviously, still necessary: for example, the stirring of a solution after adding reagents before measuring the temperature is important whether the temperature is measured by a mercury in glass thermometer or a digital probe. Also, one needs to keep aware of the science principles involved whether or not new technology is involved. For example, a little while ago I used a dynamic trolley and light-gates to demonstrate that force is proportional to acceleration. My force was a series of 1 newton weights added to a cradle with a string over a pulley tugging the 'fixed-mass' trolley. I increased the force on the weight carrier and the trolley's acceleration increased as measured by the light gates – perfect. But actually not so perfect, as when I plotted the results the line was not straight: it seemed that force was not proportional to acceleration of this fixed mass. After much scratching of my head and blaming friction in the pulley and so forth, I finally realised my basic error. For each newton weight added to the weight carrier to pull the trolley

TABLE 9.2 Science activities and possible IT tools.

Pupils' science activity	What IT tools will help?
Planning an investigation	Flowchart software Word processing
Researching/learning about a topic	Internet e.g. You Tube, Wikipedia, online tutorial, databases
Taking measurements	Sensors plus data-logging software
Making results tables	Spreadsheets
Drawing graphs	Data-logging software, spreadsheets, databases
Doing calculations	Spreadsheets, data-logging software
Searching for patterns	Spreadsheets, databases, simulations, modelling programs
Asking 'what if ...?' questions	Simulations, databases, modelling programs
Comparing pupils' results with other people's (reviewing a topic)	Social media sites e.g. wikis, blogs, data files.
Presenting information in a report	Word processing, desktop publishing, spreadsheets

along, the mass of the moving *system* (trolley plus hanging weights) increased by 100g. So the 'fixed-mass trolley' was not all that was moving, the incrementally increasing mass of the hanging weight carrier was moving too. To do this demonstration properly, using a light-gate or not, weights need to be transferred progressively from a pile on the trolley to the weight carrier that is pulling it along so that the total moving system does indeed stay as a fixed mass. However, this now scientifically sound experiment does not *look* sound to the pupils as it seems to them that the trolley is losing mass as the 100g masses are transferred from the stack on the trolley to the weight hanger (see Figure 9.1).

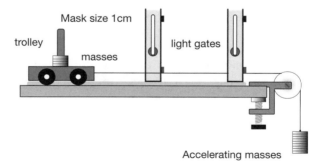

FIGURE 9.1 Experimental investigation of acceleration of a fixed mass.
Adapted from www.s3physics.org.uk

Design & technology and engineering

Looking at Table 9.1, IT can be used in design & technology and engineering for:

- Context exploration
  - Use of word processing packages and presentation software to create questionnaires
  - Use of digital photography to capture contexts
  - Use data logging equipment to carry out preliminary investigations
- Idea generation
  - Use of scanners to capture 3D form
  - Use of software to support development of brainstorms, mind maps and spider diagrams
- Idea development
  - Use of software to develop surface decoration
  - Use of CAD software to develop ever more detailed digital representations of design ideas providing accurate descriptions of both form and performance
- Idea communication
  - Use of the Internet to enable communication with others
  - Use of Photoshop software to develop detailed realistically rendered digital presentations of design proposals
  - Use of spreadsheet data to provide performance data in both table and graphical form
- Planning
  - Use of flow chart software and GANNT chart software
- Manufacture
  - Use of CAM software to drive dye sublimation printers, vinyl cutters, engravers, laser cutters, CNC lathes, milling machines and routers, and 3D printers
- Control
  - Use of programming software to embed instructions in programmable products and systems (see Table 9.3)

These activities span the spectrum from Instructional to Emancipatory. A food probe can record the temperature profile when making bread or melting chocolate or producing jam to prevent scorching – an IT version of what could be done by traditional means but easier – or a control programme can be written to automatically control the windows of a greenhouse, for example.

A question which has emerged over the last few years, as CAD/CAM (computer-aided design/computer-aided manufacturing) programs and equipment have become more affordable for schools, is how should we balance the new skills of using computer support for design and manufacture with the development of psychomotor skills that are promoted through basic hand and machine tools? Pupils are increasingly using CAD/CAM to design, for example with ProDesktop, ProEngineer, Inventor, SpeedStep, SolidWorks and Techsoft, and to make, for example with CNC lathes, mills and routers, laser cutters and computerised sewing machines. It is now possible in almost all schools to define a design that is then produced by a computer-controlled machine, just as in industry, to a level of accuracy a pupil could rarely achieve manually. And as the software improves in its usability, the time invested in becoming competent shortens and outcomes can move from 'mass production' to one-off. For example, in the USA, MIT's Fab Lab has a number of projects with community groups and developing communities that help them to participate in creating their own technological tools for finding solutions to their own problems (MIT, 2006). Pupils can now use CAD to develop designs that they could not make using traditional 'school making skills' but which they can realise using CAM. That with CAD/CAM pupils can now design and make artefacts that would otherwise be difficult to achieve is no doubt a considerable step forward in design & technology learning.

Cameo 2

My school has been collaborating with pupils on the Navaho Reservation in Arizona, USA. Using Skype and email we exchanged ideas about designing and manufacturing products and discussed different preferences which brought out the importance of considering the values of the client and the maker. They had access to a computer controlled lathe, as did we, and we exchanged Computer-Numerically-Controlled (CNC) files of our ideas as well as producing some products jointly. Most interestingly, the Americans had the idea of including as a motif a good luck spirit image of a 'mustang'.

However, the continually changing software for CAD presents challenges to pupils and teachers alike. Dr Debi Winn, head of faculty at a school in Cambridgeshire, UK notes:

Teachers often struggle to learn the programmes themselves and as teaching the programme is only a small part of the curriculum a limited time is allowed for training. This often restricts the teachers' knowledge to the basic commands and so when trying to teach a class of students and problems occur, the teacher is often unable to solve them. This is especially so if a length of time has passed between the teacher last using the program or the program has been updated. This is frustrating for both the students and the teacher, and because of this teachers can sometimes avoid teaching the more difficult CAD software. This problem is further compounded when one considers the way CAD is often taught to students. The 'traditional' method of teaching involves the entire class following either a written set of instructions or a video clip in order to make identical products at the same pace in a 'lockstep' manner. Those students that pick up the commands quicker become bored whilst they wait for the others to catch up and those that experience problems are waiting for help, which in a large class can be a several minutes. This restricts progress for both of these groups of students. This style of teaching is demotivating for both the teacher and the students and does not encourage either to take risks

(Winn, 2012, p. 6).

To tackle this problem, Debi worked with the pupils to design a computer adventure game based on wizards and requiring the pupils to use CAD to make their own items for the game such as keys, drinking cups and finally, a castle. Working in pairs, this more 'strategic' approach was shown to be much more successful than the traditional 'lockstep' learning of programme commands in producing different and more creative ideas.

In 2004, using digital technologies as part of the assessment process was instigated in England:

QCA intends now to initiate the development of an innovative portfolio-based (or extended task) approach to assessing Design & Technology at GCSE. This will use digital technology extensively, both to capture the student's work and for grading purposes. The purpose of Phase I is to evaluate the feasibility of the approach.

(Goldsmith's, University of London, 2007)

Goldsmith's, University of London responded with the e-scape project. Using portable digital devices pupils build up an e-portfolio which can be loaded up to a system to allow all learners' work to be tracked and logged in a website for subsequent assessment by Awarding Bodies (see Chapter 6).

Control

In Table 9.3, Barlex, Gardiner and Steeg (2011) attempt to capture the various strands of progression for school pupils working in design & technology with systems that enable the designing of artefacts that include embedded intelligence or control. Only hardware and software that interfaces with real hardware (simulations are excluded) and which can programme external hardware (where a PC is the controller are excluded) is listed. In other words, Barlex et al. consider the table to be centred on systems that enable the designing of real-world artefacts that include embedded intelligence, which is the domain of modern digital design & technology.

The progression in difficulty of software and in program concepts is from top to bottom. Some possible 'systems and control' projects suggested by Barlex et al. are:

TABLE 9.3 Progression in systems for controlling artefacts.

Software interface	High-level language	Device family	Program concepts	Hardware
Jigsaw blocks	Logo	PicoCricket	Simple sequence with waits (outputs)	Intelligent transducers (i/o)
Other graphic (e.g. Schemer)	Basic	Schemer	Integer variables	On/off actuators (drivers)
Flowchart	Squeak/ Smalltalk	Lego Mindstorms	Unconditional loops	Music actuator (Piezo sounder)
System/Ladder logic	Alice	Genie	Branching If… then… else… (Boolean variable)	Digital sensors
Text based [HLL]	Processing/ Wiring	PICAXE	Parallel processing Subroutines [Macro]	Analogue sensors (ADC)
Assembler Machine code	Java	PICs Cricket etc.	Arithmetic operators	Analogue output control e.g., PWM
	C++	Arduino	Variable types	Multiplexed inputs
	…	mbed	Conditional loops	Multiplexed outputs
		MS .NET Gadgeteer	Interrupts	Output protocols
		PICKit3	List processing	
			Indexing and table lookup (Arrays)	
			Structured programming	

- Design and make a device that can explore the environment in a small stream;
- Design and make a small weather station that can collect data concerning temperature, pressure, light levels and rainfall;
- Design and make a plaything to engage and amuse young children on a long car journey;

- Design and make an electronic dice to be used in a snakes and ladders game to be played by children aged between four and six years old;
- Design and make a device that will keep small valuable items at home safe from theft;
- Design an anti-theft system to be installed in a small jewellery box;
- Design and make a communication device that utilises the ability to receive and transmit infrared signals;
- Design and make a device that enables parents to listen in on a sleeping child to ensure they are breathing normally and not in distress.

(Barlex, Gardiner and Steeg, 2011, p. 3)

These examples illustrate the extensive use of IT in design & technology lessons leading Ofsted in England to state: 'Overall, ICT is more widely and better used in design and technology than in other subjects' (cited by DATA, 2013)

IT and mathematics

Just as we have seen in our consideration of the examples in other STEM subjects, IT can be used to help us teach more efficiently but particularly when doing activities that have been part of the subject for many years. It can expand the possibilities of what can be taught and it can transform what and how we teach. For example, teaching the relationship between the equation $y = mx + c$ and its graph can be done with a pencil and ruler and a pile of graph paper, but graph plotting software or a graphic calculator could allow many more possibilities to be investigated in the time available. In teaching statistics, a revelatory opportunity is possible (see Table 9.4). Is a dice loaded? If one die is thrown 100 times and there are 25 sixes, is the dice fair – could that just be chance? Using a simulation programme a pupil could re-run the number of sixes in 100 throws many times and produce a frequency chart. From that she could consider how often she might see as many as 25 sixes in a fair dice. Finally, IT can be used to do repetitive calculation and thus 'Monte Carlo' methods.

You may have noticed how many times the word 'explore' was used in Table 9.4 and this suggests that teaching mathematics is focused on investigating and experimenting with numbers. It suggests a 'trial and error' approach where a pupil can try something and the software will provide feedback that reflects what they have done – non-judgemental and impartial. In Chapter 5 we described mathematics as the 'Marmite' subject – you either love it or you hate it – and I think some of the dislike comes from what is perceived as a wholly right or wholly wrong outcome. Using IT takes away the perceived feeling of failure – if it does not work just try again. The mathematics teacher associations have for many years suggested that pupils have an entitlement to learn using IT by:

- Learning from feedback
- Observing patterns
- Seeing connections
- Working with dynamic images
- Exploring and generating data
- Sequencing logical steps

TABLE 9.4 Mathematics activities and possible IT tools.

Pupils' mathematics activity	What IT tools will help?
Explore the shape of families of graphs such as $y = a(x-b)^2 + c$ either on a tablet or graphical calculator	Graph-plotting software
Explore number patterns; find optimum solutions; solve equations numerically and graphically; investigate sequences and iteration; display statistical information on charts	Spreadsheets
Explore geometric transformations; construct geometric figures; study relationships through measuring co-ordinates, lengths, angles and areas; construct loci; develop ideas of invariance and dependency	Dynamic geometry software
Taking out the repetitive calculations often associated with statics to focus on the important statistical ideas. Specialist statistical software is often more powerful than needed at school level, but spreadsheets can be used for a range of statistical manipulations such as cross tabulation.	Statistics software
Manipulate algebraic functions, arithmetic, data handling and matrices and 3D plotting	Algebra software
On screen or using a physical floor rover or 'turtle' to explore shape and position; develop the ideas of a function and a variable; learn about algorithms	NetLogo or Scratch
Focusing on the mathematics rather than the calculation	Computation software
Independent study of topics and revision using on-line tutorials.	Email and the World Wide Web

Revised from Richardson and Johnstone Wilder (1999).

In a mathematics classroom in Uttar Pradesh in India I watched the teacher drawing on an old blackboard as his class of about 20 students, all 15-year-old boys, sat on the floor. The topic was about calculating angles within a circle. I marvelled as he drew freehand, perfectly, circle after circle with only a piece of crumbly chalk. Many teachers in the West would now use a whiteboard and software like Cabri to demonstrate a range of geometric shapes in two or three dimensions. As is set out in Table 9.4 what was once done using paper, ruler and compasses can now been done much quicker and with many more iterations using such dynamic geometry software.

The same issues return. Should the use of freehand sketches be preserved rather than use of CAD in engineering? What is the place of 'hands-on' science over simulations? What is the role of calculation – including mental arithmetic in mathematics education? In all cases there are those who argue for using IT much more in schools and those who regret the passing of some of the traditional hand skills. We return to this topic as we look to the future of STEM in Chapter 11. However, here we turn to the place of computer science in schools as a replacement for what has become in much of the UK the discredited subject of ICT.

Digital literacy and computer science in schools

The Royal Society is an influential organisation but I suspect even they were surprised by the English government's very fast response to their call to rejuvenate the teaching of computer science in schools. The lead that the UK had in the 1980s in home computing when BBC Microcomputers were introduced into schools, with a need to consider computer coding, has slipped away. In its place all pupils learn ICT, Information and Communication Technology, which concentrates on the use of Microsoft Office software; what has been described (by a pupil) as 'learning the boring bits of my Mum's job'. In 2012 Michael Gove, the English Education Secretary listened to these criticisms and looked forward to a re-vamped curriculum where 'Instead of children bored out of their minds being taught how to use Word or Excel by bored teachers, we could have 11-year-olds able to write simple 2D computer animations' (BBC News, 2012). In fact, the Royal Society were 'pushing at an open door' as Ian Livingston, a Computer Games entrepreneur and an adviser to Gove had made similar criticisms of school ICT in his Next Gen. report.

The 'boring' tag for ICT is interesting in that in only about five years, ICT has moved from a subject that pupils thought was 'cool' to one that seems irrelevant. The Royal Society's report (2012) suggests a number of reasons for this, including: its teaching by unqualified staff, the problem with keeping school computers up to date and a national curriculum that, due to its inevitably 'fixed' syllabus, finds it difficult to be 'future proof'. However, the Royal Society's main argument is similar to that of the teaching of science that should serve the needs of the citizen as well as the future scientist. The school IT curriculum needs to be appropriate for all citizens so that they have appropriate Digital Literacy, but it should also include an entitlement for all pupils to be able to study computer science.

IT and digital literacy

Teachers discussing digital literacy as part of an online discussion group suggested that digital literacy should be implemented broadly to include learners:

- Understanding how 'information technologies' (also broadly defined to include books, Internet, TV) have an impact on society (e.g., culture, ways of knowing, meaning making, ways of interacting);
- Being able to safely develop and maintain an effective Personal Learning Network (PLN) – again defined broadly, including face-to-face as well as technology-mediated information exchange/knowledge building;
- Being able to effectively investigate an issue using their PLN, bringing in search and critical appraisal skills;
- Being able to create a balanced multimedia report on an issue that they have investigated, for an intelligent and digitally literate audience.

(http://www.naace.co.uk/)

In this discussion, teachers referred to digital literacy being important in a range of contexts for diverse purposes.

Many forms of technology-enhanced learning depend on learners themselves already possessing a degree of digital literacy and fluency. While a growing number of students now develop basic skills in using smartphones, tablets and computers outside school, there is still some way to go before broad-based competence can be taken for granted. It is becoming increasingly important for learners to learn how to learn in technology-supported ways from the start, and then to be stretched to make more challenging and developing uses of technology-supported learning as they progress.

While the emphasis on computer science and programming has been welcomed in many quarters, there remains a strong school of opinion that this should be placed within a wider concept of digital literacy that should be at the heart of ICT in schools. Digital literacy recognises that it is impossible to predict what specific ICT skills pupils will need in the future. So, rather than focusing on specialist applications (e.g., CAD/CAM), digital literacy embraces broader areas of competence in the digital domain, such as problem solving, effective searching, crowdsourcing, online collaboration, and critical thinking (including being critical about ICT tools).

Activities that support students in producing, publishing (e.g., blogging), communicating and collaborating – which can be included in many parts of the curriculum beyond ICT – are a very effective way to develop digital literacy' (Adapted from Berry et al., 2012, p. 6)

Many countries are looking again at their school IT curriculum. For example, the USA has developed a new national Advance Placement course in Computer Science Principles, Israel undertook a review in the 1990s and around 20,000 students there now study computer science. Programming and computer science' was available in New Zealand from 2011 and Singapore too already has some computer science in its school curriculum including object-oriented programming, simple algorithms and logic circuits.[2] The UK has had a lead in computing since the pioneering code-breaking work of Turing and others during the Second World War and the periodic investment in school computing has led to an expertise in video games and visual effects, and a wider exploitation of IT for industry. The fact that the Royal Society report (2012) worried that such a lead would slip away has suggested a re-launch of computer science in schools. But what should that re-vamped curriculum contain?

IT and computer science

Taking the Royal Society report as a starting point, a computer science school curriculum has been suggested by the Computing at School Working Group – a group of academics, teachers, an examination board member and a computer supplier (See CSWG, 2012, for the extended curriculum suggested for ages 5 to 16 years). In a nutshell, in addition to a belief that, 'Every pupil should have repeated opportunities to design, write, run, and debug, executable programs' (CSWG, 2012 p. 11) they should know about the following six topics: algorithms, programs, data, computers, computers and the Internet. Table 9.5 lists the six topics they suggest should be covered with increasing depth and complexity with examples given for 13–14 year-old pupils.

TABLE 9.5 Topics suggested to be covered with increasing depth and complexity with examples given for 13–14 year old pupils as suggested by the Royal Society.

What 13–14 year-old pupils should know in computer science	*Computer science topic from ages 5 to 16*
■ An algorithm is a sequence of precise steps to solve a given problem. ■ A single problem may be solved by several different algorithms. ■ The choice of an algorithm to solve a problem is driven by what is required of the solution ■ The need for accuracy of both algorithm and data – garbage in, garbage out	**Algorithms** A pupil should understand what an algorithm is, and what algorithms can be used for.
■ Programming is a problem-solving activity. ■ Variables and assignment. ■ Programs can work with different types of data. ■ Simple use of AND, OR and NOT. ■ How relational operators are affected by negation. ■ Documenting programs to explain how they work. ■ Understanding the difference between errors in program syntax and errors in meaning. Finding and correcting both kinds of errors.	**Programs** A pupil should know how to write executable programs in at least one language.

(continued)

TABLE 9.5 (continued)

What 13–14 year-old pupils should know in computer science	*Computer science topic from ages 5 to 16*
■ Introduction to binary manipulation. Representations of: – Unsigned integers – Text – Sounds – Pictures [The things that we perceive in the human world are not the same as what computers manipulate]. ■ There are many different ways of representing a single thing in a computer.	**Data** A pupil should understand how computers represent data.
■ Computers are devices for executing programs. ■ Computers are general-purpose devices Not every computer is obviously a computer. ■ Basic architecture: CPU, storage, input/output. ■ Computers are very fast, and getting faster all the time (Moore's law). Computers can 'pretend' to do more than one thing at a time, by switching between different things very quickly.	**Computers** A pupil should know the main components that make up a computer system, and how they fit together (their architecture).
■ A network is a collection of computers working together. ■ An end-to-end understanding of what happens when a user requests a web page in a browser, including: – Browser and server exchange messages over the network – What is in the messages – The structure of a web page – What the server does – What the browser does – How data is transported on the Internet – Packets and packet switching Simple protocols. ■ How search engines work and how to search effectively.	**Communication and the Internet** A pupil should understand the principles underlying how data is transported on the Internet.

Significantly, the Computing at School Working Group make the case that computer science with its mathematical foundations, its scientific approach to experimentation, its design, construction and testing of artefacts and its use of a range of technologies is 'a quintessential STEM discipline, sharing attributes with Engineering, Mathematics, Science, and Technology' (CSWG, 2012 p. 4).

Raspberry Pi

Over 30 years ago cheap hobby computers were a stimulus to budding computer programmers but in the second decade of the twenty-first century what is the equivalent? In 2006, Ebden Upton and his colleagues at the University of Cambridge identified a need for a small and cheap computer for young people. Working in his spare time Ebden took three years to create the Raspberry Pi (shown in Figure 9.2). The Raspberry Pi is a credit card-sized computer that plugs into a TV and keyboard. It costs about $35. It has two USB ports and an Ethernet port for network connection and is capable of Blu-Ray quality playback. It is booted up from a SD card and can be powered from the mains or four AA batteries.

The launch of this small and cheap computer, combined with the new push for computer science in schools around the world has created enormous interest. The impetus for the development was to see cheap, accessible computers back in the hands of young people everywhere. With free open source software available, a new wave of computer programmers may start to enter higher education.

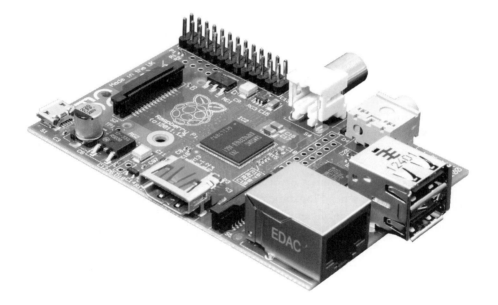

FIGURE 9.2 Raspberry Pi.

Technology Enhanced Learning (TEL)

It is time to consider Puttnam's challenge to teachers to use IT more effectively in the classroom. Since he made his unfavourable comparison with the advances in technology used by the medical profession there has been considerable changes in classrooms. At one level, the increased use may be rather superficial. Interactive whiteboards connected to the Internet bring audio-visual materials into the classroom on a daily basis, but in many ways the pedagogy has not fundamentally altered. In fact, despite the name, using interactive whiteboards has reduced classroom interaction and active learning opportunities; when used just as a 'fancy blackboard' it has locked teachers into the nineteenth century exposition pedagogy that Puttnam criticised. However, we may have reached a 'tipping point' recently in what we can expect students to have in terms of access to computing technology and we need to revisit the place of mobile phones in school.

It seems that there are the first signs of a relaxation of the prohibitions of pupils using their own ICT devices such as smartphones, tablets or notebooks in school. In the past, schools have provided the necessary hardware and controlled IT use in all aspects of pupils' learning. If pupils do bring their own device to school, what are the implications? Teachers considering this future have suggested:

- Schools may need to cope with diverse student-owned devices, develop strategies for this and employ staff who can help;
- A possible shift to less interventionist pedagogies or 'minimally invasive education' (a term linked to Self-Organised Learning Environments, discussed below);
- All teaching staff will need to develop knowledge of a range of common devices and understand their capabilities and limitations;
- A shift away from the external agency or local government authority model of provision;
- A requirement for social-based networks for teachers in all disciplines.

(Berry et al., 2012, p. 7)

If the use of smartphones or other devices are encouraged in school, rather than banned, there is a need for some changes in attitudes to authority in the classroom. Although they are proficient at 'pressing the buttons' pupils will need to be taught to understand much better ideas of information reliability and the concept of plagiarism. Project work can be set that expects the learner to generate their own learning content using their virtual pocket libraries. Pupils who are able to use social network sites can link with other pupils and schools and create a learning community of pupils and of teachers too. Research has backed this up, while also being realistic about not wanting to overload the students and being careful about the need to monitor and protect young people when given access to the Internet. The Technology Enhanced Learning (TEL) report (2012, p. 4) notes that the benefits include:

- Helping children to learn in and out of school, through activities that start in the classroom and then continue in the home or outside, enhanced by technology that reinforces, extends and relates formal and non-formal learning;
- Putting children in touch with the expertise and alternative perspectives of people other than their teachers, as well as increasing their awareness of places outside the classroom, strengthening the relevance of classroom learning;

- Collecting data 'in the wild' to take back into the classroom, enabling authentic and original investigations that ground the development of abstract knowledge in observation and experimentation in the real world;
- Unobtrusively capturing individual children's interests and learning strategies;
- Making use of communities and social interactions that happen outside the classroom.

Taking an approach to mobile learning that ensures all pupils have access, the Essa Academy in Bolton, UK has given its 900 pupils an iPod Touch. This enables them to have access to content both inside and outside school and be in charge of their own learning as described above.

When we considered the teaching of Debbi Winn in her work on design & technology computer aided design (CAD) we saw that she constructed a game that the students had to draw using 3D CAD. In a similar way, games can be used to experience different phenomena using augmented reality:

> Computer-based simulations, games and 'augmented reality' – where the real world is overlaid with information from the digital world – hugely expand the variety of problems students can study, and their ability to use this new knowledge. Simulation authoring tools such as SimQuest11, enable them to explore, for example, the physics of motion with skaters on ice, trains on railways and lorries on roads.
>
> (TEL, 2012, p. 25)

These examples show what can be done and what some schools are already doing.

I started this chapter musing on my visit to a school where mobile phones were banned. So what are the first steps? Most schools now have a Virtual Learning Environment (VLE) where pupils and parents can pick up homework assignments and class work if they miss lessons. They can download lesson PowerPoint files, upload coursework, share ideas on discussion forums and complete quizzes. It is a relatively small step to form a cross-departmental group – especially in the STEM subjects – to consider their current attitude to TEL and perhaps:

- extend the role of the VLE;
- establish a mobile phone and technology policy to protect teachers;
- research some example uses of mobile phones within the classroom;
- consider the potential benefits of bookable class sets of iPods or iPads;
- explore software for enhancing assessment strategies for all subjects.

David Puttnam would be pleased, I think, by the way that IT has revolutionised the classroom but we know that it will take a while for the exciting work being done by some schools to be the learning experience of all pupils.

Conclusion

In 1993 Larry Cuban wrote an article titled, 'Computers meet Classroom: Classroom wins'. Like Puttnam, he wondered why schools lagged behind in the use of technology when compared with other organisations and suggested 'that technological innovations have never been central to national school improvement movements, and that the dominant cultural belief about teaching, learning, and proper knowledge and about the way schools are organised for instruction inhibits computer use' (Cuban, p. 185). Given the fact many schools are so concerned about use of mobile phones that they are frequently banned, maybe Cuban's views still hold. However, we have explored in this chapter a new change in attitude that is becoming much more widespread. Not only because of pressure from the Royal Society and others, but also as the computing power of even a cheap mobile phone puts video, audio and text information in the hands of every learner and that can no longer be ignored. Rather than only being available in a special computer room or a few tablet computers that can be loaned, the library in your pocket is now available to all – and not only to the resource-rich. In India, for example, the Aakash Tablet is being mass-produced for about $70 or £50. It has Wi-Fi and thus Internet access and runs video a bit like a smartphone but bigger.

The computer is a tool that is integral to STEM activities and essential for teaching and learning in all subjects. It is in computing, digital literacy, IT, computer science, and TEL that STEM teachers need to look sideways at what other colleagues are doing but more importantly they need to be advocates to help and support teaching colleagues across the whole curriculum.

Notes

1. Information about use of calculators in maths tests can be found at https://www.gov.uk/government/news/use-of-calculators-in-primary-schools-to-be-reviewed
2. Information about the different IT curricula in the USA, Israel, New Zealand and Singapore can be found at http://press.collegeboard.org/releases/2013/national-science foundation-provides-52-million-grant-create-new-advanced-placement-comput, http://www.nextgenskills.com/israel-leads-the-way-oncomputer-science-in-schools/, http://dtg.tki.org.nz/ and http://www.nfer.ac.uk/nfer/publications/cis101/cis101.pdf
3. Table 9.2 and Cameo 2 are adapted from Learning Schools Open Educational Resources available at www.open.edu/openlearn

Background reading and references

Barlex, D., Gardiner, P. and Steeg, T. (2011) 'Learning Journeys for Computing in D&T: Embedded Control/Intelligence'. Unpublished (written for the Design and Technology Association to inform the consultation about Computing in schools carried out by the Royal Society).

Berry, M., Brooks, B., Coombs, S., Deepwell, M., Jennings, D., Schmoller, S., Slater, J., Twining, P. and Webb, J. (2012) *Better Learning Through Technology – A Report from the SchoolsTech Conversation.* Nottingham: Naace and ALT. Available at: www.naace.co.uk/schoolstechreport (accessed 10 February 2014).

Burns, J. (2012) 'School ICT to be Replaced by Computer Science Programme', BBC News, Education & Family. 11 January. Available at: www.bbc.co.uk/news/education-16493929 (accessed 5 January 2013).

CSWG (Computing at School Working Group) (2012) Computer Science: A Curriculum for School. Available at: www.computingatschool.org.uk (accessed 5 January 2013).

Cuban, L. (1993) *Teachers College Record.* 95 (2), 185–210.

DATA (2013) Available at: www.data.org.uk/ (accessed 3 December 2013).

Goldsmith's, University of London (2007) 'E-scape Portfolio Assessment: Phase 2' report. London: Department for Education and Skills and Goldsmith's, University of London. Available at: www.gold.ac.uk/media/e-scape2.pdf (accessed 10 February 2014).

Kemmis, S., Atkin, M. and Wright, S. (1977) 'How Do Students Learn?' Occasional paper No. 5. University of East Anglia: CARE.

Livingston, I. and Hope, A. (2011) 'Next Gen.: Transforming the UK into the World's Leading Talent Hub for the Video Games and Visual Effects Industries'. London: NESTA. Available at: www.nesta.org.uk/library/documents/NextGenv32.pdf (accessed 10 February 2014).

MIT (2006) Fab Lab. Available at http://fab.cba.mit.edu/ (accessed 2 February 2013).

Open University (2000) 'Overview'. Masters Programme in Education: E853 Early Professional Development for Teachers, Study Guide. Milton Keynes: The Open University. Available at: http://labspace.open.ac.uk/file.php/2938/b853_1_section1.pdf (accessed 10 February 2014).

Richardson, J. and Johnstone Wilder, S. (1999) Teaching in Mathematics, *Learning Schools Programme.* Milton Keynes: Open University/Research Machines.

Royal Society (2012) 'Shut Down or Restart? The Way Forward for Computing in UK Schools' report. London: The Royal Society. Available at: http://royalsociety.org/uploadedFiles/Royal_Society_Content/education/policy/computing-in-schools/2012-01-12-Computing-in-Schools.pdf (accessed 10 February 2014).

TEL (Technology Enhanced Learning) (2012) 'System Upgrade: Realising the Vision for UK Education' report. London: Institute of Education. Available at: http://tel.ioe.ac.uk/wp-content/uploads/2012/06/TELreport.pdf (accessed 10 February 2014).

Winn, D. (2012) *CAD and Creativity at Key Stage 3: Towards a New Pedagogy.* Unpublished PhD Thesis. Milton Keynes: The Open University.

10

Creating an environment for sustaining STEM

I think it is possible to gain quite a good impression of a school just from its environment. I don't mean where the school is located or the nature of the buildings but rather, what one 'feels' on entering. I'll give you a couple of examples. As an external examiner for a teacher education course offered in the North of England I went to a small school in the Yorkshire Dales, a particularly beautiful spot, so beautiful in fact that I stopped my car to take in the view before driving on towards the school buildings built out of an attractive weathered stone. I reported to the office, said who I was and who I wanted to see. There was much confusion and I was asked to wait. Looking around I noticed that the interior had been extensively refurbished but in the reception area there was a couple of reproduction paintings, a cabinet of trophies for different sports and a rather incongruous list of previous head boys and girls which seemed to have stopped over ten years ago. The corridors were bright and cheerful and in a 'pristine' condition although the refurbishment has taken place three years ago. I went to see quite a good design & technology lesson that was conducted in a large space with, except for safety notices, virtually bare walls. The teaching and learning environment was sterile with little on view to celebrate success, arouse curiosity or contribute to lessons and learning.

The following week I want to a school in Birmingham in the industrial heart of England that had been due to be refurbished under a Building Schools for the Future (BSF) initiative but the plans and funds had been dropped with a change in government. It was a flat-roofed building of the 1970s and quite hard to find as it was hidden at the back of a run-down housing estate. I was greeted by a smiling secretary who presented me with a visitor's badge already made out with my name on it and again I was asked to wait as she made a call to the head of department. Looking around, the reception area was full of artwork that the pupils had done, and on the wall a flat-screen TV scrolled through a series of photos of recent school trips, sport action shots and messages about forthcoming events. Walking along the corridors on the way to the department, the escorting teacher pointed out the departments we went through by the pupils' different work on display including some tessellations in the mathematics department and some photos of measuring the speed of sound in science – all done in the previous two terms. We entered the design & technology department through an arch with 'Technology' across the top. Again, I saw some safety notices but also displayed on the wall were a series of posters of working engineers and scientist of both genders and different ethnicities, some pupil graphical communication examples of ideas for a 'chocolate wrapper' and a cabinet containing some small examples of work from Year 7 to Year 10.

From the way I have described these two schools you can guess which 'environment' I thought was best for teaching and learning. In Birmingham, without overtly evangelising, the environment gave the pupils messages that STEM subjects were not only interesting and applied to life outside the school but they were also subjects that they *could* study and that they might actually find useful in their lives. Spending money on new school buildings is a very good idea, of course, and the school staff in Birmingham were understandably very bitter that they missed out, but in contrast to the pretty but sterile building in Yorkshire they showed that how the building is *used* in creating an exciting and respectful environment is much more important than how it *looks*.

In this chapter, as we have throughout this book, we are going to think about STEM beyond the one-off competitions and career initiatives, fun and interesting though they are. We will consider how to create an environment which will sustain STEM, where the place of STEM is explicit and valued, where teachers are supporting each other and working together, and where pupils see the links to help their learning.

We will look at:

- the physical environment
- the pupils' environment
- the professional environment.

The physical environment

'I hate this place – it smells!' However long one has been teaching, certain pupils will always be remembered. That frequent refrain of one student's sulky entrance to the lab still echoes in my memory many years on. She had a point. The science and technology area of that school certainly had some interesting aromas caused by the close proximity of laboratories to workshops and the mingling smells of gas, glue and gunk. The workroom environment, I admit, left much to be desired and I expect many other less vocal pupils were also affected by it. I quickly came to realise that the physical environment is very important. Not only does it affect our attitude to the subject, it also has a profound effect on learning. The layout of the room itself says much about the way that the teacher relates to pupils and how pupils relate to each other. The physical environment is intimately linked to what I call the 'pupil environment', which we will look at later. The safe distribution, use and collection of apparatus, tools and resources in an efficient and controlled manner contribute significantly to appropriate pupil behaviour. If the physical environment of the classroom is set up so that pupils can take responsibility for their work and make informed choices of tools and components as they progress through a task, they are better able to take control of their own learning. But if they have to wait for equipment, materials or attention pupils become bored and frustrated and sometimes disruptive. In creating an effective learning environment there is a very close link, therefore, between the class layout, resource management, behaviour management and the safety of all who are in the laboratory or workshop.

Primary schools in England have been world leaders in the creation of a visual environment for learning. It probably goes back to an exhibition of children's art in the 1930s that was visited by John Blackie who later became Senior Chief Primary Inspector. Over several generations of primary teachers it has now become the rule that entering a primary school is often a kaleidoscope of colour and images. But this is far more than mere decoration and secondary schools, although far better in recent years in celebrating pupils' work and using commercial and home-grown resources to support learning, have much to learn from their primary colleagues.

A web search will quickly find a range of ideas, images and resources to improve the learning environment and return links to the topic being taught. Some science and maths classroom ideas have been around for many years – such as the 'word wall' of difficult concepts – but rather than becoming hackneyed, these ideas provide a clear link between language and learning that is extremely useful.

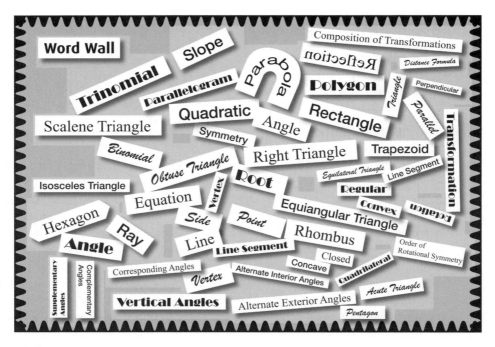

FIGURE 10.1 Mathematics word wall.

Creating a successful physical environment for learning is not only at the classroom, corridor and department level, it extends to consideration of the whole way pupils interact with the school.

I once taught in a school in Wales that was composed of a range of separate buildings. My laboratory was on top floor of a Victorian building that still had the remains of the gas pipes on the ceiling for the original lighting. The pupils sat at long teak tables and all the services were located around the edge of the room, out of way until they were needed. Although over a century old, it was the most adaptable room I ever worked in and when I had the opportunity to re-design the lab for the new school, I followed the same overall plan but added a matrix of electrical sockets across the floor (school physics labs never have enough electrical sockets). The different buildings of the old school ranged in design as they were built across the decades and as pupils moved from lesson to lesson they had to go outside to walk to the next building. It rains a lot in Wales, and pupils were always dashing with coats and hoods from place to place. The new school buildings were built as a 'shirt sleeve' environment and the difference in behaviour and attitude of the same pupils was remarkable. Carpeted areas and noise-reduction tiles brought down the acoustic 'temperature' drastically. Clean areas in science and design & technology can be improved by stimulating and informative visual displays but also can cultivate a calm and purposeful acoustic environment. A senior management team interesting in sustaining STEM could ask the following:

1. Who is responsible for display in the department and who else is involved?
2. Do pupils have some responsibility in selecting the display in communal areas?
3. How do new STEM staff gain training in display as part of their induction?
4. What are the walls used for? Pupils' work? Puzzles in maths? Do they show commercial posters of STEM careers and the practicality of the subjects in everyday life? Is there some unfinished work to debate – e.g. 'Our first ideas about forces'?
5. In the teacher's professional areas what is the tone of the notices? Is it humorous or cynical? Are there articles of interest from magazines or photocopied from journals?
6. Are all areas – including corridors – of a sensible 'acoustic temperature'? If not, what is the strategy for changing that?

The pupils' environment

What the research shows consistently is that if you face children with intellectual challenges and then help them talk through the problems towards a solution, then you almost literally stretch their minds. They become cleverer, not only in the particular topic, but across the curriculum.

(Adey, 2001, p. 17)

How do pupils learn? That seems a straightforward question, but you will already know from your day-to-day teaching that the answer is far from obvious. Are your views about how pupils learn the same as those of your colleagues both in your subject and other teachers of STEM subjects? You could ask them, perhaps informally at break-time, the following questions: How do you think pupils learn? What should we do, as teachers, to help that happen? Asking these questions in such a blunt way is likely to elicit either a flippant response or maybe a cautious one along the lines of 'Everyone learns in different ways', 'It depends who they are', 'I teach depending on the needs of the pupil'. And so on. It is almost certain that you will not get straightforward answers to your straightforward questions!

All teachers, and parents for that matter, have a 'theory' of learning. It may link to formal ideas but more often it is not a grand theory or one that is grounded in careful research, but rather is a collection of day-by-day assumptions about what teachers should do to help pupils to learn. New ideas about learning are developing and we need to test out them out against our knowledge of pupil behaviour and the views we currently hold.

The following are some views that some people, including teachers, hold about how pupils learn:

Behaviourism: Knowledge and skills can be broken down into component parts and it is the teacher's job to do this for the learner. The teacher then teaches each element and gives the pupil sufficient repetition until the learner can give a 'positive response'. The pupil will generally receive the same instruction as everyone in the class, but if assessment shows that the pupil requires further help, then an additional programme with smaller steps over a longer time scale will be provided.

Piagetianism: A child constructs meanings by getting to grips with the particular problems in hand. Private problem solving is very important and a teacher should provide the necessary stimulus material and opportunities for the individual pupil to learn something new. A pupil will not progress without plenty of practice in the activities that have already been mastered. A child will only be able to 'get' an idea when she has reached a certain stage of maturity and the teacher's job is to be aware of that and to decide when the pupil is 'ready' to move on. Some pupils are never able to 'get' certain ideas.

Social constructivism: All pupils are educable and are helped in their learning by discussion and other social interaction, including with a more experienced learner or teacher. There is no fundamental difference between the learning of children and that of adults. Rather than waiting for a pupil to be 'ready' to learn, a teacher is finding out what the pupil thinks in order to guide and support what the pupil is trying to do next. By talking with the teacher, and obtaining other support, a pupil is able to grasp ideas and new understandings that they could never arrive at on their own.

These very brief summaries relate to the three main traditions of learning theory: behaviourism, Piagetianism and social constructivism. How do these well-known ideas relate to what you actually do in the STEM classroom? Are you able to 'sign up' to any one of the theories wholeheartedly? As you read these descriptions you may have felt that each of them separately described some aspects of your ideas about learning and those of your colleagues, yet none was wholly satisfactory in its own right. For example, in teaching certain practical skills, a regime of practice and reinforcement in the 'behaviourist' tradition may be appropriate. An individual project will provide problem-solving opportunities and will be successful if the pupil is working largely within his or her capabilities, a Piagetian standpoint. That teaching methods should be selected in terms of fitness for purpose, rather than adherence to a particular dogma of good practice, is clear. Teachers tend to have their preferred way of working, which reflects a personal 'theory' but are not hidebound by particular ideologies, and will adopt a different teaching strategy if they think it will be helpful. Sometimes this is called a 'folk' theory' of learning.

Some people think that good teaching means the same thing as good explaining – keep it clear and simple and all will understand. In fact some teachers, particularly those in initial teacher training, get very upset when despite their greatest efforts, the pupils just don't grasp what they have explained. When pupils just don't 'get it', they take it as a personal failure or maybe blame the pupils. It is certainly true that a key teaching skill is the ability to explain and describe things clearly. But a belief that transmitting information clearly is *all* that is required for a 'good' teacher is insufficient. However, such a folk theory of how minds work is common across the world and also explains the position some parents take to learning and teaching. These common beliefs were investigated by Bereiter and Scardamalia who characterised a folk theory of mind as follows:

- Knowledge is 'stuff';
- The mind is a container;
- Learning involves putting stuff in the container.

(Bereiter and Scardamalia, 1995)

This tends to be reinforced by national curricula and examination syllabuses which emphasise content knowledge. Bereiter and Scardamalia suggest that the corollaries of such a view of the mind is:

- Pedagogy: a craft for stocking minds.
- Educational testing: a process for inventorying mental contents.

(Bereiter and Scardamalia, 1995)

Desforges indicates that such 'folk pedagogy' has had some success in teaching through 'show and tell', however, there are severe limitations to this approach:

> But where the 'stuff' metaphor breaks down – as it does with wisdom, creativity, knowledge creation, appreciation, a 'feel' for a subject – we are left floundering.
>
> (Desforges, 2001, p. 25)

Folk theories are indeed robust, yet the alternative ideas about teaching and learning outlined above have been considered for at least the last 60 years and linked to a growing understanding about the biology of the brain as set out by Alistair Smith, an advocate of changing the learning environment to better match what we know about how children learn:

> In the last 15 years 80% of our knowledge about the brain and how it learns has been accumulated. Understanding about the different functions of specific parts of the brain has led to a more sophisticated appreciation of what happens to the brain in learning situations. However, this new knowledge is, for the moment, playing little or no part in influencing the design of the experiences we provide for students in our classrooms. Indeed, much of what happens in classrooms throughout the country conflicts with what is known about the brain and its design.
>
> (Smith, 1996, p. 13)

Alistair Smith wrote that a decade ago and his pessimism about 'what happens in the classroom' is still valid. Smith builds on seminal work conducted by Howard Gardner a Professor at the Harvard graduate school that rejects notions of a fixed IQ and suggests that there are different sorts of intelligences:

- The personal related:
    - the interpersonal intelligence
    - the intrapersonal intelligence.
- The language-related:
    - the linguistic intelligence
    - the musical intelligence.
- The object-related:
    - the kinesthetic intelligence
    - the mathematical and logical intelligence
    - the visual and spatial intelligence
    - the naturalist intelligence.

(Gardner, 1993)

Gardner has speculated that had he used the term 'different gifts' rather than 'multiple intelligences' perhaps his work would not have received the same attention. It is suggested that because of different experiences in life, some of the intelligences will be developed more strongly than others and some will not be developed at all. Schooling and other cultural experiences can speed up or slow down this process.

In contrast to the multiple intelligences of Gardner, the American psychologist Robert Sternberg suggests that pupils exhibit about three kinds of intelligence: creative, practical and analytical. Schools, he argues, traditionally give more weight to memory and teaching analytical methods and that insufficient attention is given to the creative and practical. The common strand between Gardner and Sternberg, however, is that intelligence is considered to be multi-faceted and that schools do not give opportunities for pupils to exploit their different preferred learning styles and, as institutions, certain types of intelligence are favoured benefiting some and disenfranchising many others. Gardner and Sternberg's work have implications for the type of suitable learning environment and for the issue of differentiation of learning experiences.

So what does this understanding of how pupils learn impact on the teaching and learning environment for pupils in STEM subjects?

Consider the classroom/teaching space that you use most frequently. How are the tables or benches positioned? Is it easy to access services such as electricity and water and the places where tools, equipment and materials are kept? Compare your room with that of a colleague who teaches in a different STEM subject and see what the differences are and what they think about your room layout. There may be some similarities between a science lab and a design & technology workshop, but they will probably be quite different to a graphics studio or a textiles room. But what does the location of the tables or benches, and where they are in relation to where you often stand to teach (if you do stand), say about the expectations you have for pupil interaction?

My guess is that it is very easy to think of the times in design & technology and maths lessons when pupils are working on their own, but that individual pupil work occurs very rarely in practical work in science. The manufacture of an individual artefact that a pupil can take home is often a key part of design & technology schemes of work. But in all the STEM subjects, as in other areas of the curriculum, discussion work in pairs or small groups is vital if pupils are to address, for example, ideas about investigating patterns in mathematics, values implicit in science in society and the impact of design & technology products or materials on society and the environment. Discussion is important to enable all pupils to articulate their thinking and clarify their understanding. Of course, as well as group or pair work, the pupils will work as a whole class for presentations and evaluations and perhaps with other groups if there is a guest speaker or a whole-school STEM 'challenge' or competition. In some schools, the timetable is collapsed at certain times of the year to allow for a concentrated period of work with even larger groupings.

The extent to which pupils interact in your lessons has much to do with how you think pupils learn and how you wish to be viewed as a teacher. Environmental psychology is a discipline that draws on areas of knowledge such as geography, architecture, sociology, anthropology, design and ergonomics and suggests that everyday objects are not only physical but have an impact on how we relate to the world. The ability of a pupil to sit and work, to move around the room, to have control over the tools (both physical and cognitive) they choose when problem solving and the nature and usefulness of display material have a profound effect on their creativity and ability to work constructively with others. The layout of a teaching room should help pupils to understand the classroom environment and support what is expected of them.

Chapters 3 to 9 in this volume suggest that pupils learning can be enhanced by exposure to and appreciation of the connections between the STEM subjects. It may be convenient for schools to compartmentalise knowledge and understanding into specialist subjects in specialist rooms but real life is obviously not like that and, at the very least, teaching a subject in the light of another helps pupils connect up their thinking. Schools that have embraced such a coordinated approach to STEM have noted the following learning benefits:

- STEM learning is fun and therefore motivating; it helps learners to see the relevance of what they are learning, especially in mathematics and science.
- Co-operative learning is effective and develops personal learning and thinking skills (PLTS).
- When learning in one subject area is reinforced in others it aids understanding.
- STEM projects help teachers to understand the work of their colleagues in other departments better, resulting in schemes of work that are prepared in a coordinated and collaborative way, which increases the efficiency of teaching.
- Targeted STEM interventions can affect results […] and offer opportunities to stretch gifted and talented students.
- STEM enhancement and enrichment activities with built-in reflective opportunities have an impact on […] attainment.
                    (Specialist Schools and Academies Trust (SSAT), 2009, p.6 abridged)

We know that building a positive, supportive learning environment and maintaining positive self-esteem is important, although often in a busy school environment with fragmented periods this is not always easy to achieve. As we have seen, the physical environment is important as well as the social in order to put learners in what Gardner would call 'the right frame of mind'. Displays in the classroom aid the learning of those pupils who have particular visual and spatial intelligence and help to set the right learning conditions for all. As we see, there is a close inter-relationship between learning, the interconnectedness of the problems that they face and the physical space that pupils work in.

Building on the evidence from the Specialist Schools and Academies Trust (SSAT), ideas about learning, and knowledge about how the brain responds to different situations, Alistair Smith suggests that to help pupils learn we need to set up conditions of low stress but high challenge in our classes. Smith summarises how to create a successful pupil environment into nine principles:

1. The brain develops best in environments with high levels of sensory simulation and cognitive challenge.
2. Optimal conditions for learning involve sustained levels of cognitive challenge with low threat.
3. Higher order intellectual activity may diminish in environments the learner considers emotionally or physiologically hostile (remember the student and the 'smelly' lab!).
4. The brain thrives on immediacy of feedback and choice.
5. There are recognised processing centres in the hemispheres of the brain. This suggests structured activities.
6. Each brain has a high degree of plasticity, suggesting developing and integrating classroom with other experiences.
7. Learning takes place at a number of levels. This requires a range of strategies and personal goals.
8. Memory is a series of processes rather than locations. To access long-term memory is an active not a passive process.
9. Humans are 'hard-wired' for a language response. Discussion is a vital part of learning.

(Adapted from Smith and Call, 1999, p.33–34)

The professional environment

In this final section we turn to the professional environment of the teacher. Here I don't mean the state of the staff room, the quality of the coffee at break-time (although they certainly have an impact) or even conditions of service. The professional environment that I am considering is how, from the newest member of staff to the senior management, the school creates, manages and sustains an environment that addresses staff needs and aspirations, and allows STEM activities and the associated curriculum to become embedded. Creating the right physical environment and nurturing the pupils' environment are very important, but for ensuring the sustainability of STEM in a school, addressing the professional needs of staff, in particular teaching staff, are vital.

Tim Brighouse, a Professor of Education and a local government Chief Education Officer for over 15 years used to say 'Teachers get exhausted where the rest of us merely tire'. The 'rest of us' includes headteachers and other members of the senior staff in school who often have 'down time' during the day that classroom teachers rarely have even in those periods set aside for planning and assessment. Keeping staff motivated and enthusiastic when they have such an intense and often stressful workload is a key function of the leadership of a school. Brighouse suggested that staff require four conditions to create the successful professional environment that enables them to teach effectively:

1. Responsibility
2. Circumstances that enable change to happen
3. New experiences
4. Respect

Responsibility

There is a difference between work, which is about things to do and which there is often far too much of, and responsibility, which we quite like and which is about having the final say and looking to improve how something might be done. So there is a real difference between jobs to be done and the responsibility to do it and ensuring the right person at the right level has the appropriate responsibility is key in embedding STEM and ensuring it is sustainable long term. I don't only mean just teaching staff here. Technicians and classroom assistants also need to know the nature and extent of their responsibilities.

Responsibility is often formally established through the job description for staff appointments. I often sit on appointment panels and I think that most descriptions of jobs responsibilities are too numerous and too diffuse, and wonder if they are drawn up to allow flexibility when a school is not certain what they want the candidate to actually do. Two or three lead responsibilities and three or four secondary ones makes it clear what is required and is much more likely to attract a candidate who has a clear vision of what they could make of the job. Below is an example of a job description for a senior subject teacher of science that I think illustrates this point well.

Job description for a senior subject teacher of science

Job purpose

To promote learner enjoyment and achievement through outstanding teaching that creates an irresistible climate for learning for all learners. To share your skills and experience with other teachers.

Key responsibilities:

- Take a lead role in the continuing improvement of teaching and learning in the science faculty.
- Provide high-quality personalised professional development for teachers within the school.
- Support curriculum leaders in planning and resourcing high-quality differentiated schemes of work.

You will also have these secondary responsibilities:

- Embrace whole school initiatives, including Assessment for Learning, Accelerated Learning and the use of ICT.
- Promote learner self-esteem and a positive academic self-concept.
- Work effectively as a member of the subject team to improve the quality of teaching and learning.
- Have a thorough and up-to-date knowledge of all the national curriculum and examination courses.
- To keep up-to-date with research and development in pedagogy both within the subject and as a teacher/learner.

The responsibilities will be reviewed annually as part of our Performance Management process and may be subject to amendment or modification at any time after consultation with the post holder.

Some points I think are worth emphasising. There is a particular emphasis on supporting other staff in science, working as part of a team and keeping up to date in both subject developments and in new teaching strategies. This job description also matches well against the framework for teacher's professional knowledge discussed in Chapter 2.

Teachers of STEM subjects are first and foremost teachers of young people but they are also subject teachers and feel responsible for keeping up to date as knowledge and processes expand exponentially. For example, in Chapter 9 Dr Debi Winn introduced her game method of teaching CAD which not only makes learning of the software package more efficient and more fun but she also realised that it would help colleagues who were reluctant to teach CAD as they felt their knowledge of CAD and the new computer controlled workshop machines was inadequate. Answering questions in science such as 'Do mobile phone give you brain tumours?' and 'Why are GM crops called "Frankenstein Foods" in the media?' are similarly challenging. It is increasingly easy to access information through the use of new technology and pupils can more easily be coached to access information for themselves, but it is important to create an environment that facilitates different teachers sharing their knowledge and enthusiasm, one where ideas and resources are shared not only formally through schemes of work but also through communal noticeboards or coffee-time conversations. In terms of sharing STEM information and ideas, it is vital to create an environment where this is permissible. I have worked in both large and small schools and found that large schools shared a cross-subject STEM ethos less well simply due to where staff chose to meet at break-time: big subject departments stuck together, small subject groups went out to seek company. I know that teachers who have a responsibility to 'provide high quality personalised professional development for teachers within the school' have to work hard to avoid being labelled 'Billy Wizz' and 'Super-Teacher' by some cynical colleagues and the quickest way to gain credibility and change attitudes is through informal cooperative arrangements promoted by a careful consideration of where teachers can congregate at break-and meal-times. Having clear responsibilities and understating how they relate to those they work with is so important to create a successful supportive professional environment that reduces stress.

Circumstances that enable change to happen

Having clear responsibilities is an important first step, but for teachers to be effective the leadership of the school needs to create the right circumstances to make change happen. At the basic level this is an obvious 'give me tools and I'll do the job' plea. Both authors of this book have spent time in classrooms in rural India and it is encouraging to see what good teaching goes on in some science and mathematics classrooms with extremely limited resources. So much more could have been achieved, however, with more books, materials and equipment. Having adequate resources is necessary for any teacher, anywhere. Teaching STEM subjects in a way that develops understanding is best done through interacting with tools and materials so that learning can be 'minds-on' as well as 'hands-on'. As we saw in Chapter 1, the tradition of practical work in STEM (including mathematics) has been established in schools since the 1960s. Through the influence of ideas such as those of Jean Piaget, pupils became a 'scientist for the day' and learnt from discovery. But over the decades the possibility of such a hands-on approach has mirrored the prevalent economic climate and the money spent on schools has sometimes not been adequate to provide new science equipment or the latest CAD/CAM machines in design & technology. Some headteachers have tried to influence the curriculum and pupils' entitlement to engage across STEM when they have felt that the limited resources possible could not be stretched sufficiently and it is encouraging to see even world leaders stress the importance of STEM education for all.

I think there are four important circumstances that enable change to happen for STEM to be embedded in schools. One is being able to work in teams and learning from each other. We are convinced that encouraging teamwork not only shares work and expertise but it also provides a richer and more purposeful learning environment for pupils. Teachers need to look sideways.

In order to bring about this kind of change, leaders in school need to ask the following questions:

- Is it possible, at the department level, for team teaching if it is needed?
- How can the head of department and the teacher responsible for subject development (such as in the above job description) have the support to build teamwork?
- Are there noticeboards which enable *everyone* to keep up-to-date with the latest research and developments in the pedagogy of their subject?

- How can teachers be given the circumstances to 'look sideways' at the teaching in other STEM subjects?
- How can experts outside the school contribute effectively to the STEM curriculum?
- What support do such visitors need?

Ensuring that staff, working in a coordinated and collaborative way, know what is happening with and across STEM subjects seems to us to be the one key factor that would improve pupil learning, attainment and, just as important, a positive attitude and open mind. The composition of the team, and so the ideas, need not be solely from school staff. Due to funding from other organisations, it is often possible for external experts to contribute to a team approach, e.g., STEM Ambassador or taking pupils out to engage with other adults in learning STEM in 'real-world' contexts.

STEM learning takes place in the real world. Schools work with outside partners from industry, commerce, government services, higher education and other schools. Examples suggested by the SSSA include:

- working with environmental agencies to develop a more sustainable school;
- bringing space craft into the school;
- visits to hydro-electric power generation plants;
- working with the motor industry to help careers awareness;
- bridge building with engineering consultants;
- involving STEM ambassadors in school life;
- working with a water company and a university to solve a problem on a sewage treatment plant;
- companies providing challenges that can be worked on in clubs;
- working with primary partners on STEM;
- visiting a botanical garden to see how tropical environments are maintained.

Schools report that learners enjoy being out of school and seeing how science, design & technology, engineering and mathematics are used in the real world. This reinforces and extends what they learn in the classroom. [...] Companies get a chance to inform learners about their work. This long-term strategy helps them to recruit and demonstrate their commitment to the community.

(Specialist Schools and Academies Trust (SSAT), 2009, p.7 abridged)

However, as is discussed in Chapter 11, the benefit of such work needs to be firmly embedded in the school curriculum to be effective and it is well to remember the obvious point that external experts are not teachers, and need to be supported so that their contribution can be an effective and a positive experience both for the pupils and for them.

The second circumstance that enables change to happen brings together teamwork and conditions for interaction and links back to our above discussion of the physical environment. We are all influenced by our social and physical environment. The classroom walls, school bookshelves and noticeboards in staff areas influence attitudes to teaching just as it influences the learning of pupils. Conversations can be dominated by school politics or (and!) they can be informal debate about projects and pupils' progress. Noticeboards which have dusty and curling union posters give one a certain type of feel to a school, a changing series of cuttings from the Times Educational Supplement – humorous as well as the 'cutting edge' – give quite another. A department might have access to journals and other hard-copy resources from subject associations whereas other communal areas might provide the more general resources. Creating such an environment need not be a huge drain on resources as subject association membership, for example, can cheaply provide a great range of resources and information and so the professional impact can be marked.

The third circumstance that enables significant change is the huge support that non-teaching colleagues offer. Getting right the technical resource that supports preparation in science and design & technology can make probably the most significant difference between a lesson that is mediocre and one that runs like clockwork and is an exciting and successful learning experience. The professional development of technicians is important and in most schools is now firmly in the staff development plan. Some school science technicians in the UK have enrolled for courses leading to professional recognition such as Registered Science Technician (RSciTech) through the Science Subject Association (ASE) which requires knowledge and competences such as:

- application of knowledge and understanding
- personal responsibility
- interpersonal skills
- professional practice
- professional standards.

Other staff that support teachers in providing photocopy and audio visual resources, or can give support to finding illustrations and materials for the electronic whiteboard, for display in class or Open Educational Resources (OER) for free sharing on the Virtual Learning Environment need to be properly supported, trained and adequately resourced too.

There is one fourth and final point to be made. Probably the most significant circumstance that the leadership of a school can do to enable change to occur is to give STEM subjects the permission to experiment and try out new ideas. How can a senior management team encourage this and enable those good ideas to be shared? David Hargreaves suggests that one of the principal tasks of senior management is to know how to manage 'knowledge creation' – how to encourage and nurture such new ideas. Hargreaves uses a five-step gardening metaphor to set out what managers need to do, which I have adapted here:

- Step 1: Generating the ideas – Sowing

  Creating a professional environment – a school culture which promotes 'tinkering' – so that teachers actively try out new ideas or adapt old ones and take carefully-calculated risks. Enabling teachers to try something new is important (see the section on new experiences below) but often teachers find it difficult to explain why something that they do 'works'. The knowledge is tacit. By enabling teachers to work together or even team-teach creates the shared experience which generates and transmits tacit knowledge. Also, dialogue and collective reflection across the STEM team enables externalisation to turn tacit knowledge into explicit knowledge which can be shared with others.

- Step 2: Supporting ideas – Germinating

  In a school that supports new ideas – new ideas will come, and just as likely (more likely?) from the newly qualified teacher as much as the more experienced. Such ideas may need protection from the cold frost of cynicism.

- Step 3: Selecting the most promising ideas – Thinning

  Not all new ideas can be picked up and enacted at the same time but the ones that are selected need to be done so with a clear rationale. The criteria for selection of the best must be clear and those whose ideas are not pursued immediately should not lose face.

- Step 4: Developing ideas into knowledge and practice – Shaping and Pruning

  This is difficult – showing that the new idea is worthwhile and really works. Also, if something is not working any more it is the responsibility of the senior staff to move practice forward and to take on the new methodology. This may, for example, be by embedding the new content or teaching strategy in a scheme of work.

- Step 5: Disseminating knowledge and practice – Showing and Exchanging

  An effective school management team will create channels of communication in a school so that the outcomes of knowledge creation are shared across all staff.

  (Hargreaves, 2001, pp. 29–33 abridged and adapted)

In Chapter 4, we talked about respecting STEM subjects other than your own and appreciating their value and educational intentions as being essential for STEM to flourish. It is clear that creating and disseminating knowledge of teaching should be across the whole school and be considered a two-way street.

Hargreaves' steps 1 to 5 are often facilitated through appropriate use of IT. Some schools have their own professional development wiki with links out to Open Educational Resources sites such as ORBIT from Cambridge University or OpenLearn from The Open University. The school sites, linked to their own virtual learning environment provide a forum to discuss aspects of professional knowledge (see Chapter 2) and Technology Enhanced Learning (TEL) (see Chapter 9). In terms of creating an appropriate professional environment for both staff and pupils, the use of a school wiki and the availability of social network sites like Twitter for transmitting important messages have seen the once-ubiquitous school tannoy system mercifully consigned to the dustbin.

When results and high-stakes inspections are so important, it is a brave headteacher who will support their staff when they wish to move away from the orthodox and try something new in their teaching practice. It is exciting and motivating when one is allowed to take risks with one's teaching – it is reasonable, however, that the senior management is told about it first.

New experiences

Everyone needs new experiences to be intellectually stimulated. That happens, of course, in the classroom. I must have taught Ohm's Law a thousand times but on every occasion, even when I set about teaching in a similar way, the reaction of the class would be different and the experience would be new. As we saw in the small print of the job description above 'The responsibilities will be reviewed annually [...] and may be subject to amendment or modification at any time after consultation with the post holder'. It is important that all staff teaching STEM subjects have clear responsibilities which enable them to 'look sideways' at what others are doing but changing those responsibilities for teaching younger and older students helps to keep staff fresh and work interesting. Being able to contribute to the teaching of electronics and control and systems in design & technology and to computer science is also a stimulating new experience for a physical science teacher.

School leaders know that they have created a healthy professional environment when a colleague comes to ask to run a STEM challenge during a lunch hour, as part of an after school club or as part of a project with a particular group of pupils. Today a quick online search shows a range of possible group challenges, such as designing a CAD Formula 1 car, designing a robot and creating video game and others run annually by multinational companies like BP and Toyota. Although we would suggest that STEM is much more than just these extra-curriculum peripheral events, it is certainly the case that such activities gives a buzz to STEM teaching in any school and, if carefully selected, appeals to both boys and girls (see Chapter 8).

New ideas and new experiences can also come through teacher professional development. These can also be brought about by systematic appraisal procedures where a school is able to contribute to formal qualifications meaning teachers feel valued and establishing a professional environment that recognises and supports such individual need for teacher development which can be aligned with the collective department and school agenda.

New experiences need not be lonely ones. In one school I taught at 'knotworking' was used as an interesting technique to kick off something new, and brought people together – from both inside and outside the school – to collaborate on a project. A member of the design & technology department had heard of Young Foresight as an approach to stimulate creativity in design & technology and in STEM generally. Young Foresight is a 12-week programme for 14 year olds that stimulate their creativity by challenging the orthodox in design & technology. It does this in seven ways.

1. Pupils design but do NOT make.
2. Work is done in groups.
3. Designs are for products and services for the future, not for now nor for an immediate market.
4. Mentors from industry work with teachers to support the pupils.
5. Design ideas are based on the use of new and emerging technologies.
6. Ideas are presented to pupils' peers, their teacher and mentor and to others.
7. Pupils develop their own design briefs for the needs and wants of people in the future and the possible new markets that might exist or could be created.

In introducing Young Foresight schools must ensure that the learning is:

- clarified to the pupils so they know what is expected at each session;
- active, and that all participate;
- personally relevant;
- in groups so that discussion is encouraged;
- involves problem-solving so that, in their groups, pupils can face up to conflicting demands and unanticipated difficulties;
- important and relevant to the pupils so that they engage with the problems and feel that opinions matter – they are valued.

Yrjö Engeström and his colleagues (see Engeström et al., 2012), use the idea of 'knotworking' to describe how a group of people can come together to do various strands of activity to tackle a particular task or problem. Knotworking, the tying and untying of a knot from separate threads of activity, is not linked to any specific individual or fixed organisational entity, such as a department, as centre of control or authority. Rather the 'knot' brings together interested participants from different communities of practice to solve a particular problem.

At the school I taught at, the Young Foresight was an attempt to re-ignite creative thinking so the knot was created not only from teachers of design & technology but also from art and design, science as well as two STEM Ambassadors, engineers from a local camera company. Once the Young Foresight initiative was established and up and running, the 'knot' was untied as it had served its purpose. Knotworking is a useful technique for STEM as it recognises that there are a range of stakeholders which can all contribute to the different strands of activity needed.

Respect

Probably every generation of teachers, and in Africa and Asia as well as the USA and Europe, has felt a certain lack of respect from the society of which they are a part. Never well paid, teachers are often blamed for the ills of society. A vital factor in creating a professional environment where teachers are committed to working to improve the teaching and learning in STEM is for the senior management team of a school to make sure it knows what is being done and ensuring such commitment is recognised. All teachers are good with people; to last any time in the profession they must be. Senior staff must be the best. It is the task of the senior school leaders to ensure that they recognise the importance of interpersonal relationships and are seen around the school by pupils and staff. Quite simply, they should set aside some time each day for thanking people. However, just as important is that respect is not just top down it is also peer to peer. To be able to look sideways to work with colleagues within one's own department and across STEM subjects one needs to be respectful of that privilege.

An environment that creates respect between staff so that the seeds of new ideas can grow links naturally into rules for the classroom that creates similar respect between pupils. Although formal school rules are important so that all know what is expected of them, far more important are the 'rules' of how certain activities are carried out that encourages respect between pupils. I was in a school in Wales recently and the following was on the wall:

Our rules for brainstorming:

■ Every suggestion is written down
■ Use words already on the sheet to spark off other ideas
■ No one's suggestion is discussed [initially]
■ No one's suggestion is ignored or 'rubbished'.

I remember one teacher near retirement complaining that in his experience parents believe that if the child does well it's because they are clever, if they do badly it's because they were badly taught. One of the great pleasures of teaching is that one does have an opportunity to impact in a positive way on pupils' lives and generally pupils do recognise that. Establishing an environment for both teachers and pupils where values are identified and shared, aims and objectives agreed and teaching methods approved encourages respect between staff and pupils. Some schools make this opening up of the needs of pupils and the responses by teaching and other school staff formal through a policy of hearing the 'student voice' through School Councils or Parliaments. Others informally ensure that all pupils, whatever their interests and talents, are recognised and built on through their project work in science or design & technology (see Chapter 6). STEM subjects draw on and are relevant to 'real life' and respect is not only important at the inter-personal level but also at the level of appreciating the contribution to STEM of other domains of knowledge. As we saw in Chapter 4, other subjects respecting STEM subjects other than their own and appreciating their value and educational intentions is essential for STEM to flourish.

Conclusion

STEM is much more than one-off projects and challenges, off-timetable activities to enliven the post-exam period or a thinly-veiled excuse to entice young people into the manufacturing industries. Rather the drawing together the teachers of Science, Technology, Engineering, and Mathematics so that pupil work in one area can support and enhance their understanding in another is both efficient in classroom time and supports the way that we know young people learn. We have seen in Chapter 2 that whether teachers coordinate to support teaching in two areas, collaborate to work on a joint project or integrate their work in a club or for special project, staff need to look sideways at what colleagues are doing. If the STEM subject silos that have existed for so long in secondary schools are to be made much more 'porous' then a whole school approach is needed that addresses the physical environment of the school, the learning needs of pupils and the professional needs of their teachers. Sustaining the change is important.

In times of change the learners will inherit the earth, while the knowers will find themselves beautifully equipped to deal with a world that no longer exists
(Eric Hoffer in Smith, 1996, p. 15)

Background reading and references

Adey, P. (2001) 'In Need of Second Thoughts', *Times Educational Supplement,* 23 February.

Barlex, D. (2000) *Young Foresight Book One Teacher Guide*, Young Foresight Limited. Available at: www.nationalstemcentre.org.uk/elibrary/resource/9188/book-one-teacher-guide (accessed 10 February 2014).

Bereiter, C. and Scardamalia, M. (1995) 'Re-thinking Learning'. In D. R. Olson and N. Torrance (eds) *The Handbook of Education and Human Development: New Models of Learning, Teaching and Schooling.* New York: Blackwells.

Building Schools for the Future (BSF). Available at: www.education.gov.uk/schools/adminandfinance/schoolscapital/funding/bsf (accessed 10 February 2014).

Desforges, C. (2001) 'Familiar Challenges and New Approaches: Necessary Advances in Theory and Methods in Research on Teaching and Learning', Nuttall/Carfax memorial Lecture, Southwell: British Educational Research Association.

Engeström, Y., Kaatrakoski, H., Kaiponen, P., Lahikainen, J., Laitinen, A., Myllys, H., Rantavuori, J. and Sinikara, K. (2012) 'Knotworking in Academic Libraries: Two Case Studies from the University of Helsinki', *Liber Quarterly,* 21 (4).

Gardner, H. (1993) *Frames of Mind: The Theory of Multiple Intelligences.* London: Fontana.

Hargreaves, D. (2001) *Creative Professionalism: The Role of Teachers in the Knowledge Society.* London: Demos.

OpenLearn. Available at: www.open.edu/openlearn/ (accessed 30 June 2013).

ORBIT. Available at: http://orbit.educ.cam.ac.uk/wiki/Home (accessed 30 June 2013).

Smith, A. (1996) *Accelerated Learning in the Classroom.* Stafford: Network Educational Press.

Smith, A. and Call, N. (1999) *The ALPS Approach.* Stafford: Network Educational Press.

Specialist Schools and Academies Trust (SSAT) (2009) *Leading Practice in STEM*, London: Specialist Schools and Academies Trust.

11

Future visions for STEM

Introduction

This chapter is of necessity speculative. It will consist of two main parts. The first part will deal with possible futures for the individual subjects comprising STEM in which they operate more or less independently of one another, as if the STEM acronym had a full stop between each of the letters – S.T.E.M. The second part will consider possible futures in which there is a dynamic and synergic relationship between two or more of the contributing subjects. Across these two parts will be comments from some of the delegates who attended the World ORT Hatter Technology Seminar entitled Integrated Approaches to STEM, which took place October 29th – November 2nd 2012 in England. Taken as a whole, the delegates represented an international STEM 'dream team'. Overlaid on each part will be a consideration of the extent to which the subjects are seen as components of general education as opposed to vocational education and also the nature of the pedagogy that is used for teaching. In the final part we encourage you to develop your own personal future vision of STEM.

S.T.E.M.

There appears to be little doubt that science and mathematics will continue to be regarded as significant subjects for all students but especially for those who wish to enter a technical career. In most countries they are compulsory subjects to the age of 16 years and sometimes beyond. There are no signs that they will not continue to be gatekeeper subjects and hence they will continue to enjoy high status.

Considering science

As we have seen, significant members of the science education community make arguments for science to be seen as an essential element of general education for all.

They argue, convincingly, that a vocational rationale can only apply to a small minority of students. However, one problem facing science education as a part of general education for all is a poor record in 'modernity'. Much of the content of science curricula involves science that was discovered well over one hundred years ago. Such 'old' science, whilst lacking appeal to young people and being conceptually challenging, is necessary to understand much contemporary science. Young people will hear from the media about the findings of modern science e.g., black holes, the Higgs Boson, global warming, intelligent matter, genetic modification of food – but such matters even if they do find their way into syllabuses may only receive scant treatment. The 2012 proposed programme of study for science for a revised national curriculum in England contains minimal twentieth century science. So an interesting question for the future of science education is how to engage with contemporary science? One possible way is for curricula and associated examination specifications to have a small open section concerned with a contemporary aspect of science to be decided jointly by the teacher and the student. This would support a choice made on the basis of student interest. The student would carry the major burden of finding out about the science. There is unlikely to be a shortage of information about such science and the role of the teacher becomes that of critical friend advising the student on how best to present his or her understanding of the science in question, demonstrating as appropriate their knowledge and under-standing of the key underpinning 'old' science that the contemporary science has developed from. Note that this is not the 'traditional' role of the teacher, that of a knowledgeable person passing knowledge on to someone who is as yet unaware of that knowledge. Such a change in pedagogy may be strange at first for both the student and the teacher. In some cases it might be possible for students to communicate with the professional scientists who are developing the modern science that they are interested in. In a few cases it might be possible for a student to engage in practical work. Of course the issue of assessing such work is a significant challenge.

Twenty First Century Science, developed by the Nuffield Foundation, University of York Science Education Group in partnership with the examination awarding body OCR and the publisher Oxford University Press, goes some way towards dealing with this issue by setting case study tasks. The awarding body provides a set of information derived from various popular media articles about a particular aspect of science. In 2011, for example, these were concerned with air pollution and health. The precise title of the study is left to the student by means of the question 'Do you have a question about air pollution and health that you would like to find out more about?' The student is expected to use the information supplied by the awarding body and other information they find for themselves to consider and answer their own question. The awarding body provides comprehensive guidance concerning the assessment of students' responses. Although the students have considerable control over the way they respond to the task they are completely constrained with regard to the topic they have to consider. It would be interesting to find out if the OCR approach could be made more general and students be given the freedom to choose their own area of interest. Of course, students are likely to be interested in the possibilities and implications of deploying the science technologically. Now the student's interest has led her to erase the 'full stop' or 'point' between the 'S' and the 'T' in S.T.E.M, reflecting the relationship between science and technology in the world outside school. We will return to this matter in the second part of this chapter.

Capitalising on student's personal interests is a motivational strategy used by many teachers in many subjects. Sometimes personal interests can be inspired by national achievements. At the Sha'ar Ha Negev High School in the south of Israel a teacher named Ella Yonai uses the national pride in Israel's space achievements in her science teaching. Interestingly, Ella Yonai advocates an aspirational approach to engage students aged 14 years in science education. The aspiration is that the student, wherever they are from, could one day be part of their country's space programme and become an astronaut. If this is something students wish to pursue then understanding science will be important to them. Ella has developed a science programme around meeting the needs of a space traveller. This is summarised in Table 11.1. Each topic is taught in a two-hour class but within the school timetable. Ella hopes that this programme will be able to bring students closer to science (and also technology), and believes that learning in such a hands-on way, creating and exploring science, will help the students find the practical connection they look for in mathematics, physics or chemistry lessons. And she believes that at the end of the school year when it is time to choose a specialty in high school, some students who had never consider it before, may choose a scientific or a technological direction.

Considering mathematics

So what will happen to mathematics if it existed as an isolated subject within S.T.E.M? It will certainly retain its position as a gatekeeper subject and be the focus of high-stakes testing. And given that mathematics curricula are unlikely to change significantly in many countries, as we discussed in Chapter 5, it will remain the 'Marmite' of the curriculum: loved by some hated by others, in all probability the majority. There is no lack of intention on the part of teachers and curriculum developers to improve the school mathematics experience of young people but there is reluctance, almost inhibition, to do anything radical. The approach of the Kahn Academy, whilst innovative in enabling pupils to access mathematics tuition in out of school hours in the USA and beyond, does little to change what is actually being learned. It is not a curriculum development exercise. Proposed changes to the mathematics curriculum to combat the 'Marmite syndrome' in England have been welcomed by government ministers but are slow in development. So is there anywhere where radical development is taking place? It turns out there is – in Estonia. The project is the brainchild of Conrad Wolfram. He argues for a fundamental reform of the mathematics curriculum summing up his approach with the strapline 'Stop teaching calculating, start teaching math!' Wolfram argues his case forcibly and eloquently in a TED Talk on page 242.

TABLE 11.1 Ella Yonai's 'being a space traveller' approach to science teaching.

Main topic	Motivation	Sub topics and Activities
Size and scale in the universe	*When you go to space it's important to know how you measure distance*	■ Distance and speed conversion to different scales. ■ Measuring distance in parallax method. ■ Introduction to the solar system by the distances between planets.
The conditions in space	*When you go to space it's important to know how it feels*	■ Forces and how they affect masses. ■ Gravity and the difference between planets. ■ Why do we orbit? ■ How is it like, being weightless? ■ Designing clothing or tools that help to deal with high or low gravity.
Planets and other bodies in the solar system	*When you go to space it's important to know what you see around you*	■ Students research about different planets and present to each other. ■ Using 'cellestia', 'stelarium' (computer programs) for a tour of the solar system and the night sky.
Cooking up a comet	*When you go to space it is important to know what things are made of.*	■ The 'ingredients' of planets. ■ Matter and the periodic table. ■ Making a comet in class.
Nutrition	*When you go to space it's important to know what to eat*	■ The influence of space travel on the human body. ■ How we consume food in space conditions. ■ The food pyramid, making a menu for a space traveler.
Astronomy innovation	*When you go to space it's important to know the news there*	■ Selected topics in current astronomy. ■ Latest space missions. ■ Practicing critical reading of simple astronomy related articles.
The way to space	*When you go to space it's important to know how you get there*	■ The physics of rockets. ■ Investigating rocket motion by building simple rockets and launching them. ■ Fuel sources and drive in outer space.
Conclusion and final assignment		■ Students in teams select one topic relevant to space travel for a project.

Mathematics can be defined as a four step process:

1. Posing the right question (one that has a relation to the real world).
2. Formulate the question in mathematical terms.
3. Using computation to gain an answer.
4. Transform the answer into real world terms in order to verify the first point.

(Wolfram, 2010)

He complains that most of mathematics education deals with computation using outdated (i.e., by hand) methods and that in today's world we should use computers for this task. This would take much less time and allow the majority of time to be spent on the other three aspects. He counters some of the arguments made by critics which are: get the basics first; computers dumb down mathematics; hand calculating procedures teach understanding. With regard to the basics he argues that 'the basics' are not the calculating but in fact points 1, 2 and 4 above, and to facilitate this we should provide the best tools for calculating. In response to 'dumbing down' he argues that when correctly applied, using computers will achieve the opposite as computers will enable conceptual understanding. As for using hand calculating procedures to teach understanding, he asserts that a much better way to learn about procedures is through programming, arguing that programming demands that you *understand* the problem. Conrad believes that this approach cannot be achieved by incremental reform. He argues that it requires a complete change in the way mathematics is taught and uses the analogy of jumping across a chasm. If you try to do it slowly you will fall into the abyss. You have to 'start with a very high initial velocity (of course solving the differential equations correctly before you do) and jump over and (hopefully) get to the other side' (Wolfram, 2010). (See Figure 11.1) And Estonia is taking this bold step. Jaak Aaviksoo, Minister of Education and Research in Estonia, has said:

> In the last century, we led the world in connecting classrooms to the Internet. Now we want to lead the world in rethinking education in the technology-driven world. [...] We believe in the enthusiasm and potential of the Internet generation— they are ready for computer-based mathematics. It will also give them a competitive advantage in the labor market.
>
> (Computerbasedmath.org, 2013)

Rather than learning topics like solving quadratic equations or factorising polynomials, students in Estonia will be using the power of computer-based mathematics to solve real-world mathematics problems like 'Should I insure my mobile?', 'How long will I live?', or 'What makes a beautiful shape?', with all their rich and challenging contexts. Such an approach would certainly sit well with using mathematics in STEM and promote the use of mathematics within the other subjects. Will the rest of the world follow Estonia's lead? At the moment, the

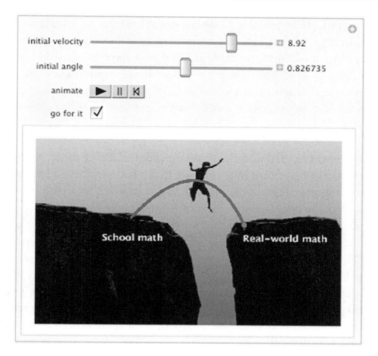

FIGURE 11.1 Moving from school math to real-world math as envisaged by Conrad Wolfram.
Source: Wolfram (2010)

impediments are significant, not the least being the professional development required for mathematics teachers. This development is certainly one to watch.

Considering technology

Compared with science and mathematics, the status of technology education in England could not be more different. The status of design & technology education was challenged by the expert panel appointed by the UK government to advise on a review of the national curriculum. Members of the panel cited weak epistemological roots and a lack of disciplinary coherence as reasons to downgrade the subject and to remove it from the prescribed national curriculum. The government rejected this advice but, ironically, the programme of study suggested in February 2012 was such a hotchpotch that it seriously lacked disciplinary coherence and compounded the expert panel's view of weak epistemology. Senior figures from industry and members of the Design and Technology Association immediately lobbied the Minister responsible for the suggested programme of study to be completely scrapped. Sir Richard Olver, chairman of one of the UK's biggest engineering/technology companies BAE Systems, was particularly critical. Olver, who is also chair of E4E, an organisation of 36 engineering institutions, was reported in the *Guardian*, that draft proposals for design & technology:

did not meet the needs of a technologically literate society. Instead of introducing children to new design techniques, such as biomimicry (how we can emulate nature to solve human problems), we now have a focus on cookery. Instead of developing skills in computer-aided design, we have the introduction of horticulture. Instead of electronics and control, we have an emphasis on basic mechanical maintenance tasks…In short, something has gone very wrong.

(Olver, 2013a)

The advice was heeded and the resultant programme of study published five months later was such a significant improvement that it is almost beyond recognition compared with the original suggestions. The day had been saved for design & technology

But in other countries the position of technology education is still contested. In Argentina, Marcos Berlatzky and colleagues have noted that although technology became a compulsory component of education at both primary and secondary levels in 1995, the implementation has been very uneven and influenced by different conceptions of technology within the educational system. Three particular conceptions have been identified. First, technology is seen as a cross-curricular space embedded in all other subjects. This is based on the idea that technology is present in all forms of human activity and hence can be taught as an aspect of other subjects. This conception does not require technology to have specialist teachers or a physical space with associated resources dedicated to the teaching, or an allocation of time on the timetable. This inevitably leads to a highly fragmented student experience in which it is difficult to achieve coherence. Second, technology is seen as a set of cases of the application of science. This approach leads to the teaching being directed towards and limited to the teaching of scientific concepts. It does not acknowledge the idea of technological knowledge beyond the sciences and as such presents a very restricted, some would say inadequate and erroneous, view of technology. Third, technology is seen as a body of knowledge different from other areas with its own unique paradigm which requires specialist teachers and dedicated spaces. This approach necessitates the identification of dominant features within the paradigm. So far two such features have emerged. In the first, design is seen as dominant. This concerns not only the invention and production of objects or products, but incorporates a broader look at the definition of solutions to transform situations that may include services or, even, production processes. In the second feature, a systems view dominates which transcends particular technologies and can be used whatever technological discipline is under consideration. It remains to be seen whether either of these paradigms becomes the prevailing orthodoxy or whether they will be able to coexist comfortably within a technology curriculum that sees itself as providing a unique body of knowledge.

Having three quite distinct and different manifestations of technology within the school curriculum will doubtless make the 'T' in STEM difficult to achieve for teachers and not easy to understand for other possible stakeholders.

The other aspect of the 'T' in STEM in England fared better at the outset than design & technology through effective high profile lobbying. Giving the MacTaggart

Lecture at the Edinburgh International Television Festival in 2011, Eric Schmidt of Google commented 'I was flabbergasted to learn that today computer science isn't even taught as standard in UK schools. Your IT curriculum focuses on teaching how to use software, but gives no insight into how it's made'. The Royal Society produced an influential report ('Shut down or restart: The way forward for computing in UK schools', 2012). The Royal Academy of Engineering in collaboration with British Computing Society (BCS) and its Computing at School group, developed a proposal for a programme of study and put it in the public domain as it was submitted to the Minister. This has led to the change of name of the subject from 'ICT' to 'Computing' (see Chapter 9), and the inclusion of computer science in the English Baccalaureate set of valued qualifications.

Considering engineering

There is little doubt that school education that will lead some young people to become engineers is seen as important. Sir Richard Olver is reported to have said the UK was at 'crisis point' (2013b). 'We have to double our output of engineers from the education system now. We have to increase engineering graduates from 20,000 to 40,000 each year...for the economy to stand still. This is just to keep the lights on and the infrastructure ticking over'. We have seen in Chapter 7 that in England, positioning engineering as a subject in the school curriculum has proven difficult. Its status has varied considerably recently, particularly for pupils aged 14–16 years. The report from the parliamentary Science and Technology Committee, 'Educating tomorrow's engineers: the impact of Government reforms on 14–19 education' has voiced concern as indicated by the following extracts:

> However, we are concerned that important subjects such as Design and Technology (D&T) are being adversely affected as schools focus on the EBac. Although the EBac leaves curriculum time to study other subjects, schools are likely to focus more on the subjects by which their performance is measured and less on non-EBac subjects. Therefore, the Government must consider how to reward schools and recognise performance in non-EBac subjects when it reviews the school accountability system.

> The rationalisation of vocational qualifications following the Wolf Review was generally welcomed, the EBac includes a focus on science and maths education and UTCs have met with approval from the engineering community. However, the devil is in the detail and some of the individual effects of such changes could be detrimental to engineering education, for example the recent changes to the Engineering Diploma following the Wolf Review. We consider that the Government's approach towards engineering education in some aspects has not been effective.

> (Science and Technology Committee, 2012)

In 2013, the UK government announced a new Technical Baccalaureate measure. This 'TechBacc' will be a performance measure marking achievement by young people aged 16 to 19 in three areas:

1. A high-quality Level 3 vocational qualification
2. A Level 3 'core maths' qualification
3. An extended project

The government is currently consulting on which vocational qualifications will be identified as high quality. It seems certain that the engineering qualifications being developed by the Royal Academy of Engineering will be seen as such. The introduction of the TechBacc as a performance table measure indicates the increasing importance that the UK government is placing on vocational education involving engineering.

In the USA, the position of engineering as a school subject would seem to be more secure but, as we have seen in Chapter 7, only at the expense of sequestering it into the science curriculum with the attendant problem of identifying teachers with the necessary knowledge and skills to teach this component. The extent to which this is adopted by teachers and plays out in classrooms has yet to be seen. National pronouncements have a long journey to take before they reach the classroom in the USA and the influence of both state and district legislature can influence the outcomes considerably.

The development of a vocational pedagogy

Recently, there has been an increased interest in describing vocational pedagogy. This has led to three distinguished academics in education, Bill Lucas, Ellen Spencer and Guy Claxton, to write a guide to vocational pedagogy (City & Guilds Centre for Skills Development, 2012).

In their chapter concerning learning and teaching methods that 'work', Lucas et al. present seven principles for vocation education, shown in Table 11.2, and a set of effective methods, shown in Table 11.3. Inspection of Table 11.2 reveals that these principles would not go amiss in academic education and similarly many of the methods listed in Table 11.3 would seem appropriate for academic study. Perhaps this sort of writing will lead to a blurring of the boundaries between vocational and academic courses to the benefit of STEM education, even when there is little interaction between the individual subjects.

So what are we to make of this? If STEM subjects are seen as separate, with little if any interaction then their fate will be determined by their individual status at different times in different countries. Any opportunities to gain mutual benefit through curriculum relationships will be lost. In this scenario there is no doubt that in the foreseeable future science and mathematics will continue to be highly significant as academic subjects that are gatekeepers to progress into further and

TABLE 11.2 Principles of vocational education.

Play the whole game – use extended projects and authentic contexts.

Make the game worth playing – work hard at engaging learners giving them choices wherever possible.

Work on the hard parts – discover the most effective ways of practising.

Play out of town – try things out in many different contexts.

Uncover the hidden game – make the processes of learning as visible as possible.

Learn from the team and the other teams – develop robust ways of working in groups and seek out relevant communities of practice.

Learn from the game of learning – be in the driving seat as a learner, developing your own tried and tested tactics and strategies.

From Lucas, Spencer and Claxton (2012)

TABLE 11.3 Effective methods for vocational education.

Learning by watching

Learning by imitating

Learning by practising ('trial and error')

Learning through feedback

Learning through conversation

Learning by teaching and helping

Learning by real-world problem-solving

Learning through enquiry

Learning by thinking critically and producing knowledge

Learning by listening, transcribing and remembering

Learning by drafting and sketching

Learning by reflecting

Learning on the fly

Learning by being coached

Learning by competing

Learning through virtual environments

Learning through simulation and role play

Learning through games

From Lucas, Spencer and Claxton (2012)

higher education. However there are indications that in schools in England, mathematics will feature significantly within vocational qualifications that act as gatekeepers and such qualifications will include engineering. Whether science will feature in such a general way in vocational qualifications seems unlikely. However, in schools in the USA there is the possibility that engineering will become part of the science curriculum for pupils aged 5–18 years although the extent to which this might happen is not clear. The status of technology is less clear. As a relative newcomer to the school curriculum it has yet to establish a secure position and in many countries it has still to establish a particular position among several possibilities. This makes future gazing particularly difficult. Future scenarios will depend on local conditions and whilst in one country technology may be seen as a general academic subject that has its own fundamental body of knowledge, principles and concepts not provided elsewhere in the curriculum, this may not be the case in another country, where it might be seen simply as a vehicle for making science and mathematics more palatable. The current interest in computing as a separate discipline within technology in England provides an interesting example of a STEM subject being transformed and reinvigorated without the need to forge relationships across the STEM piece.

STEM

Now we consider the future of STEM in which there is deliberate acknowledgement and encouragement of curriculum relationships between the contributing subjects. This does not imply that in such a curriculum all learning activities will involve all of the subjects in some overall integrated programme, rather that opportunities of different sorts will be taken to make links between one or more of the individual subjects and capitalise on the synergy that produces with regard to student understanding and learning.

A view from Israel

Ronit Peretz is a science and mathematics teacher at Rabin High School in Kiryat Yam in Israel and the regional moderator of the Science for All curriculum. At my invitation she commented on STEM in Israel. Peretz began by reminding us of the Israeli government's support for science and technology education, quoting the Science and Technology Education Higher Committee's report 'Tomorrow 98'. She said, 'Science and technology are part of the general education necessary today and will be required even more in the future, to any person who can contribute to society'. This leads her to acknowledge the necessity of educating the next generation of scientists and technologist but reminds us that this is not sufficient:

> One of the goals of science education in high schools in Israel is educating students for active involvement and commitment to society and environment.

As future citizens we expect our students to participate in decision-making based on scientific knowledge and values in order to raise the quality of life and environment in which we live.

(Peretz, 2012)

Peretz is clear that this has implications, 'So, we, the teachers of Science and Technology, have to adapt our way of teaching for those changes in order to promote those goals and prepare the future citizens (our students)'. Peretz argues for the importance of relating science to technology as follows:

When science and technology subjects are taught as separate disciplines, students are not aware of the link between the different contents and are not able to develop a systematic comprehensive view of the world around them. Therefore, it is very important to teach science and technology in a broader context regarding mathematics and engineering. Integrating STEM subjects: Sciences, Technology, Engineering and Mathematics, together into one interdisciplinary subject – STEM – unlike learning them independently, can break down the barriers between the school and the outside world and reduce the gap between learning at school and the real life. STEM education can provide opportunities for students to understand in general the scientific and technological principles as well as the relationships between science (the natural environment), technology (artificial environment) and society. Understanding these relationships can teach them a lot about their lives, the possibilities and benefits on one hand and problems or limitations on the other, so they will be able to discuss issues and reach responsible decisions about their present and future life based on their knowledge. Using interdisciplinary teaching-learning processes will expose the students to genuine daily life problems, dealing with them and finding solutions. This will make the study of science and technology more relevant to the student's life and they will better understand the scientific – technological world around us.

(Peretz, 2012)

Ironically perhaps, the new programme to meet this challenge is called 'Science for All'. It is now being offered at the high-school level in Israel for non-science major students as an alternative to the traditional natural science courses. The processes of teaching and learning in Science for All are organised around integrative interdisciplinary topics that are relevant to the student's world, and include active and cooperative learning and involve project-based learning, which will allow students to apply their acquired knowledge in designing, development and technological implementation. Peretz believes that such learning provides an opportunity to deal with practical difficulties and challenges and contributes to the development of analytical thinking skills, creativity, entrepreneurship, innovativeness, communication and teamwork – skills needed for coping in the future life and at work. In addition, integrating projects in cooperation with the industry, the army or the academy inside or outside the curriculum will expose the students to the various options inherent in the study of science and technology and can encourage them to these fields. Peretz believes that this approach should not be limited to secondary/high school but should begin much earlier, from nursery/kindergarten upwards. However, she is aware of the challenges that come with this approach, writing as follows:

> One of the challenges in implementing such a program is recruiting the appropriate teachers. The teachers of science, technology and mathematics are usually specific discipline experts, and dealing with all STEM aspects together may not be so trivial for them and they also may feel discomfort about questions of students in class. Thus, obviously, teacher training is required through courses, seminars, and workshops dealing with the appropriate pedagogical approach. Another challenge is the development of an appropriate teaching model of such a subject – one central teacher or maybe several teachers from different disciplines teaching in coordination around the same theme or project.
>
> (Peretz, 2012)

A view from Brazil

Vitor Soares Mann is Chief of Science and Biotechnology's Laboratories and Professor of Introduction to Technology at Instituto de Tecnologia ORT of Rio de Janeiro, Brazil. At my invitation he wrote about STEM in his country. He cited two ways forward for STEM activities which incorporate interaction between the contributing subjects. The first way is in formal classes:

> At the level of formal classes, it is necessary to challenge the usual bureaucratic approach like the restriction of time and respect to the disciplines program. So, the role of the teacher is planning and suggesting to students some activities that include an integrated view. When we study pollution, for example, it would be the teacher's function to plan the activities, among which practical activities, that provide a complex understanding about the subject. In this case, it is necessary that the study begins with a brief presentation/discussion, involves the development of monitoring/assessment activities, the construction of systems for remediation that provide some possible solutions to the problem, leads to the reformulation of initial discussion and the preparation of an individual report (instrument for the assessment of learning). The activities of monitoring and evaluation (measure the air quality for example) provide to students a better understanding of the theme, the establishment of theoretical and practical concepts. Already the construction of simple and efficient systems for the purification of natural resources, as the construction of carbon filters for water purification, encompasses the use of scientific and technological knowledge as tools for solving practical problems. The integration of Science, Technology, Engineering and Mathematics is the essential key to the development of these activities; they are the knowledge basis needed to design these

experiments and to understand your results. In this first level of use of the STEM philosophy the teacher meets a centralizing role, fitting himself the task of guiding the learning process and the content to be learned.

(Mann, 2012)

The second way is through the informal curriculum:

In non-formal environments such as a science club, the STEM philosophy gains another dimension, a second level. In such environments, where the didactic of learning is free from bureaucratic issues, the teacher loses his centralizer role and restricts himself to co-operator function. It is student's responsibility to design and develop activities, which immeasurably enriches the learning process. If the classroom teacher's commitment highlights the importance of integration between Science, Technology, Engineering and Mathematics, in non-formal environments students discover the relevance of this integration in practice. When they develop a hydroponic project, for example, they must discover science (biology and chemistry) to understand plants and their needs, technology to solve problems, engineering to design their systems and the importance of mathematics along process, in system design and in its maintenance (preparation of the nutrient solution for plants where they associate biology, chemistry and mathematics). Students experience a real integration between knowledge and this integration is required because without it their projects are unviable. Thus, as it happens in life, during a science club we can allow students to 'break their heads' and discover alone how the interdependence between the different types of knowledge is a natural and complex phenomenon. When they are developing their projects autonomously, the students restructure their understanding of the world, transforming themselves in participatory and creative subjects.

(Mann, 2012)

Vitor is clear on the need for both approaches:

In short, we can understand that the STEM philosophy can be adapted to two different, but equally important, pedagogical conditions. It is accountability of the formal environment ensure students an egalitarian educational basis, allowing everyone to have access to the same content. The informal environment plays a complementary role, using the previously established knowledge in formal education to offer students a context of greater autonomy. Consequently, we must understand the two scenarios as complementary, one environment of security and stability and other of creativity and innovation. Although methodologically different, these environments are capable of absorbing STEM philosophy as an ideology, as a social responsibility; the responsibility to provide students a complex and integrating formation, committed to the construction of critical subjects.

(Mann, 2012)

A widening approach from the USA – STEAM

Some argue that concentrating on the STEM subjects alone, albeit in ways that encourage links between the subjects, is insufficient. Hence there is a small, but growing 'STEAM' movement where STEAM stands for Science, Technology Engineering, Arts and Mathematics. One proponent of STEAM is Harvey White, a highly successful businessman in wireless communications who argues that the Arts should be an essential feature of education for economic prosperity. On his website (http://steam-notstem.com/) he argues the case for STEAM:

> Together we can demonstrate that Arts is a necessary adjunct to STEM 'by connecting the dots' for all constituents:
>
> - Arts education is a key to creativity, and
> - Creativity is an essential component of, and spurs innovation, and
> - Innovation is agreed to be necessary to create new industries in the future, and
> - New industries, with their jobs, are the basis of our future economic wellbeing.
>
> A win-win situation – low cost – job growth and insuring the future. If we do not connect these dots Arts education will continue to be virtually extinct in our schools – and the US's economic future will be damaged.
>
> (White, 2012)

White cites the Chinese curriculum which relatively recently (1994) required art, defined as music and fine art, to be present in senior secondary school programmes. He also condemns the current USA education system as being fit for purpose only for times past and contrasts American parents' attitudes to those of their Chinese counterparts as sounding warning bells.

> A *Newsweek* article compared what Chinese and American parents thought was the most important skills their children will need to drive innovation. The most important skill for 42% of Chinese parents, was 'creative approaches to problem solving' (vs 18% of American parents) while for 52% of American parents 'math and computer science' was the most important skill needed to drive innovation (vs. 9% of Chinese parents).
>
> (White, 2012)

He cites Education Secretary Arne Duncan speaking to the Arts Education Partnership National Forum in April 2010: 'The arts can no longer be treated as a frill...arts education is essential to stimulating the creativity and innovation that will prove critical to young Americans competing in a global economy' (Arne Duncan, 2010).

Some art teachers might question this utilitarian approach to arts education but at a time of economic austerity and budget cuts, entangling arts education with STEM education will be seen by some as a pragmatic necessity. Given the difficulty encountered in enabling interaction between STEM subjects we must wonder if introducing another player into the equation is likely to lead to success. However, the argument that creativity is important for the STEM subjects to be used for innovation is compelling for some teachers so it will rest with them to open lines of communication across the so called arts-science divide.

So what are we to make of this? Clearly, there are movements in various countries to encourage teachers out of their subject silos and into more dynamic curricular relationships across the STEM subjects, although it is acknowledged that this will not be an easy task. However, underlying our thoughts about the future of STEM in which the subjects are connected must be the nature of the schools in which such work takes place. It is not difficult to imagine unconnected STEM subjects operating in conventional schools. This is the status quo. Vitor Soares Mann is particularly condemning of the unchanging school.

Schools remain in an ideological bubble and ignore social demands required by our development. According to the Brazilian Institute of Geography and Statistics in 2009, 27.4% of Brazilian households had Internet access, and according to forecast of Brazilian Communications Minister Paulo Renato, in 2012 we will reach the level of 50% of Brazilian homes (or even more) with Internet access. And how is the school adapting this new reality? The answer is simple: the school is not adapting anything new. The school remains the same, untouched and absolute, teaching abstract content and underrating non-academic information, giving them the air of vulgar information. Conceptual and ideological changes of our educational proposal are inevitable. It is necessary that the Brazilian education contemplate a serious and skilful project of scientific and technological literacy. Our citizens need to be educated to enjoy the scientific and technological revolution in which they participate and to which they contribute. To understand and interact inside our society a critical subject needs to understand the science and technology as social phenomena. Soon a rapidly developing country like Brazil needs competent, autonomous and clarified subjects, capacitated to contribute to the healthy development of our society.

(Mann, 2012)

Keri Facer, in her book *Learning Futures, Education, Technology and Social Change*, tries to meet Vitor's concerns by reconceptualising schools as places where communities build their *own* future. Keri is particularly concerned that advances in cognitive enhancement, prosthetic development and genetic manipulation will have significant and as yet unknown impact on our society and by implication on education. These areas are clearly STEM-related. At the end of the book Keri outlines nine conditions to enable future-building schools. Of these, one is particularly STEM relevant: develop an ethical code for the educational use of digital and biotechnologies. Here Keri argues that schools would no longer be recipients of new socio-technical practices developed in the world outside school but would rewrite the relationship between education and socio-technical change as one of active design, critique and engagement. Just imagine what that would mean for teaching and learning in the STEM subjects. Keri envisages these changes as having the potential to influence the nature of schools within 20 years. How many schools will change in response to Vitor's concern as to the inadequacies of current schools and in line with Keri's future vision remains to be seen. The situation in England of a rapidly changing educational landscape with possibilities for many different types of school, many of which are not required to teach to the national curriculum, indicates that significant change and variation are possible. This leads us to the final section in which we ask you to consider your vision for the future of STEM and as part of this consideration you will need to take into account concerns as to the adequacy of current schooling and how these might be dealt with in the future.

Your vision

Clearly we, as the authors of the book cannot and should not define a future vision for STEM. Any such attempt would be futile and the fact is that it is *your* vision for the future of STEM in *your* school that is important and only you can decide on, and work towards, that. So a question must be asked: are you keen to develop significant links with other subjects? Or do you prefer to operate mainly within your subject but be on 'good terms' with other STEM subjects, knowing something about their curriculum programmes and teach in the light of STEM but without engaging in anything likely to disrupt current practice? Both positions are tenable and the one you adopt will, to some extent, depend on the prevailing ethos in your school. Whichever position you choose to adopt, a first step will be to find out about STEM subjects other than your own and audit your findings with regard to possible links. This is best started through informal conversations which can lead to the identification of opportunities to explore. The nature, scope and frequency of these opportunities will define your vision for the future of STEM at the present. To develop this into a longer-term vision it will be necessary to enact these opportunities and reflect on their potential for further development. This will almost certainly require further and wider conversations particularly with your school's senior leadership team (see Chapter 10). In this way you will establish your personal vision for the future of STEM as it relates to your school. Given that schools, schooling and educating young people will manifest themselves in various guises in the future, another important consideration will be the flexibility of your vision as the nature of your school changes or perhaps you move to another school with a different ethos and ways of working. Indeed your vision of the future of STEM may influence the sort of schools that you wish to work in as you move through your career.

Of course, national events in education will influence your vision. For example, new educational policy might privilege only some STEM subjects and not others and this might impact the significance given to using learning from different STEM subjects within other STEM subjects. And of course the ramifications of any new policy will play out in examination specifications and means of assessment. We believe that it is important that you use your vision of STEM to be proactive and to inform how you react to these influences. The voice of professional STEM educators should inform both policy and practice with regard to teaching, learning and assessment and this voice will be all the more powerful if it is driven by clear visions for the future of STEM. Articulating these visions into a coherent form will not be easy or straightforward as the future is not certain. Keri Facer is particularly strong on this.

> The socio-technical developments of the next 20 years will not evolve smoothly and inevitably along one predictable trajectory. They will emerge messily and unevenly out of the aspirations, struggle and compromises between different social actors. We cannot determine the future that will unfold. We can, however, create schools that are public places and democratic laboratories that can play a powerful role in tipping the balance of that change in favour of sustainable futures for all our students.
>
> (Facer, 2011)

We believe that your future vision of STEM should contribute to the aspirations, struggle and compromises that will take place.

Most of this book has concentrated on the nature of STEM subjects, curriculum development, curriculum politics and the role of teachers. It is important in our thinking about STEM education, as it is playing out now and as it may play out in the future, to consider the young people at the centre – the students. Their response to the STEM curriculum, be it in silos or connected across subjects, is crucial. Recent work by sociologists is revealing that the assumptions underpinning STEM initiatives to increase engagement with STEM subjects may be invalid and that student responses are dependent on many factors, only some of which are now coming to light. We will describe two pieces of work that are significant. First is the work of Clare Gartland of University Campus, Suffolk (Gartland, 2014). Clare has looked at the way ambassadors from higher education interact with school students. Her work questions the prevailing wisdom that young people of similar ethnicity and gender, as school students, will necessarily provide role models to emulate. School students can sometimes be suspicious of the 'marketing approach' and can feel alienated because they are seen as lacking appropriate ambition. Gartland's work shows that a much more nuanced approach is required with ambassadors working more closely with teachers in subject-specific contexts as opposed to simply providing 'look what I've done – you can do it too' sessions. Second is the work of Louise Archer in the ASPIRES project. Beginning in 2009, this is a five-year longitudinal study of pupils when they are aged 10/11, 12/13 and 13/14 years old.

In phase 1 the project surveyed 9,319 Year 6 (10-year-old) pupils from 279 primary schools in England and carried out 170 interviews (92 children and 78 parents). In phase 2 the project surveyed 5,634 pupils in Year 8 (from the original 9,319 pupils) from 69 secondary schools and carried out interviews with 85 children. Phase 3 investigating the pupils in Year 9 is on-going. The research revealed that the emerging identity of the children influenced their aspirations with regard to science careers. The majority of the children enjoyed science lessons at school, agreed that they learned interesting things in science and had enthusiastic teachers who expected them to do well yet those that aspired to be scientists were in a small minority. Louise and her colleagues argue that the family environment, popular perception of science and gender shape science aspirations. Of particular interest is the family environment and their findings that science capital and 'family habitus' are very important (Archer et al., 2012). Science capital refers to the extent to which there are science-related qualifications within the family, interest in science and contacts with the science community. Habitus is related to this but extends further embracing family values, practices and a sense of 'who we are' and 'what we do'. For some children becoming a scientist is actually unthinkable, going against all that is likely to be expected of them. So a challenge for STEM educators is to make science, and science-related careers a 'thinkable' option. Hence Louise and colleagues argue that gaining interest is not enough and there needs to be a shift of emphasis from interest to participation. Some of the enhancement and enrichment activities described in Chapter 8 are very participation based, but a problem here is that it is usually students from families with existing science capital that participate. To make STEM aspirations 'thinkable' for all may require more diverse post-16 routes in science and mathematics. There is some evidence that this is being developed for mathematics but little as yet for science. It will also be important to challenge perceptions of science as a subject only for 'clever' people, mainly males. We have seen that the 'science for all' agenda is strong in many countries but often this is seen as 'science for citizenship' as opposed to science-related career aspiration. Interestingly, in arguing for a redistribution of science capital, Louise and her colleagues suggest improved careers advice, embedding careers awareness into the curriculum and the importance of working with families, particularly those with little science capital who cannot imagine their children entering a STEM-based career. In developing your vision for the future of STEM it will be important to take this sort of work into account so that your enthusiasm and advocacy for STEM subjects, however well-intentioned, does not fall on stony ground.

Whatever your vision, we find ourselves returning to the ever-important idea of conversation – with colleagues in your own discipline, colleagues from other disciplines, senior leaders in your school, students and their families, the wider school community and within and across the various professional bodies that represent and engage with STEM education. These conversations alone will be insufficient to implement your vision but without them we believe that however attractive and worthwhile the vision, it will not become a reality. Looking sideways at what your colleagues are doing and talking to them about what you are doing is vital. Such conversations are the starting point for change.

Background reading and references

Archer, L., DeWitt, J., Osborne, J., Dillon, J., Willis, B. and Wong, B. (2012) Science Aspirations and Family Habitus: How Families Shape Children's Engagement and Identification with Science. *American Educational Research Journal*, 49(5), 881–908.

ASPIRE. Available at: www.kcl.ac.uk/sspp/departments/education/research/aspires/ASPIRESpublications.aspx (accessed 10 February 2014).

Computerbasedmath.org (2013) Comments made by Jaak Aaviksoo, Minister of Education and Research in Estonia in 'Estonia Named First Computer-Based Math Education Country', Press release. Available at: www.computerbasedmath.org/computer-based-math-education-estonia.html (accessed 10 February 2014).

Department for Education (2013) 'New TechBacc Will Give Vocational Education the High Status it Deserves' press release. Available at: www.education.gov.uk/inthenews/inthenews/a00224304/techbacc-accounced (accessed 10 February 2014).

Facer, K. (2011) *Learning Futures, Education, Technology and Social Change*. London and New York: Routledge/Taylor & Francis Group.

Gartland, C. (2014) *STEM Ambassadors and Social Justice in HE*. London: Trentham Books (forthcoming).

House of Commons (2013) 'Educating Tomorrow's Engineers: The Impact of Government Reforms on 14–19 Education' report. Available at: www.publications.parliament.uk/pa/cm201213/cmselect/cmsctech/665/665.pdf (accessed 10 February 2014).

Lucas, B., Spencer, E. and Claxton, G. (2012) 'How to Teach Vocational Education: A Theory of Vocational Pedagogy' report. City & Guilds Centre for Skills Development. Available at: www.skillsdevelopment.org/PDF/How-to-teach-vocational-education.pdf (accessed 10 February 2014).

OCR (2011) Twenty-First Century Case Study. Information for Teachers. Available at: www.ocr.org.uk/Images/80722-unit-a144-controlled-assessment-teacher-guidance-case-study-accredited.pdf (accessed 10 February 2014).

OCR Media Pack (2011) Available at: www.ocr.org.uk/qualifications/gcse-twenty-first-century-science-suite-science-a-j241-from-2011/ (accessed 26 November 2013).

Olver, R. (2013a) Quoted text from a conference in March 2013, reported in the *Guardian*. 1 April. Available at: www.theguardian.com/education/2013/mar/31/school-curriculum-cookery-horticulture-before-technology (accessed 10 February 2014).

Olver, R. (2013b) Taken from keynote speech at City University Chancellor's Dinner, 10 April, London: City University.

Royal Society (2012) 'Shut Down or Restart: The Way Forward for Computing in UK Schools' report. Available at: www.royal.society.org/education/policy (accessed 10 February 2014).

Schmidt, E. (2011) Quoted in the MacTaggart Lecture at the Edinburgh International Television Festival. 26 August. Available at: www.geitf.co.uk/GEITF/mactaggart-hall-of-fame (accessed 10 February 2014).

STEAM. Available at: http://steam-notstem.com/ (accessed 10 February 2014).

White, H. (2011) 'Our Education System Is Not So Much "Broken" As It Is Totally Outdated!' Available at: http://steam-notstem.com/articles/our-education-system-is-not-so-much-broken-as-it-is-totally-outdated/ (accessed 10 February 2014).

Wolfram, C. (2010) 'Stop Teaching Calculating, Start Teaching Math', TED Global 2010 Talk. Available at: http://computerbasedmath.org/resources/reforming-math-curriculum-with-computers.html (accessed 10 February 2014).

Index

Page numbers in **bold** indicate tables and in *italic* indicate figures.